Quick
Cakes

FOR BUSY MUMS

Karen Taylor

Celebration cakes you can make and decorate at home

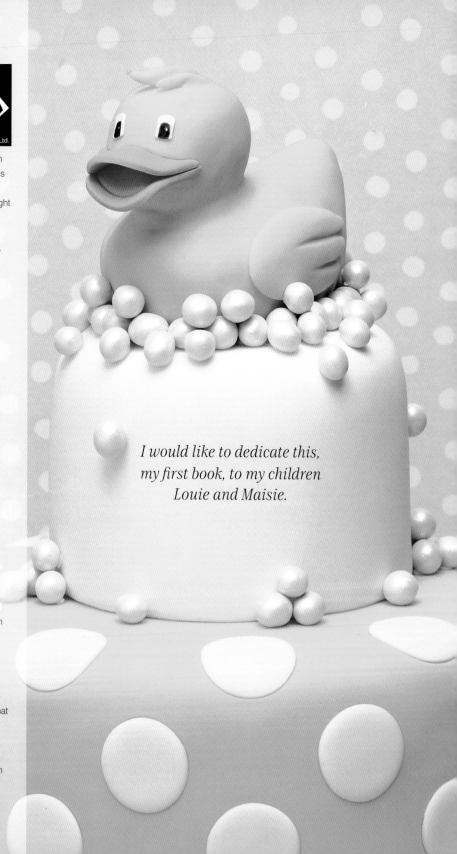

First published in July 2014 by B. Dutton
Publishing Limited, The Grange, Hones
Business Park, Farnham, Surrey, GU9 8BB.
Copyright: Karen Taylor 2014
ISBN-13: 978-1-905113-47-7
All rights reserved.

Publisher: Beverley Dutton
Group Editor: Jennifer Kelly
Art Director/Designer: Sarah Ryan

Book publishing

Copy Editor: Frankie New
Graphic Designer and Photography Stylist: Louise Pepé
Graphic Designer: Abbie Johnston
Photography: Alister Thorpe

Magazine publishing

Editor: Jenny Royle
Copy Editor: Adele Duthie
Senior Graphic Designer: Zena Deakin
PR and Advertising Manager: Natalie Bull

Wallpaper supplied by wallpaperdirect.co.uk
Printed in China by 1010 Printing Ltd.

Important Information

The Author and Publisher have made every effort to
ensure that the contents of this book will not cause harm
or injury or pose any danger. Please note that some
inedible items, such as floral wires, ribbon and cocktail
sticks, have been used in the projects in this book. All
such inedible items must be removed before the cakes
are eaten. Similarly, any non-food-grade equipment and
substances must not come into contact with any food that
is to be eaten. Neither the Author nor the Publisher can
be held responsible for errors or omissions and cannot
accept liability for injury, damage or loss to persons or
property, however it may arise, as a result of acting upon
guidelines and information printed in this book.

*I would like to dedicate this,
my first book, to my children
Louie and Maisie.*

Introduction

I always wanted my first book to have something for everyone – cake designs for a wide range of occasions that are achievable whether you're a beginner or a more experienced cake decorator.

Using just a few basic skills, the cakes in this book can be recreated following the simple step-by-step instructions and photographs. If you are new to cake decorating, I recommend that you look through the first sections of this book which take you through the basics. I believe that if you can master these skills and techniques, you'll consistently achieve great results.

I have used a broad range of techniques, from simple figure modelling to more creative decorations, such as the intricate quilling on the Ruby Anniversary Cake. For some of the projects, I also introduce an alternative modelling method which uses a mixture of crisped rice cereal and marshmallows to create larger, more sculptural shapes whilst ensuring they remain light and tasty. With designs for cookies and cupcakes to complement each project, there is also plenty of choice depending on the occasion or on how much time you have.

One of the reasons I love cake decorating is that the possibilities are endless, so let your creativity flow, develop the ideas in this book and experiment with new ones. I have thoroughly enjoyed putting all of these projects together and I hope that they will inspire you to recreate them in your own way.

Karen.

Contents

Essential Edibles and Equipment 6–7

Recipes and Baking Charts 8–17

Fillings 18

Basic Techniques 19–27

Icings and Pastes.. 28–30

PROJECTS

Rub-a-Dub-Dub Baby Shower Cake 32–37

Pitter Patter Christening Cake 38–41

'Bright as a Button' Birthday Cake 42–48

Baby Elephant First Birthday Cake 49–55

Toy Soldier Birthday Cake 56–63

'What a Hoot!' Birthday Cake 64–75

Crafted with Love Valentine's Cake 76–81

'Hoppy Easter' Cake 82–87

First Pint 18th Birthday Cake 88–95

Designer Handbag Cake 96–103

Pompom Wedding Cake 104–109

Ruby Anniversary Cake 110–113

Red-nosed Reindeer Christmas Cake 114–120

Templates 121–125

Gallery 126–127

Suppliers 128

Essential Edibles and Equipment

If you're a busy baker, it is important to have everything you need to hand before you begin in order to save time. You will need the same basic items for most of the projects in this book, so I have listed them here. Any other specific edibles or equipment are given at the beginning of each cake project. All of the items are readily available from sugarcraft suppliers, see page 128.

1 Cake drums (boards) and cards
2 Clear alcohol, e.g. gin or vodka
3 Clear, sterilised ruler
4 Cornflour in a muslin dusting bag
5 Craft knife
6 Dowels
7 Dresden tool
8 Dried spaghetti
9 Edible glue (SK)
10 Food-grade plastic bags
11 Icing sugar in a shaker
12 Marzipan spacers
13 Non-stick board
14 Non-stick rolling pins, large and small

15 Non-toxic glue stick
16 Paintbrushes
17 Palette knives, large and small
18 Pastry brush
19 Piping nozzles
20 Quilting tool
21 Scribing tool
22 Serrated knife
23 Sharp, plain-bladed knife
24 Shell/blade tool
25 Small paper piping bags
26 Small scissors
27 Smoothers
28 Sugar shaper
29 Turntable
30 White vegetable fat

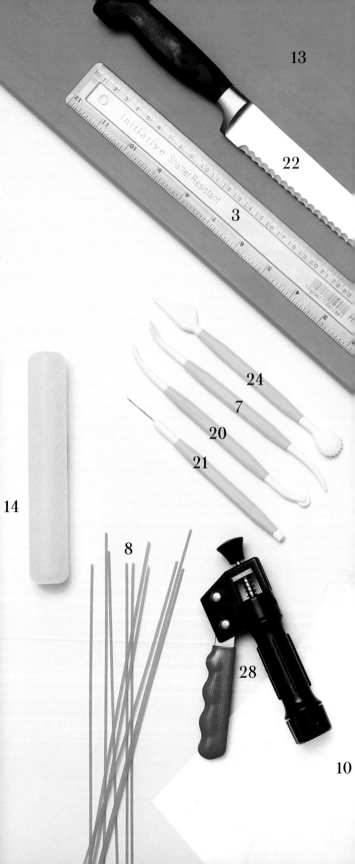

Recipes and Baking Charts

A well-decorated cake should taste as good as it looks and I have been using these tried-and-tested recipes for years to make deliciously moist celebration cakes. I have also provided useful charts to help you easily adapt the recipes for different-sized cakes.

Traditional fruit cake

This recipe makes a lovely, moist fruit cake which is suitable for wedding, christening, anniversary or Christmas cakes. It is best to make your fruit cake at least 6–8 weeks before it is served to allow it to mature.

1　Soak the mixed fruit in brandy overnight.

2　Preheat the oven to 140°C/120°C fan/275°F/gas mark 1.

3　Grease and line a cake tin with parchment paper (see page 19).

4　Place the butter and sugar in an electric mixer or large mixing bowl and beat together until light and fluffy.

5　Add the eggs, treacle, vanilla and a little flour to the mixture and beat gently. Fold in the remaining flour until it is all combined.

6　Mix in the cherries, almonds, mixed spice and mixed fruit, saving the brandy to feed the cake once it has cooled.

7　Spoon the mixture into the tin and bake for the recommended time or until a skewer inserted in the centre comes out clean.

8　Leave the cake to cool in the tin before removing it.

9　Carefully make a few small holes in the top of the cake with a clean skewer then pour a little of the brandy over and allow it to soak in. This can be repeated every four weeks, until you are ready to decorate the cake.

INGREDIENTS	15cm (6")		20.5cm (8")		25.5cm (10")		30.5cm (12")	
	ROUND	SQUARE	ROUND	SQUARE	ROUND	SQUARE	ROUND	SQUARE
Butter	90g (3oz)	145g (5oz)	175g (6oz)	285g (10oz)	340g (12oz)	510g (1lb 2oz)	595g (1lb 5oz)	800g (1lb 12oz)
Soft brown sugar	90g (3oz)	145g (5oz)	175g (6oz)	285g (10oz)	340g (12oz)	510g (1lb 2oz)	595g (1lb 5oz)	800g (1lb 12oz)
Eggs	1	2	3	5	6	9	11	14
Black treacle	2tsp	2tsp	1tbsp	1tbsp	1tbsp	2tbsp	2tbsp	2tbsp
Vanilla extract	1tsp	2tsp	3tsp	4tsp	5tsp	6tsp	7tsp	8tsp
Plain flour	130g (4½oz)	225g (8oz)	260g (9oz)	400g (14oz)	450g (1lb)	650g (1lb 7oz)	680g (1lb 8oz)	900g (2lb)
Mixed spice	½tsp	1tsp	2tsp	2½tsp	3tsp	3½tsp	4tsp	4½tsp
Mixed fruit	285g (10oz)	450g (1lb)	650g (1lb 7oz)	935g (2lb 1oz)	1.2kg (2lb 10oz)	1.5kg (3lb 6oz)	1.9kg (4lb 4oz)	2.5kg (5lb 10oz)
Cherries	45g (1½oz)	70g (2½oz)	90g (3oz)	115g (4oz)	145g (5oz)	225g (8oz)	285g (10oz)	340g (12oz)
Ground almonds	15g (½oz)	30g (1oz)	30g (1oz)	45g (1½oz)	60g (2oz)	70g (2½oz)	100g (3½oz)	130g (4½oz)
Flaked almonds	15g (½oz)	30g (1oz)	30g (1oz)	45g (1½oz)	60g (2oz)	70g (2½oz)	100g (3½oz)	130g (4½oz)
Brandy	75ml (2½fl oz)	75ml (2½fl oz)	145ml (5fl oz)	150ml (5¼fl oz)	210ml (7½fl oz)	220ml (7¾fl oz)	280ml (9¾fl oz)	300ml (10½fl oz)
Baking time	3–3½hrs		4–4½hrs		5–5½hrs		5½–6hrs	

Vanilla sponge cake

I use an all-in-one method to make a deliciously light sponge cake. This basic recipe can be altered to make a variety of flavoured sponges.

1 Preheat the oven to 200°C/180°C fan/400°F/gas mark 6.

2 Grease and line two cake tins of the same size, or just one tin if you are making a 10cm (4") cake (see page 19).

3 Beat the flour, caster sugar, butter, eggs and vanilla extract together in an electric mixer until the mixture is well combined and fluffy in appearance. Split the mixture equally between two cake tins (except for a 10cm (4") cake which is baked in one tin).

4 Bake in the centre of the oven for the recommended time or until the cake springs back to the touch.

5 Turn the cake out of the tin immediately and leave to cool.

Flavour variations

Chocolate cake

Reduce the amount of self-raising flour in the recipe by half the amount of cocoa powder added (see below). Sieve the recommended amount of cocoa powder with the flour. For example, to make a 20.5cm (8") round chocolate cake you will need 285g (10oz) of self-raising flour and 115g (4oz) of cocoa. Add 1tbsp of milk per 60g (2oz) of cocoa added.

Lemon cake

Add finely grated lemon zest to the mixture towards the end of mixing. When the cakes are cooled and sliced, juice the lemons and mix the juice with 30g (1oz) of golden caster sugar per lemon. Using a spoon, drizzle this over each layer of sponge.

Toffee cake

Make in the same way as the vanilla sponge but replace the caster sugar with dark soft brown sugar.

INGREDIENTS	10cm (4")		15cm (6")		20.5cm (8")		25.5cm (10")		30.5cm (12")	
	ROUND	SQUARE	ROUND	SQUARE	ROUND	SQUARE	ROUND	SQUARE	ROUND	SQUARE
Self-raising flour	115g (4oz)	115g (4oz)	175g (6oz)	225g (8oz)	340g (12oz)	450g (1lb)	550g (1lb 4oz)	700g (1lb 8oz)	800g (1lb 12oz)	900g (2lb)
Caster sugar	115g (4oz)	115g (4oz)	175g (6oz)	225g (8oz)	340g (12oz)	450g (1lb)	550g (1lb 4oz)	700g (1lb 8oz)	800g (1lb 12oz)	900g (2lb)
Butter (or margarine)	115g (4oz)	115g (4oz)	175g (6oz)	225g (8oz)	340g (12oz)	450g (1lb)	550g (1lb 4oz)	700g (1lb 8oz)	800g (1lb 12oz)	900g (2lb)
Eggs	2	2	3	4	6	8	10	12	14	16
Vanilla extract	½tsp	½tsp	1tsp	1tsp	2tsp	2tsp	3tsp	3tsp	1tbsp	1tbsp
Baking time	15–20mins		15–20mins		20–30mins		30–40mins		40–50mins	
Cocoa powder	30g (1oz)	30g (1oz)	60g (2oz)	90g (3oz)	115g (4oz)	145g (5oz)	175g (6oz)	200g (7oz)	225g (8oz)	260g (9oz)
Lemons	½	½	1	1	2	2	3	3	4	4
Dark brown sugar	115g (4oz)	115g (4oz)	175g (6oz)	225g (8oz)	340g (12oz)	450g (1lb)	550g (1lb 4oz)	700g (1lb 8oz)	800g (1lb 12oz)	900g (2lb)

Vanilla cupcakes

When making cupcakes, I use the same recipe as for the vanilla sponge cake but I cream the butter and sugar first before adding the rest of the ingredients. This helps to prevent the cupcake cases coming away from the cakes once baked.

Ingredients

175g (6oz) butter (or margarine)

175g (6oz) caster sugar

3 medium eggs

175g (6oz) self-raising flour

Makes 12

1   Preheat the oven to 180°C/160°C fan/350°F/gas mark 4.

2   Cream the butter (or margarine) and sugar together in an electric mixer.

3   Slowly add the eggs, then the flour and vanilla and mix until fully combined. Make sure you scrape the bowl with a spatula between mixing.

4   Place the cupcake cases in a muffin tin and spoon approximately 50ml (1¾fl oz) of mixture into each one. Bake in the oven for 20–25 minutes.

5   Once the cakes are baked and spring back to the touch, take them out of the tin immediately. Leave to cool before decorating.

top tip

If you are making mini cupcakes, you only need to fill each of the cases with 10ml (¼fl oz) of mixture. Reduce the baking time to 15–20 minutes.

Sponge cakes for projects

Cake Project	Bakeware	Butter/ margarine	Caster sugar	Self-raising flour	Eggs	Vanilla extract	Baking time
Rub-a-Dub-Dub Baby Shower Cake	10cm (4") round tin and 2 x 20.5cm (8") round tins	115g (4oz) 340g (12oz)	115g (4oz) 340g (12oz)	115g (4oz) 340g (12oz)	2 6	½tsp 2tsp	15–20mins 20–30mins
'Pitter Patter' Christening Cake	2 x 20.5cm (8") round tins	340g (12oz)	340g (12oz)	340g (12oz)	6	2tsp	20–30mins
'Bright as a Button' Birthday Cake	10cm (4") round tin and 2 x 20.5cm (8") round tins	115g (4oz) 340g (12oz)	115g (4oz) 340g (12oz)	115g (4oz) 340g (12oz)	2 6	½tsp 2tsp	15–20mins 20–30mins
Baby Elephant First Birthday Cake	Tiffin/crinoline tin or 15cm (6") round tin and 1.2l (2pt) pudding basin	285g (10oz) 115g (4oz) 175g (6oz)	285g (10oz) 115g (4oz) 175g (6oz)	285g (10oz) 115g (4oz) 175g (6oz)	5 2 3	2tsp ½tsp 1tsp	30–40mins 15–20mins 15–20mins
Toy Soldier Birthday Cake	10cm (4") square tin and 2 x 20.5cm (8") square tins	115g (4oz) 450g (1lb)	115g (4oz) 450g (1lb)	115g (4oz) 450g (1lb)	2 8	½tsp 2tsp	15–20mins 20–30mins
'What a Hoot!' Birthday Cake	10cm (4") round tin, 2 x 15cm (6") round tins and 2 x 20.5cm (8") round tins	115g (4oz) 175g (6oz) 340g (12oz)	115g (4oz) 175g (6oz) 340g (12oz)	115g (4oz) 175g (6oz) 340g (12oz)	2 3 6	½tsp 1tsp 2tsp	15–20mins 15–20mins 20–30mins
Crafted with Love Valentine's Cake	2 x 20.5cm (8") heart-shaped tins	340g (12oz)	340g (12oz)	340g (12oz)	6	2tsp	20–30mins
'Hoppy Easter' Cake	Tiffin/crinoline tin or 15cm (6") round tin and 1.2l (2pt) pudding basin	285g (10oz) 115g (4oz) 175g (6oz)	285g (10oz) 115g (4oz) 175g (6oz)	285g (10oz) 115g (4oz) 175g (6oz)	5 2 3	2tsp ½tsp 1tsp	30–40mins 15–20mins 15–20mins
First Pint 18th Birthday Cake	2 x 15cm (6") square tins	225g (8oz)	225g (8oz)	225g (8oz)	4	1tsp	15–20mins
Designer Handbag Cake*	20.5cm (8") square tin	340g (12oz)	340g (12oz)	340g (12oz)	6	2tsp	20–30mins
Pompom Wedding Cake	10cm (4") square tin, 2 x 15cm (6") square tins, 2 x 20.5cm (8") square tins and 2 x 25.5cm (10") square tins	115g (4oz) 225g (8oz) 450g (1lb) 700g (1lb 8oz)	115g (4oz) 225g (8oz) 450g (1lb) 700g (1lb 8oz)	115g (4oz) 225g (8oz) 450g (1lb) 700g (1lb 8oz)	2 4 8 12	½tsp 1tsp 2tsp 3tsp	15–20mins 15–20mins 20–30mins 30–40mins
Ruby Anniversary Cake	2 x 25.5cm (10") hexagonal tins	550g (1lb 4oz)	550g (1lb 4oz)	550g (1lb 4oz)	10	3tsp	30–40mins
12 cupcakes	12 cupcake cases and 12-hole muffin tin	175g (6oz)	175g (6oz)	175g (6oz)	3	2tsp	20–25mins
12 mini cupcakes	12 mini cupcake cases and baking tray	60g (2oz)	60g (2oz)	60g (2oz)	1	½tsp	15–20mins

*Cakes for carving should be made using a Madeira sponge cake recipe which is much firmer than a traditional sponge.
For the Designer Handbag Cake, add 175g (6oz) of plain flour to the vanilla sponge recipe along with the self-raising flour.

Please note that the Red-nosed Reindeer Cake project uses a fruit cake recipe. However, if you'd like to make this cake with sponge, follow the recipe on page 10.

Basic vanilla biscuits

Ingredients

200g (7oz) unsalted butter

200g (7oz) caster sugar

1tsp vanilla extract

1 egg, lightly beaten

400g (14oz) plain flour

Makes approximately 20–25

1   Place the butter, sugar and vanilla extract into an electric mixer and cream them together until well-combined and creamy. Avoid over-mixing as this will cause the biscuits to spread as they are baking.

2   Add the egg until well combined, then turn the mixer down to the lowest setting and add a little of the flour. Gradually add all the flour and mix until a dough is formed.

3   Preheat the oven to 190°C/170°C fan/375°F/gas mark 5.

4   Roll the dough out on a lightly floured surface to 5mm (¼") thick. Line a large baking tray with parchment paper, place the biscuit dough onto the tray and refrigerate for 30 minutes.

5   Cut out the biscuits using your chosen cutters. If you are using a template, place the template on the dough and cut around it with a sharp knife.

6   Place the cookies on two baking trays lined with parchment so they are not touching then bake in the oven for 10–15 minutes, depending on the size of the biscuits. The biscuits should be slightly brown around the edges when baked.

Crunchy gingerbread biscuits

Ingredients

185g (6½oz) unsalted butter

4tbsp golden syrup

2tbsp black treacle

150g (5¼oz) soft brown sugar

450g (1lb) plain flour

1tbsp ground ginger

1½tsp cinnamon

1tsp bicarbonate of soda

1tbsp milk

Makes approximately 25

1   Place the butter, golden syrup, treacle and sugar into a saucepan and heat gently until the sugar has dissolved and the butter melted. Leave to cool slightly.

2   Sieve the dry ingredients into a mixing bowl. Pour in the melted mixture and stir well. Add the milk to the mixture. Combine to make a dough, adding more milk if necessary.

3   Place the dough in a food-grade plastic bag and chill for 20 minutes in a refrigerator.

4   Preheat the oven to 190°C/170°C fan/375°F/gas mark 5.

5   Roll out the dough on a lightly floured surface to 5mm (¼") thick. Line a large baking tray with parchment paper, place the biscuit dough onto the tray and refrigerate for 30 minutes.

6   Cut out the biscuits using your chosen cutters. If you are using a template, place the template on the dough and cut around it with a sharp knife.

7   Place the cookies on baking trays lined with parchment paper then bake in the oven for 10–15 minutes, depending on the size of the biscuits.

Crisped rice cereal mix

This is ideal for making larger models for cakes as it is lighter than modelling paste or sugarpaste and won't cause the cake to collapse. I have used this mix to make the rubber duck on page 34 and the pint of beer on page 88.

Ingredients

100g (3½oz) marshmallows

25g (just over ¾oz) butter

90g (3oz) crisped rice cereal

Makes 175g–190g (6oz–6¾oz)

1   Place the marshmallows and butter into a saucepan and heat gently until melted. Stir well to avoid the mixture sticking.

2   Measure the rice cereal into a large mixing bowl, then pour the melted marshmallow mix over the cereal until it is all coated.

3   Leave to cool slightly before moulding it into the required shape.

top tip

If it is difficult to mould, dust your hands with icing sugar to stop the mixture sticking to them.

Chocolate truffles

Ingredients

½ tin condensed milk

30g (1oz) butter

100g (3½oz) milk chocolate

12 digestive biscuits

2tbsp desiccated coconut

Makes 25–30

1   Gently heat the condensed milk, butter and chocolate in a pan until melted.

2   Blitz the digestive biscuits in a food processor, or place them in a large food-grade plastic bag and crush them with a rolling pin.

3   Place the crushed biscuits in a large bowl and mix in the melted mixture and the coconut. Leave to cool slightly.

4   Take a teaspoonful of the mixture at a time and roll it into a ball with your hands. If you wish to coat the truffles, do this straight away. Allow to firm.

Macaroons

Ingredients

SK Instant Macaroon Mix

SK Quality Food Colour (QFC) Dusts of your choice

Vanilla buttercream (see page 18)

Makes 18

1   Preheat the oven to 130°C/120°C fan/250°F/gas mark ½.

2   Add a small amount of dust food colour if desired to 120g (4¼oz) of macaroon mix and combine well. Mix in 25ml (just over ¾fl oz) of hot, pre-boiled water that is approximately 45–50°C in temperature.

3   Mix for four minutes in the electric mixer using the beater attachment at medium speed, or until smooth.

4   Fit a large piping bag with a plain Savoy nozzle and fill with the macaroon mix. Pipe 18 2.5cm (1") discs onto a lined baking tray.

5   Place the first tray on top of a second baking tray and bake in the preheated oven for approximately 15–20 minutes. Once baked, allow them to cool on the tray.

6   Sandwich two macaroon halves together with a layer of buttercream coloured to match.

top tips

Use heavy-duty baking trays or stack two trays together, lined with baking parchment or re-usable baking liner, so that the macaroons don't cook too quickly.

It is best to make macaroons in the morning or evening, so the humidity in the air is less likely to cause problems with the mixture.

A very clean oven will perform better and improve results.

Fillings

Cake fillings bring flavour and moisture to a sponge cake and should complement the recipe. Preserves and buttercreams are the most popular choice for fillings, and ganache is often used in chocolate cakes. I prefer to cut my sponges into four layers, so there are two layers of preserve and a layer of buttercream in the middle.

Vanilla buttercream

Ingredients

250g (8¾oz) butter

300g (10½oz) icing sugar

1tsp vanilla extract

Makes 525g (1lb 2½oz) buttercream

1   Beat the butter in an electric mixer whilst gradually adding the icing sugar. Add the vanilla extract once all the icing sugar is combined.

2   Beat on a higher speed until the buttercream becomes light and fluffy.

This can be used straight away or stored in an airtight container in the fridge for up to three or four days. Buttercream that has been kept in the fridge will need to be brought up to room temperature or warmed slightly in order to be able to spread it easily. To freeze buttercream, seal in an airtight container; bring to room temperature and re-beat before use.

Flavour variations

Lemon: Add the zest of two lemons instead of the vanilla extract.

Chocolate: Add 125g (4½oz) of melted chocolate instead of the vanilla extract.

Toffee: Add 2tbsp of *dulce de leche* caramel to the buttercream instead of the vanilla extract.

Ganache

Ingredients

450g (1lb) double cream

500g (1lb 1¾oz) high-quality chocolate couverture (at least 53% cocoa solids)

Makes 850g–900g (1lb 14oz)

1   Pour the cream into a saucepan and slowly bring to the boil.

2   Place the chocolate in a large bowl and pour the boiled cream over the top.

3   Stir carefully until all the chocolate has melted and combined with the cream. Leave to cool.

4   Spoon the mixture into the bowl of an electric mixer and beat the ganache for 2–3 minutes to thicken. Avoid over-beating as this will cause the ganache to split.

If you don't need to use it immediately, cover the ganache and place in the fridge after step 3. When you are ready to use the ganache, bring it to room temperature and then re-beat in a mixer. The ganache can be kept in the fridge for up to a week.

top tip

If you would like to make a white chocolate ganache, follow the same method but only use half the amount of cream.

Basic Techniques

Good preparation is the key to a successful finished cake and the following techniques are invaluable if you want to create a special cake for any occasion.

Lining a cake tin

It is important to line your cake tin properly in order to achieve a well-formed cake that is easy to release. The following method can be used for any regular-shaped tin.

Edibles

White vegetable fat

SK Professional Food Colour Pen

Equipment

Cake tin

Baking parchment

Scissors

Round

1 Lightly grease the inside of a cake tin with white vegetable fat.

2 Place the cake tin onto some baking parchment and draw around it using a food colour pen.

3 Cut around the shape with scissors and place it in the base of the tin.

4 Cut out a strip of parchment paper that is long enough to fit around the circumference of the tin and as deep as the sides of the tin.

5 Place the strip around the inside of the tin, making sure the edge of the parchment paper is flush with the base of the tin.

Marzipanning a fruit cake

Edibles

Fruit cake (see recipe on page 9)

Marzipan (see page 24 for amount)

Apricot jam

Equipment

Serrated knife

Cake drums (boards)

Small spirit level

Marzipan spacers

Pastry brush

Cake smoothers

top tip

I would normally leave a marzipanned cake to dry overnight before covering it with sugarpaste – this gives the cake a firmer surface and a better finish.

1   Level the top of the fruit cake with a serrated knife and turn over onto a cake drum.

2   Place a spare cake drum on top of the cake and place the spirit level on it to ensure the cake is level.

3   Boil the apricot jam to make a glaze, then use a pastry brush to spread the warm apricot glaze over the fruit cake.

4   Roll a long, thin sausage of marzipan, wrap it around the base of the cake to fill the gap and trim to size. Fill any holes in the cake with small pieces of marzipan, if necessary.

5   Dust the work surface with icing sugar and knead the marzipan until smooth and pliable. Place spacers on either side and roll out the marzipan to the thickness of the spacers using a non-stick rolling pin. Turn the paste regularly to create an even circle of paste that is big enough to cover the cake.

6   Fold the marzipan over the rolling pin, lift and place over the top of the cake.

7   Use a smoother to smooth over the top of the cake first to prevent any air bubbles, then use your hands to smooth the marzipan down the sides of the cake.

8   Smooth down the sides of the cake with a smoother and trim away any excess marzipan from around the base of the cake with a palette knife.

9   Polish the top and sides of the cake with smoothers for a neat finish.

10   Brush the marzipanned cake with cooled, boiled water just before covering with sugarpaste in order for it to stick and seal.

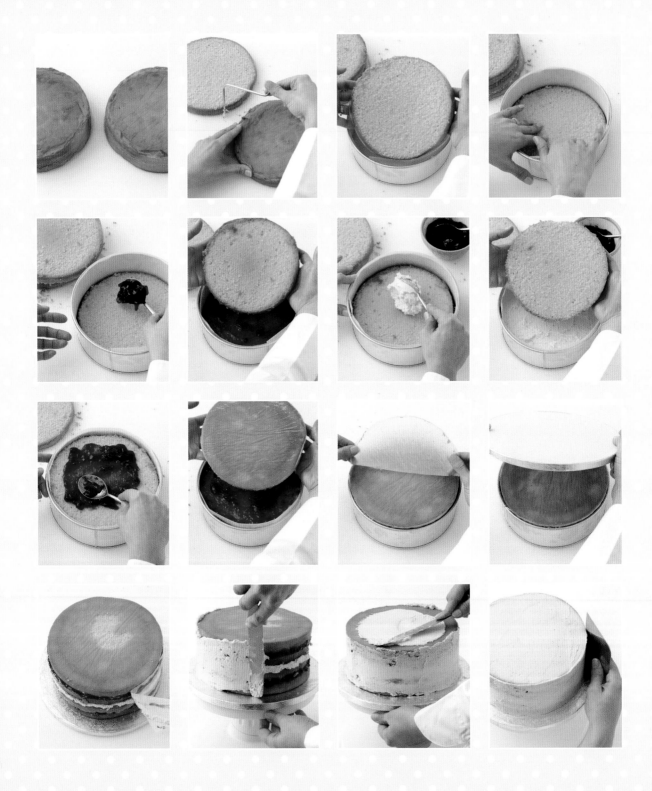

Preparing a sponge cake for covering

Edibles

2 x sponge cakes, with a sheet of baking parchment on the base

Jam

Buttercream

Equipment

Serrated knife or cake leveller

Baking parchment

Cake tin

Cake drum

Turntable

Palette knife

Side scraper

Small spirit level (optional)

1   Leave the baking parchment on the bottom of two sponges and cut each one into two equal layers using a cake leveller or a serrated knife.

2   Re-line one of the cake tins with baking parchment and place one of the bottom layers of cake into the tin with the parchment paper facing downwards: this will be the top of the cake.

3   Spread the cake with a thin layer of jam and place another layer on top. Press it down gently to ensure it is flat then spread with a layer of buttercream. Place the third layer on top, spread with jam then position the final layer on top, so the baking parchment faces upwards.

4   Place the cake in the fridge to chill for around 30 minutes.

5   Remove the cake from the fridge and remove the baking parchment from the top. Turn the cake out onto the required size cake drum and peel away the rest of the parchment.

6   Place the cake on a turntable and use a palette knife to spread a thin layer of buttercream over the surface of the cake: this will seal in the crumbs and help achieve a smooth finish. Pull a side scraper around the sides of the cake to make sure the surface is even.

7   Place in the fridge for 10 minutes to firm slightly.

top tip

To ensure your cake is level place a cake drum on top of the cake then place a spirit level on the drum: this is particularly important for stacked cakes.

Basic Techniques

23

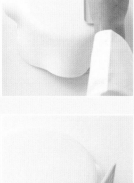

Covering a cake with sugarpaste

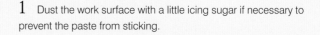

Edibles

Icing sugar in a shaker

Sugarpaste

Equipment

Marzipan spacers

Large non-stick rolling pin

Cake smoothers

Palette knife

1   Dust the work surface with a little icing sugar if necessary to prevent the paste from sticking.

2   Take the required amount of sugarpaste (see below) and knead it well until it is soft and pliable.

3   Place the spacers either side of the paste and use a large non-stick rolling pin to roll out the paste, turning regularly to give an even circle that is big enough to cover the cake.

4   Fold the sugarpaste over the rolling pin, lift and place over the top of the cake.

5   Use a cake smoother to smooth over the top of the cake first to prevent any air bubbles and then use your hands to smooth down the sides of the cake.

6   Smooth down the sides of the cake with a smoother and trim away any excess paste from around the base of the cake with a palette knife.

7   Polish the top and sides of the cake with smoothers for a neat finish.

CAKE SIZE	ROUND	SQUARE
10cm (4")	280g (9¾oz)	350g (12¼oz)
15cm (6")	450g (1lb)	570g (1lb 4oz)
20.5cm (8")	800g (1lb 12oz)	900g (2lb)
25.5cm (10")	1.13kg (2lb 8oz)	1.35kg (3lb)
30.5cm (12")	1.7kg (3lb 12oz)	1.81kg (4lb)
35.5cm (14")	1.81kg (4lb)	1.92kg (4lb 4oz)

Covering a cake drum (board)

A covered cake drum gives a neat finish and can enhance the cake design. Depending on the shape of the cake, there are two different ways to cover a cake drum.

Edibles

Icing sugar in a shaker
Sugarpaste

Equipment

Cake drum (board)
Large non-stick rolling pin
Palette knife
Cake smoother

Method 1

I would use this method for regular shaped cakes, e.g. round or square, where the cake has been iced on the cake drum.

1   Dampen the visible parts of the cake drum around the cake with a little cooled, boiled water.

2   Roll out a strip of sugarpaste to 3mm ($^1/_8$") thick on a work surface dusted with icing sugar. The strip should be wide enough and long enough to cover the visible board.

3   Cut a straight edge along one side of the strip and place it onto the cake drum with the cut edge against the base of the cake. Cut to size and smooth over the join at the back with your fingers.

4   Cut away any excess paste from around the edge with a palette knife and smooth over the cut edge with the palm of your hand or a cake smoother.

Method 2

I would use this method for novelty-shaped cakes, such as the Designer Handbag and 'Hoppy Easter' cakes in this book. The cake drum is covered completely and the iced cake is placed on top.

1   Dampen the cake drum with a little cooled, boiled water.

2   Roll out the sugarpaste to 3mm ($^1/_8$") thick on a work surface dusted with icing sugar.

3   Fold the rolled paste over the rolling pin, lift and place centrally over the dampened cake drum.

4   Smooth over the paste with a cake smoother, trim away any excess with a palette knife and smooth the edge with the palm of your hand or a cake smoother.

top tip

Leave the cake drum to dry overnight if you have time, before placing the cake on top.

Basic Techniques

Dowelling and stacking a tiered cake

You should always dowel cakes with two or more tiers to prevent them from sinking or toppling over. This may seem a daunting task to those who are new to cake decorating, but by following these simple steps you can achieve a stable stacked cake.

The biggest cake should always be placed on a cake drum for the base tier, and any other tiers need to be iced on double-thickness cake boards that are the same size as the cakes so they are not visible.

Edibles

Two or more iced cakes

SK Professional Food Colour Pen

A small amount of royal icing

Equipment

Plastic cake dowels (washed in hot, soapy water and dried)

Dowel template (available from any good sugarcraft supplier)

Craft knife

Spare cake board

Small spirit level

1   Place the dowel template centrally on top of the largest tier and use it to work out where the dowels need to be placed. Use the end of a dowel to mark on the position of four dowels, making sure they are within the diameter of the second tier cake.

2   Insert a dowel into the cake and use a food colour pen to mark it level with the top of the icing.

3   Remove the dowel and carefully score around the line with a sharp knife. Snap the dowel along the line.

4   Use the height of this dowel to cut three more dowels to size.

5   Insert all four dowels at the marks on the sugarpasted cake.

6   Place a spare cake board on top of the cake and position a small spirit level on it to ensure the dowels are level. If they are uneven, remove and cut them to the same size.

7   Spread a little royal icing over the centre of the dowelled cake with a palette knife and carefully place the next tier on top.

8   If you are stacking three or more tiers, repeat the process to dowel all the cakes excluding the top tier.

top tip

If you have time, leave the cakes overnight before stacking them as this gives the icing time to firm up slightly and makes stacking easier.

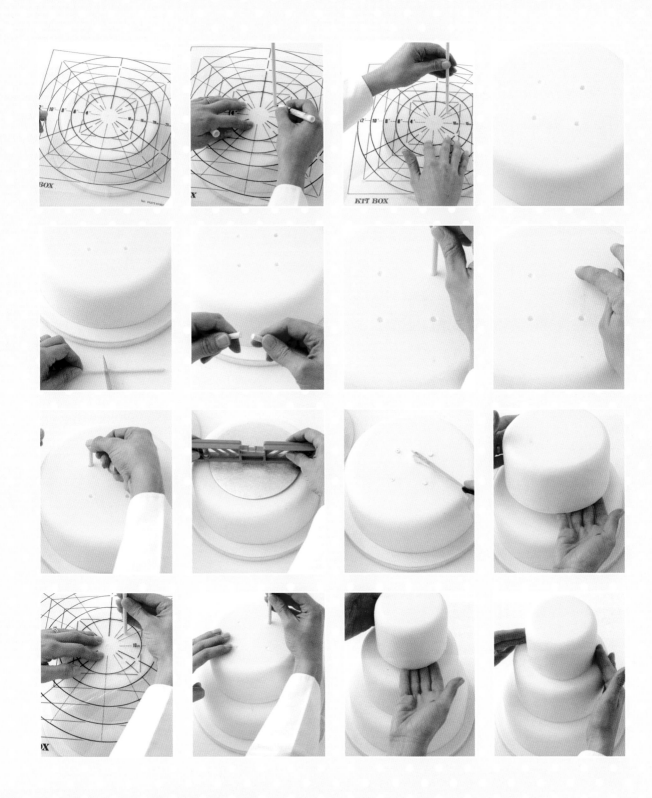

27

Icings and Pastes

Sugarpaste (rolled fondant)

Sugarpaste is an ideal covering for all cakes as it's very soft and pliable. Readymade sugarpaste is available in a wide variety of colours, but can also be coloured using paste food colours. Sugarpaste dries out when exposed to the air, so it is best to keep any spare paste or trimmings sealed in a food-grade plastic bag whilst you work.

Marzipan

This nut paste is traditionally used to cover and seal fruit cakes but can also be used on sponges. Covering a cake with a layer of marzipan then sugarpaste helps to give the cake a neater finish.

Flower paste (gum paste)

Flower paste is a ready-to-use paste that can be rolled out paper-thin without breaking and gives a smooth finish. I recommend using SK Sugar Florist Paste (SFP) which is widely available from sugarcraft suppliers (see page 128).

Modelling paste

Modelling paste can be made up of a mixture of sugarpaste and flower paste in equal parts, but you can also buy it readymade, e.g. SK Mexican Modelling Paste (MMP) and SK Sugar Dough which I use regularly in this book. This stronger paste is ideal for making models where you require the paste to hold its shape and dry quicker than sugarpaste.

Royal icing

Learning to work with royal icing is an essential skill in cake decorating. It is very versatile and can be used for icing cakes and cookies, piping inscriptions, making run-outs, stencilling and more. Royal icing can be bought readymade or in powder form, such as SK Instant Mix Royal Icing and SK Art-ice 2-in-1 Cookie Icing Mix, to which you just add water. If you are unable to get hold of these, then you can always make your own following the recipe below.

Recipe

Edibles

15g (½oz) dried egg albumen powder

75ml (2½fl oz) cooled, pre-boiled water

500g (1lb 2oz) icing sugar

Equipment

Large electric mixer

1   Place the egg albumen into a small bowl. Add the water and stir until dissolved. Leave to stand for at least 30 minutes.

2   Sieve the icing sugar into a bowl. Pour the egg mixture into the bowl of your mixer and gradually add the icing sugar, beating between each addition. Mix on a low speed until the icing is firm and forms stiff peaks.

3   Store the icing in an airtight container or in a bowl covered with a damp cloth. Royal icing will keep in the fridge in a sealed container for 4–5 days and you will need to re-beat it before use.

Consistencies

Soft-peak

Soft-peak consistency is achieved by adding a little cooled, pre-boiled water to the royal icing to make it softer and easier to pipe. To test the consistency, dip a palette knife into the icing, then lift it up. If the icing forms gentle peaks, it is at the correct consistency. Beat further if the icing does not form peaks. I use this consistency for piping decorative lines and outlines for iced cookies.

Run-out

Run-out royal icing has a runny, creamy consistency and is used to cover (or flood) areas with icing. To achieve this consistency, add a few drops of cold, pre-boiled water to the icing. To test the consistency, pick some icing up on a spoon, hold it over the bowl of icing and let it run off the spoon. The icing should sit for a few seconds before disappearing back into the rest of the icing. The consistency is important because if the icing is too thin it will run over the edge of cookies or run-out decorations; if it is too thick it will not settle and dry flat.

top tip

It is important that your utensils are extremely clean, as any grease will affect the consistency of the icing. To ensure you have no grease in your mixer, pour boiling water into the bowl to clean it thoroughly and remove any unwanted residue, then dry before use.

How to make a piping bag from baking parchment

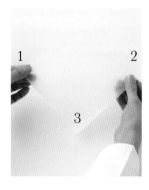

Paper piping bags and triangles can be bought readymade, but you can always make your own if you prefer.

Equipment

43cm (17") square of baking parchment

Sharp knife

1   Fold the parchment square in half corner-to-corner and cut through the fold with a sharp knife.

2   At this stage you will have two large triangles for making large piping bags. Fold in half and cut again if you want to make smaller piping bags.

3   Hold the triangle with the longest straight edge facing away from you. Hold onto point 1 with your left hand and bend point 2 inwards with your right hand towards your body at point 3.

4   Bring point 1 across and around the cone so that all the points meet at point 3.

5   Adjust by moving back and forth slightly until you get a sharp point at the tip of the cone. Fold all the points over with your left hand. Make a small cut at the fold and fold this over to secure the bag.

6   To fill, pick up a small amount of royal icing with a palette knife and place it in the bag. Pull the knife against the side of the bag as you remove it. Fill $^2/_3$ full with icing and fold down the top of the bag.

PROJECTS

Rub-a-Dub-Dub Baby Shower Cake

Brighten up a baby shower with this bath-time-inspired cake, complete with an adora-bubble rubber ducky. The polka dot design uses a quick and easy sugarpaste technique to add a playful twist to a plain tier. You can also create a complete party spread with the matching rubber ducky mini cupcakes and iced cookies.

Edibles

10cm and 20.5cm (4" and 8") round sponge cakes, filled and crumb-coated (see page 23)

1.35kg (3lb) SK Sugarpaste: 350g (12¼oz) Bridal White, 1kg (2lb 3¼oz) Sunshine Yellow

70g (2½oz) crisped rice cereal mix (see recipe on page 16)

1 pack each SK Sugar Florist Paste (SFP): Pale Blue, White

SK Quality Food Colour (QFC) Paste: Orange

SK Quality Food Colour (QFC) Lustre Dust: Pearl

SK Designer Metallic Lustre Dust Food Colour: Silver Sparkles

SK Professional Food Colour Pen: Black

SK Instant Mix Royal Icing

SK Edible Glue

Equipment

Basic equipment (see pages 6–7)

25.5cm (10") round cake drum (board)

10cm (4") round cake card

4 plastic cake dowels

Round cutters: 9mm (³/₈"), 2.5cm (1"), 3.5cm (1³/₈")

Piping nozzle: no. 2

70cm (27½") x 9mm (³/₈") width satin ribbon: pale blue

90cm (35½") x 15mm (⁵/₈") width satin ribbon: pale blue

Template (see page 121)

Cakes and cake drum

1   Position the 10cm (4") cake onto the corresponding cake card and the 20.5cm (8") cake centrally on the 25.5cm (10") cake drum. Cover the 20.5cm (8") cake and drum with Sunshine Yellow sugarpaste and the smaller cake with Bridal White sugarpaste (see pages 24–25).

2   Use a 2.6cm (1") round cutter to mark out evenly spaced circles around the 20.5cm (8") cake. Leave the cakes to dry overnight.

3   Insert four dowels into the 20.5cm (8") cake (see page 26) and use a little royal icing to secure the 10cm (4") cake centrally on top.

4   Roll out the remaining Bridal White sugarpaste thinly and cut out enough 2.5cm (1") circles to cover those marked on the cake. Carefully secure the white circles over the marks on the cake with edible glue and smooth down the edges to make them flush with the surface of the cake.

5   Secure the 9mm (³/₈") wide ribbon around the base of the cake with a little royal icing.

Rubber duck

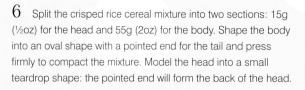

6 Split the crisped rice cereal mixture into two sections: 15g (½oz) for the head and 55g (2oz) for the body. Shape the body into an oval shape with a pointed end for the tail and press firmly to compact the mixture. Model the head into a small teardrop shape: the pointed end will form the back of the head.

7 Pinch a 5g (just under ¼oz) ball of Sunshine Yellow sugarpaste into a thick disc. Place the disc on the rounded end of the body and place the head on the sugarpaste. Use a Dresden tool to smooth down the paste between the head and the body.

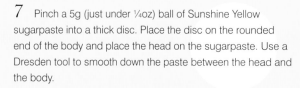

8 Use pinches of Sunshine Yellow sugarpaste to fill in any gaps or indents in the head and body. Cover the whole duck with pieces of paste and smooth over with your hands to create an even shape. Leave to dry for a couple of hours.

9 Roll out 100g (3½oz) of Sunshine Yellow sugarpaste to 3mm (⅛") thick then brush some clear alcohol over the surface of the duck. Fold the rolled-out sugarpaste over a small rolling pin and lay it over the top of the duck, smoothing down from the top. Shape the paste around the head and down over the body, then use a Dresden tool to push the paste into the neck.

10 Shape a 2g (¹⁄₁₆oz) ball of Sunshine Yellow sugarpaste into a teardrop, make two cuts into the thinner end and roll each section into a point. Lay the tuft on top of the head so that the pointed ends are facing the front, then use a Dresden tool to smooth over the joins and secure it in place.

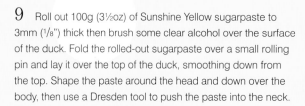

11 Colour 12g (½oz) of White SFP with Orange paste food colour, then roll out the paste thinly and cut out two 3.5cm (1⅜") circles with a cutter. Press a smaller 2.5cm (1") round cutter into one of the circles to indent the paste, ensuring not to cut through it. Use a 3.5cm (1⅜") cutter to cut away the top of both circles to make them crescent-shaped for the beak. Brush a little edible glue along the edge of each crescent, then stick the plain piece on top of the indented piece and secure the edges. Open up the beak slightly and attach to the front of the head with edible glue.

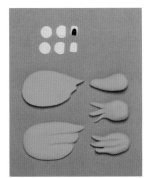

12 Roll out a small amount of White SFP and cut out two 9mm (³/₈") circles. Cut away the rounded edges from the sides and bottom of each circle to make the eyes. Use a Black food colour pen to draw the pupil on each eye and a touch of edible glue to attach the eyes just above the beak.

13 Roll out 10g (¼oz) of Sunshine Yellow sugarpaste to a 3mm (¹/₈") thickness, use the template and a craft knife to cut out the first wing, then turn the template over and cut out the second wing. Smooth around the edges, then mark two feather lines across each wing with a Dresden tool. Attach to either side of the duck's body with edible glue.

Bubbles

14 Take 50g (1¾oz) of Pale Blue SFP and pinch out approximately 60 pea-sized balls. Place them all into a food-grade plastic bag and add approximately ½tsp of Silver Sparkles dust food colour and ½tsp of Pearl lustre dust. Shake the bag well to coat all the balls in dust. Tip them out into a sieve to remove any excess dust then place on a piece of kitchen paper.

15 Place the duck onto the 10cm (4") cake and secure in place with a little royal icing. Fit a piping bag with a no. 2 nozzle and fill ²/₃ with white royal icing. Secure one bubble at a time around the base of the duck with a dot of royal icing. Attach a few of the bubbles around the bottom of the 10cm (4") cake to finish.

16 Attach the 15mm (⁵/₈") wide pale blue ribbon around the edge of the cake drum with a non-toxic glue stick, being careful that the glue does not come into contact with the cake.

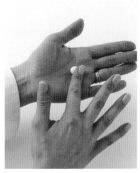

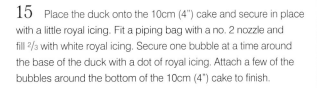

Ducky Mini Cupcakes

Edibles

20 mini cupcakes, baked in SK Mini Dotty Cupcake Cases: Yellow (see recipe on pages 12–13)

Apricot glaze (see page 20)

100g (3½oz) SK Sugarpaste: Lullaby Blue

1 pack each SK Sugar Dough: Orange, Yellow

SK Professional Food Colour Pen: Black

Equipment

Basic equipment (see pages 6–7)

3.5cm (1³/8") round cutter

Texture mat: bubbles

Makes 20

1   Roll out the Lullaby Blue sugarpaste to a 3mm (¹/8") thickness, place the texture mat onto the paste and gently roll over the mat with a small rolling pin to emboss the pattern. Remove the mat and cut out 20 x 3.5cm (1³/8") circles of paste with the cutter.

2   Brush the top of the cupcakes with a little apricot jam or buttercream and place the circles of paste on top. Smooth down the edges slightly on each one and set aside to dry.

3   Shape a small ball of Yellow Sugar Dough into a pointed teardrop for the duck's body and roll a smaller ball for the head, then secure the head to the body with edible glue.

4   Roll out a small amount of Orange Sugar Dough thinly and cut out a 4mm (³/16") square for the beak. Place the back of the craft knife from corner to corner and fold the paste over. Attach to the head with edible glue. Mark two dots for the eyes with a Black food pen. Repeat to make 19 more small ducks.

5   To finish, secure one duck on top of each cupcake with edible glue.

Ducky Cookies

Edibles

25 basic vanilla biscuits (see recipe on page 15)

Apricot glaze (see page 20)

600g (1lb 5¼oz) SK Sugarpaste: Sunshine Yellow

1 pack each SK Sugar Dough: Orange, White

SK Professional Food Colour Pen: Black

Small amount of SK Instant Mix Royal Icing

Equipment

Basic equipment (see pages 6–7)

SK Ducky Cookie Cutter

Piping nozzles: nos. 1.5, 2

1.2cm (³/₈") round cutter

Template (see page 121)

Makes 25

1   Make the biscuit dough following the recipe on page 15, cut out 25 duck shapes using the cookie cutter and bake according to the recipe instructions. Leave to cool.

2   Brush each of the cookies with cooled, boiled apricot glaze. Roll out the Sunshine Yellow sugarpaste to a 3mm (¹/₈") thickness and cut out 25 ducks using the cookie cutter. Place a piece of paste onto each cookie and smooth over the edges. Cut away the beak part of each duck with a craft knife.

3   Roll out a small amount of Orange Sugar Dough to 3mm (¹/₈") thick and use the beak part of the cookie cutter to cut out 25 orange beaks. Attach the beaks to the cookies with edible glue.

4   Roll out a little White Sugar Dough and cut out 25 x 1.2cm (³/₈") circles of paste for the eyes. Cut away the rounded edges from the sides and bottom of each circle to make the eye shape. Attach an eye to each duck and mark on the pupil with a Black food colour pen.

5   Fit a piping bag with a no. 1.5 nozzle and fill ²/₃ with white royal icing. Mark out the word 'Baby' onto each cookie using a scribing tool and the template then pipe over the lines to finish.

'Pitter Patter' Christening Cake

Celebrate a new addition to the family with a beautiful cake that is so simple to make. Stencilling is a quick and easy way to create a detailed design and has been used here to form the focal point of the cake top.

Edibles

20.5cm (8") round sponge cake, filled and crumb-coated (see page 23)

1kg (2lb 3¼oz) SK Sugarpaste: Bridal White

SK Quality Food Colour (QFC) Dust: Blue

125g (4½oz) SK Instant Mix Royal Icing

Equipment

Basic equipment (see pages 6–7)

25.5cm (10") round cake drum (board)

Footprints stencil

Piping nozzles: nos. 1.5, 2

Food-grade plastic syringe

83cm (32½") x 15mm (⅝") width satin ribbon: baby blue

92cm (1yd) x 39mm (1½") width sheer ribbon: baby blue striped

Templates (see page 121)

1   Position the cake centrally on the cake drum and cover with Bridal White sugarpaste (see pages 24–25). Leave to dry overnight.

2   Make up 125g (4½oz) of royal icing to stiff-peak consistency by adding 18ml (1tbsp) of cooled, pre-boiled water and mix following the instructions on the packet. Fit a small paper piping bag with a no. 2 nozzle and fill ⅔ with the icing. Place the remaining icing into a bowl and cover with a clean, damp cloth to prevent it from drying out.

3   Place the cake on a turntable. Starting at the back of the cake, continuously pipe lots of small teardrops to create a snail-trail border around the base.

4   Colour the remaining royal icing with a little Blue dust food colour and add 1.25ml (¼tsp) of cooled, boiled water to loosen the consistency of the icing slightly.

5   Position the footprint stencil in the centre of the cake, take a little blue royal icing on a small palette knife and spread the icing over the stencil, starting at the edge and working inwards. Once the footprints are covered, pull the palette knife across the whole stencil in one movement to remove any excess icing

and leave an even layer. Carefully lift the stencil up to remove it, then leave to dry.

6   Once the footprints have dried, copy the words 'Pitter' and 'Patter' onto a piece of greaseproof paper to make the templates. Place the templates onto the cake one at a time and use a scribing needle to mark out the inscription on the cake. When you lift off the paper, you will be left with guidelines that mark out where you need to pipe.

7   Fit a small piping bag with a no. 1.5 nozzle and fill $^2/_3$ with blue royal icing. Carefully pipe over the marks in the icing, starting with 'Pitter…' at the top and then '…Patter' underneath the footprints. Leave to dry.

8   Wrap the wide sheer ribbon around the cake and tie it at the front in a neat bow. Secure the narrow baby blue ribbon around the edge of the cake drum using a non-toxic glue stick, being careful that the glue does not come into contact with the cake.

top tip

I use a food-grade plastic syringe to measure out small amounts of water: this allows you to be very accurate and only add small drops at a time.

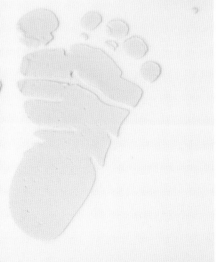

Footprint Cookies

Edibles

24 basic vanilla biscuits (see recipe on page 15)

500g (1lb 1¾oz) bag of SK Instant Mix Royal Icing

SK Quality Food Colour (QFC) Dust: Blue

Equipment

Basic equipment (see pages 6–7)

SK Footprint Cookie Cutter

Piping nozzles: nos. 0, 2, 4

Makes 24

1   Make the biscuit dough following the recipe on page 15 and cut out 24 footprint shapes using the cookie cutter. Flip the cutter to make 12 left feet and 12 right feet. Bake according to the recipe instructions (see page 15).

2   Make up some royal icing to soft-peak consistency following the packet instructions. Colour 450g (1lb) of the icing using a little Blue dust food colour to make it pale blue.

3   Fit a small paper piping bag with a no. 2 nozzle and fill ²/₃ with pale blue icing. Pipe a circle outline around each big toe, then pipe a separate outline around the sole of the foot. Remember to reverse the outline for the right and left feet. Leave the outlines to dry.

4   Fit another piping bag with a no. 4 nozzle, let down the remaining icing by adding a few drops of water and fill the bag ²/₃ full with the icing. Pressure-pipe a dot of pale blue icing on each of the remaining four toes by squeezing the bag with the nozzle on the surface.

5   Using the same bag of runnier icing as in step 4, work from the edge of each outline in towards the middle to flood inside the outline of the foot, then repeat for the big toe. Leave to dry completely in a warm, dry atmosphere.

6   Fit another paper piping bag with a no. 0 nozzle and fill with the remaining white icing. Pipe 'Pitter..' freehand onto the left feet and 'Patter..' onto the right feet and leave to dry.

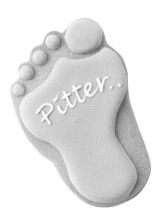

'Bright as a Button' Birthday Cake

Little ones will love this cute and colourful birthday cake, complete with its own friendly rag doll. As a busy baker, the specially designed silicone sugarcraft moulds used here allow you to make lots of detailed decorations in no time at all.

Edibles

10cm and 20.5cm (4" and 8") round sponge cakes, filled and crumb-coated (see page 23)

1.2kg (2lb 10¼oz) SK Sugarpaste: 300g (10½oz) Ballerina Pink, 600g (1lb 5¼oz) Bridal Rose, 300g (10½oz) Vintage Ivory

1 pack each SK Sugar Dough: Green, Light Pink, Soft Beige, White, Yellow

1 pack SK Sugar Florist Paste (SFP): Cream

SK Professional Dust Food Colour: Bulrush (dark brown)

Small amount of SK Instant Mix Royal Icing

SK Edible Glue

Clear alcohol, e.g. gin or vodka

Equipment

Basic equipment (see pages 6–7)

25.5cm (10") round cake drum (board)

10cm (4") round cake card

3 plastic cake dowels

Garrett frill cutter (PME)

Square cutters: 1.6cm (⅝"), 2cm (¾")

Piping nozzles: nos. 0, 1

Round cutter: 7mm (¼") (KB)

SK Great Impressions 7-in-1 Button Mould

Funky alphabet upper and lower case cutters (FMM)

90cm (35") x 15mm (⅝") width grosgrain ribbon: ivory stitched with pink thread

Template (see page 121)

Cakes and drum

1 Place the 10cm (4") cake onto the corresponding cake card and the 20.5cm (8") cake centrally on the 25.5cm (10") cake drum.

2 Mix together the Ballerina Pink and Bridal Rose sugarpaste to make a baby pink colour. Cover the 20.5cm (8") cake and cake drum with baby pink sugarpaste and the 10cm (4") cake with Vintage Ivory sugarpaste (see pages 24–25). Leave both cakes to dry overnight.

3 Once the cakes are dry, insert three dowels towards the back of the 20.5cm (8") cake (see pages 26–27). Position the 10cm (4") cake over the dowels so it sits towards the back of the larger cake and use a dab of royal icing to secure in place.

Buttons

4 Mix together 40g (1½oz) of Light Pink Sugar Dough with 30g (1oz) of White Sugar Dough to make a pale pink paste. Mix 15g (½oz) of Green Sugar Dough with 30g (1oz) of Yellow

Sugar Dough and 105g (3¾oz) of White Sugar Dough to make a light green paste. Mix 40g (1½oz) of Vintage Ivory sugarpaste with 20g (¾oz) of Cream SFP and place all the paste in food-grade plastic bags to prevent them from drying out.

5   Dust the whole button mould with a little cornflour in a dusting bag. Push pea-sized pieces of paste one at a time into one of the button shapes. Once you have filled a shape, use a palette knife to trim away any excess paste from the back of the button. Repeat these steps until you have made all the buttons in the mould, turn the whole mould over and gently tap with a small rolling pin to release the paste.

6   Use the mould to make the required number of buttons from the pink, cream and green paste as shown on the chart (see below). Leave the buttons to dry and brush with clear alcohol to remove any cornflour from the paste.

7   Make up a small amount of royal icing and colour it dark brown with a little Bulrush dust food colour. Fit a small paper piping bag with a no. 0 nozzle, fill ⅔ with brown royal icing and pipe small lines between the holes of each button to achieve a stitched effect.

Rag doll

8   To make the doll's body, take 48g (1¾oz) of Soft Beige Sugar Dough and shape it into a cone that is approximately 5.5cm (2¼") long. Push a 7cm (2¾") length of dried spagetti into the top of the body, leaving a small piece sticking out. Take another 40g (1½oz) of Soft Beige Sugar Dough and roll it in your palms to make an oval shape for the head.

9   Divide 13g (½oz) of Soft Beige Sugar Dough into two equal pieces for the legs. Roll each piece of paste into a sausage,

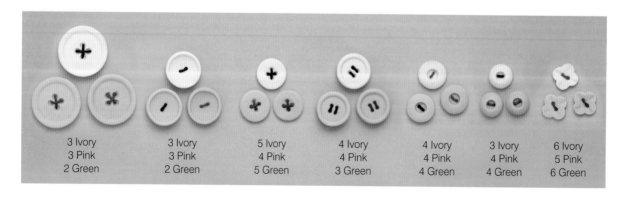

3 Ivory	3 Ivory	5 Ivory	4 Ivory	4 Ivory	3 Ivory	6 Ivory
3 Pink	3 Pink	4 Pink	4 Pink	4 Pink	4 Pink	5 Pink
2 Green	2 Green	5 Green	3 Green	4 Green	4 Green	6 Green

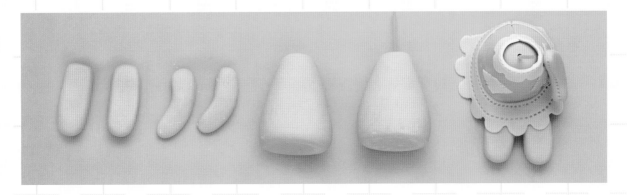

then flatten the top and sides of each leg to shape. Use a quilting tool to mark seams around each leg and attach the top of each leg to the base of the body with a little edible glue.

10   Roll out some pale pink paste thinly and cut out the dress shape with a craft knife following the template on page 121.

11   Fit the Garrett frill cutter with the largest central circle and roll out a small amount of light green paste. Place the cutter on the paste and cut out a frill ring. Make a cut in the ring and position the frill around the bottom of the dress. Secure in place with a little edible glue and use a quilting tool to make two seam lines along the frill.

12   Cut a 2cm (¾") square out of the remaining circle of paste and attach it to the front of the dress with a little edible glue. Use a Dresden tool to mark two lines across each side of the square so the patch looks like it has been stitched to the dress.

13   Roll out a small amount of cream paste, cut out another Garrett frill ring of the same size and cut out a section from the ring that fits across the top of the dress. Attach the frill to the dress and use the quilting tool to mark a seam around the top of the collar. Cut a 1.6cm (⅝") square from the leftover paste, attach the square to the front of the dress and mark two lines as for the first patch.

14   Paint a line of edible glue down the back of the doll, wrap the dress around the body and stick it down at the back. Glue three small buttons down the back of the dress to hide the join.

15   Divide 7g (¼oz) of Soft Beige Sugar Dough into two equal pieces, roll the paste into sausages and flatten them slightly to make the arms. Round off the ends and bend each arm a little at the elbow. Run a quilting tool around the sides to make a seam line, then attach the top of each arm to the sides of the body with edible glue.

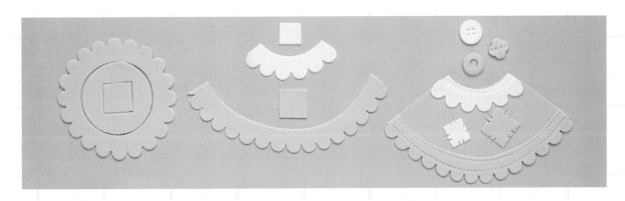

16 Gently push the head down onto the spaghetti and secure in place with a little edible glue.

17 Thinly roll out a small amount of Light Pink Sugar Dough and cut out two 7mm (¼") circles for the cheeks using the round cutter. Use edible glue to attach the cheeks to either side of the doll's face.

18 Roll out a small amount of cream modelling paste, cut out another two 7mm (¼") circles and glue to the face for the eyes.

19 For the hair, take 8g (¼oz) of both Light Pink and light green Sugar Dough and another 8g (¼oz) of cream paste. Roll each piece out very thinly and then cut five 1cm (⅜") wide strips in varying sizes from the Light Pink paste, seven from the light green paste and five from the cream paste. The strips should be between 3cm (1⅛") and 6cm (2⅜") long. Run the quilting tool along the edges of each strip and finish the ends with either a diagonal cut or a 'V'-shaped cut to represent ribbons.

20 Attach two green 6cm (2⅜") ribbons to either side of the head with edible glue. Secure more of the longer strips around the back of the head and cut them to size with a craft knife. Overlap with shorter ribbons of paste and glue two small buttons at the join.

21 Use the brown royal icing and a no. 0 nozzle to pipe a cross over each eye. Fit another paper piping bag with a no. 1 nozzle and fill ⅔ with white royal icing. Pipe a white line across the face for the smile.

Finishing touches

22 Roll out a small amount of light green Sugar Dough into a long strip that is approximately 2mm (1/16") thick. Use a sharp knife to cut out a strip that is 1cm wide x 47cm long (3/8" x 18½"). Run the quilting tool along the edges and cut each end at an angle.

23 Wrap the ribbon of paste around the base of the 10cm (4") ivory cake, making sure that the ends overlap towards the right-hand side at the front of the cake. Secure in place with a little edible glue and attach a pink button at the point where the ends cross over.

24 Use a no. 1 nozzle to pipe a little dot of white royal icing onto the back of each button and secure randomly around the base of the 20.5cm (8") cake.

25 Roll out the leftover Sugar Dough thinly and use the alphabet cutters to cut out your chosen name. Use a scribing tool to release the letters from the cutters. Attach in place on top of the base tier using edible glue.

26 Attach the ivory ribbon around the edge of the cake drum with a non-toxic glue stick, being careful that the glue does not come in contact with the cake.

'Bright as a Button' Cupcakes

Edibles

12 cupcakes baked in SK Dotty Cupcake Cases: Pink (see recipe on page 12)

350g (12¼oz) vanilla buttercream (see page 18)

SK Sugar Dough: Green, Pale Pink, White, Yellow

Small amount of SK Instant Mix Royal Icing

SK Professional Dust Food Colour: Bulrush (dark brown)

Equipment

Basic equipment (see pages 6–7)

Large piping bag

Large star nozzle

Makes 12

1 Bake 12 cupcakes in SK Pink Dotty Cupcake cases following the recipe on page 12 and leave to cool.

2 Make several buttons in the same way as for the main cake, using each colour of Sugar Dough (see page 44). Leave to dry slightly on a board dusted with icing sugar, then brush with clear alcohol to remove any excess cornflour. Pipe on the stitches using Bulrush-coloured royal icing (see page 44).

3 Fit a large piping bag with a large star nozzle, fill with vanilla buttercream and start piping around the outside edge of each cupcake. Pipe in towards the middle to finish the swirl.

4 Decorate each cupcake with three buttons while the buttercream is still soft.

Baby Elephant First Birthday Cake

Elephants are a popular theme for young children's nurseries and toys and I was inspired to make this cake for the arrival of my first nephew. The cake is baked in a tiffin tin and the head is made of crisped rice cereal mix so you can easily create the rounded, cuddly shape of the elephant. This cute cake is sure to be a hit with little ones and grown-ups alike, making it a great choice for a first birthday party.

Edibles

Sponge cake, baked in a tiffin tin (see page 13)

150g (5¼oz) buttercream (see page 18)

Two quantities of crisped rice cereal mix (see page 16)

SK Sugarpaste: 150g (5¼oz) Bridal Rose, 500g (1lb 1¾oz) Bridal White, 1kg (2lb 3¼oz) Dove Grey, 150g (5¼oz) Iced Mint, 1kg (2lb 3¼oz) Lullaby Blue, 50g (1¾oz) Sunshine Yellow

5g (just under ¼oz) SK Sugar Dough: Black

SK Quality Food Colour (QFC) Paste: Blue

SK Cellulose Gum (CMC)

SK Edible Glue

Equipment

30.5cm (12") round cake drum

Plastic dowel rod

Round cutters: 9mm (³/₈"), 1.3cm (½"), 1.5cm (⁵/₈"), 3.5cm (1³/₈")

Piping nozzle: no. 4

Polystyrene cone: 14cm (5½") high

80cm x 4cm (31½" x 1½") width sheer ribbon: yellow gingham

1m x 15mm (39" x ½") width sheer ribbon: yellow gingham

Templates (see page 122)

Cakes and cake drum

1   Cover the cake drum with Bridal White sugarpaste (see page 25).

2   Place the cake onto a spare cake drum and use a sharp knife to neaten the bottom of the cake, carving inwards slightly to round off the base. Carve away a small section of sponge from the front of the top of the cake, then crumb-coat it (see page 23).

3   Mix all the Dove Grey sugarpaste with all the Lullaby Blue sugarpaste to make a light blue colour. Roll out 1kg (2lb 3¼oz) of the paste to a thickness of 6mm (¹/₃") and cover the cake all in one go. Use a Dresden tool make an arc shape across the tummy.

4   Push a plastic dowel down into the centre of the body, leaving 7cm (2¾") sticking out of the top.

Head

5   Work the crisped rice cereal mix into a large ball for the head. Shape the top to make it slightly narrower, then leave to dry.

6 Make a hole in the centre of the base of the head with a plastic dowel. Take 130g (4½oz) of Bridal White sugarpaste and use a little at a time to fill in any dents in the head to give it a smooth surface.

7 Roll a piece of Bridal White sugarpaste into a long sausage shape that tapers at either end. Attach this to the face for the mouth and smooth down the paste at the edges to secure.

8 Roll out 300g (10½oz) of light blue paste to a thickness of 3mm (⅛") and cover the head, smoothing from the top down. Trim around the bottom and shape around the mouth. Use a Dresden tool to mark two arcs for the cheeks.

9 Using the eye template and a craft knife, cut away two circles of paste from the face to leave sockets for the whites of the eyes. Roll out 10g (¼oz) of Bridal White sugarpaste to a thickness of 6mm (⅓") and cut out two eyes using the template. Secure the whites into the gaps using edible glue.

10 Roll out a small amount of light blue paste thinly and cut out one of the eye shapes. Make two curved cuts down the paste to split it into three pieces. Attach each side piece above the eyes to make the eyelids.

11 Colour a small pea-sized ball of Bridal White sugarpaste with Blue paste food colour to make a mid-blue colour. Roll it out thinly and cut out two 1.5cm (⅝") circles of paste. Roll out a small amount of Black Sugar Dough and cut out two 1.3cm (½") circles of paste. Attach these on top of the light blue circles with edible glue, then stick them onto the whites of the eyes. Roll out a tiny amount of Bridal White sugarpaste, cut out two very small circles of paste using a no. 4 piping nozzle and attach to the eyes.

12 Add ½tsp of CMC to 180g (6¼oz) of light blue sugarpaste and knead well. Roll the sugarpaste into a thick sausage shape making it thickest at one end. Cut the wider end at an angle so that it will sit flush on the face, then bend the end of the trunk up to the right. Push a paintbrush into the end of trunk to shape it.

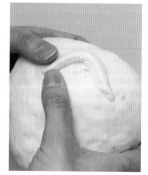

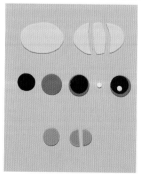

13 Mark horizontal lines across the trunk using a Dresden tool. Attach the trunk to the centre of the face using edible glue and smooth over the join. Hold in place for a few minutes until it is secure.

Legs

14 Knead 1tsp of CMC into 660g (1lb 7¼oz) of light blue sugarpaste, then split it into four equal pieces and keep them tightly sealed in a food-grade plastic bag. Take one piece at a time and model each into a thick leg shape, making them wider at the base. For the two back legs, cut the thinner end at a slight angle so it will fit around the bottom of the body. Attach to the front of the elephant with edible glue.

15 Make the two front legs in the same way, but cut the paste at a greater angle on the thinner end so they sit flush to the body. Roll out 10g (¼oz) of Bridal Rose sugarpaste thinly and cut out four 3.5cm (1⅜") circles. Attach one to the base of each leg with edible glue. Secure the front legs ¾ of the way up the body so the feet are resting on the back legs.

16 Add a little more Blue paste colour to a small amount of the light blue paste to make a slightly darker shade. Roll out the paste thinly, cut out ten 1.3cm (½") circles and cut each one in half using a craft knife. Attach five halves around the base of each leg for the toes.

Ears

17 Roll out 100g (3½oz) of Bridal Rose sugarpaste thinly. Use the template to cut out two inner ear shapes from the paste and set to one side.

18 Add 1tsp of CMC to 200g (7oz) of light blue paste and roll it out to a thickness of 3mm (⅛"), making the paste thinner on one side. Place the template on the paste so that the straight edge is on the thicker side (this edge will be attached to the head). Cut out the ear using a craft knife, smooth the edges with your fingers and attach the pink inner ear in the centre. Set to one side to firm up slightly, then repeat to make the other ear.

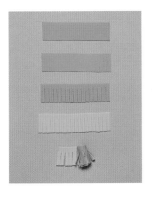

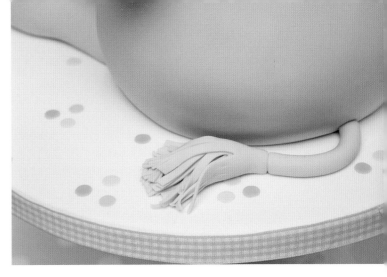

19 Attach the head to the top of the body with edible glue, filling any gaps between them with pieces of light blue paste.

20 Attach the ears to the sides of the head one at a time, using edible glue to secure them in place. Place a folded piece of kitchen paper into each ear to help shape them and hold the ear in place for a few minutes until secure.

Hat

21 Knead ½tsp of CMC into 100g (3½oz) of Iced Mint sugarpaste then roll it out to approximately 2mm (¹/₁₆") thick. Cut out the hat following the template and dust the back of the paste with icing sugar. Wrap it around the cone former, securing the edges together at the back with a little edible glue. Set aside to dry.

22 Thinly roll out a small amount of Bridal Rose, Bridal White and Sunshine Yellow sugarpaste. Cut out several circles of each colour using the 9mm (³/₈") round cutter. Attach the circles to the hat in groups of three, using a little edible glue to secure them in place.

top tip

If you don't have a polystyrene cone former you could make one using the hat template and a piece of cardboard.

23 For the brim, roll out a small amount of Sunshine Yellow sugarpaste into a long, thin strip and cut it to 1cm (³/₈") wide. Wrap this around the bottom of the hat, securing with edible glue.

24 Roll out 10g (¼oz) of Sunshine Yellow and 10g (¼oz) of Bridal Rose sugarpaste thinly and cut each piece into a 2.5cm x 10cm (1" x 4") rectangle. Use a craft knife or a small pair of scissors to make cuts ¾ of the way down the paste and approximately 5mm (¼") apart. Stick the yellow paste on top of the pink using edible glue. Roll the paste up tightly from one end and secure with edible glue. Attach to the top of the hat and let the paste pieces fall naturally.

25 Once fully dry, brush edible glue around the base of the hat and attach it to the head at a slight angle.

Tail

26 Roll 6g (just under ¼oz) of light blue paste into a thin sausage that is approximately 7cm (2¾) long, then attach it to the back of the elephant with edible glue.

27 Roll out 24g (just over ¾oz) of light blue paste into a fine 5cm x 10cm (2" x 4") rectangle. Cut down into the paste, leaving a 1cm (³/₈") strip across the bottom. Roll the paste up tightly and shape the bottom to make it the same size as the end of the tail. Trim and attach to the end of the tail.

Finishing touches

28 Roll out a small amount of Bridal Rose, Iced Mint and Sunshine Yellow sugarpaste thinly. Cut out several circles of each colour using the 9mm (³/₈") round cutter. Attach randomly around the covered cake drum with a little edible glue.

29 Tie the 4cm width (1½") sheer yellow gingham ribbon around the elephant's neck, secure with a bow towards the left side and trim the ends at an angle.

30 Attach the 15mm (½") yellow gingham ribbon around the edge of the cake drum with a non-toxic glue stick, being careful that the glue does not come into contact with the cake.

First Birthday Cupcakes

Edibles

12 cupcakes baked in SK Colour Block Cupcake Cases: Deep Pink, Lemon Yellow, Wheatgrass Green (see page 12)

150g (5¼oz) buttercream (see page 18)

SK Sugarpaste: 50g (1¾oz) Bridal Rose, 300g (10½oz) Bridal White, 25g (just over ¾oz) Iced Mint, 50g (1¾oz) Sunshine Yellow

SK Edible Glue

SK Cellulose Gum (CMC)

Equipment

Basic equipment (see pages 6–7)

7cm (2¾") round cutter

Piping nozzle: no. 4

Domed formers, e.g. food-grade plastic cupcake domes

Template (see page 122)

Makes 12

1 Roll out the Bridal White sugarpaste to approximately 2mm (¹/₁₆") thick. Cut out 12 circles of paste using the 7cm (2¾") round cutter and set them to one side.

2 Roll out the Bridal Rose and the Sunshine Yellow sugarpaste thinly, then use the template and a craft knife to cut out six pink and six yellow fondant shapes. Place these centrally on top of the white circles and smooth over with your hands. Place the circles over cupcake domes or an alternative domed former, and leave to dry.

3 Fill a sugar shaper with a small amount of Iced Mint sugarpaste. Fit with the large rope disc and extrude a length of paste. Cut it into 3cm (1⅛") lengths, hold the ends of each length and twist them to create the candle shape. Leave them to dry. Pinch out 12 small balls of Bridal White sugarpaste, flatten them between your finger and thumb and push a green twisted candle into each one.

4 For the flames, take a pea-sized ball of Sunshine Yellow sugarpaste and roll it into a point at one end. Bend it in the middle slightly and attach it to the top of the candle with a little edible glue. Secure to the centre of the sugarpaste topping.

5 Thinly roll out a small amount of Bridal Rose, Bridal White, Iced Mint and Sunshine Yellow sugarpaste. Using the end of a no. 4 piping nozzle, cut out several tiny circles of paste and attach them in groups of three over the sugarpaste covering.

6 Pipe a small dome of buttercream in the centre of each cupcake and place the sugarpaste circles over the top.

Toy Soldier Birthday Cake

This timeless design combines a nostalgic feel with modern techniques to create a cake that will bring joy to young and old alike. The smart soldier and toy train are made in a way that allows you to easily recreate the look of a traditional wooden toy from sugar. Little ones will also love the troop of toy soldier cookies which make perfect take-home treats.

Edibles

10cm and 20.5cm (4" and 8") square sponge cakes, filled and crumb-coated (see page 23)

SK Sugarpaste: 1kg (2lb 3oz) Lullaby Blue, 330g (11½oz) Vintage Ivory

1 pack each SK Sugar Dough: Black, Blue, Golden Bear Brown, Red, Soft Beige

1 pack SK Sugar Florist Paste (SFP): Cream

Small amount of SK Instant Mix Royal Icing

SK Professional Food Colour Pen: Black

Equipment

Basic equipment (see pages 6–7)

25.5cm (10") square cake drum (board)

10cm (4") square cake card

3 plastic dowels

Round cutters: 9mm (³/₈"), 1.3cm (½"), 1.5cm (⁵/₈"), 2.2cm (¾"), 2.7cm (1")

Upper case alphabet cutters (PC)

1.2m (1yd 11") x 15mm (⁵/₈") width ribbon: red and white gingham

Cakes and drum

1   Position the 10cm (4") cake on the corresponding cake card and the 20.5cm (8") cake centrally on the 25.5cm (10") cake drum. Cover the 25.5cm (10") cake and the drum with Lullaby Blue sugarpaste and the 10cm (4") cake with Vintage Ivory sugarpaste (see pages 24–25). Leave cakes to dry overnight.

2   Insert three dowels into the 20.5cm (8") cake (see page 26), spread a little royal icing over the top of the dowelled area and secure the 10cm (4") cake on top.

3   Use a ruler and a scribing tool to mark a line around the circumference of the 20.5cm (8") cake that is approximately 5cm (2") up from the base. Roll out some Red Sugar Dough to 3mm (¹/₈") thick and cut it into a 2.5cm x 5cm (1" x 2") rectangle. Brush the back of the rectangle with edible glue and attach it vertically to the far left-hand side of the front of the cake.

4   Fit the sugar shaper with the largest circle disc and fill with Vintage Ivory sugarpaste. Extrude 5cm (2") lengths of paste and attach them vertically either side of the first red strip.

5 Roll out the Blue Sugar Dough to 3mm (¹/₈") thick and cut out a 2.5cm x 5cm (1" x 2") strip of paste. Brush with edible glue and attach it next to the second Vintage Ivory strip of paste, ensuring to stick them closely together.

6 Repeat the steps to cover all the sides of the cake with alternate blue and red strips that are each separated by a length of ivory sugarpaste. Once you have finished, extrude four lengths of Vintage Ivory sugarpaste that are as long as the side of the cake. Secure each length above the striped border of paste and smooth over any joins for a neat finish.

7 Fill the sugar shaper with Red Sugar Dough, extrude a length of paste to fit around the base of the 10cm (4") cake and secure in place with a little edible glue.

Toy soldier

8 Mix 15g (½oz) of Vintage Ivory sugarpaste with 15g (½oz) of Cream SFP to make cream-coloured modelling paste. Seal the paste in a food-grade plastic bag and set to one side.

9 Roll out a small amount of Black Sugar Dough to 3mm (¹/₈") thick and cut out two 1.5cm (⁵/₈") circles and four 1.3cm (½") circles. Shape the 1.5cm (⁵/₈") circles into ovals for the feet and attach two of the smaller circles on top of each foot with edible glue. Push a 7cm (2¾") length of dried spaghetti into each foot.

top tip

If you are transporting the cake, then you can use cocktail sticks instead of dried spaghetti in order to give the model extra strength, but make sure any inedible parts are removed before the cake is served.

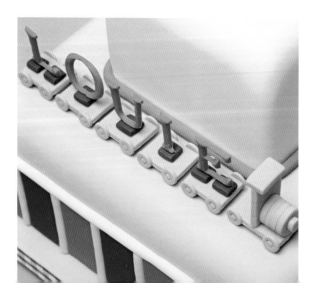

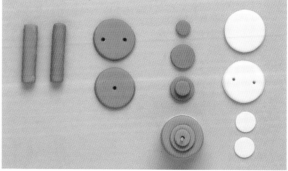

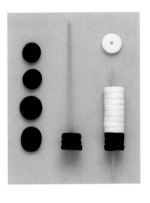
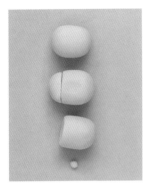
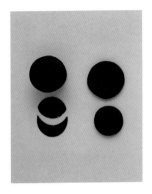

10 Roll out the cream-coloured modelling paste to 3mm (1/8") thick and cut out 16 1.3cm (1/2") circles. Use a piece of dried spaghetti to make a hole in the centre of each circle, then cut out a 2.7cm (1") circle and put to one side. Thread eight small cream circles down each piece of dried spaghetti so they sit on top of the feet. Stand the two feet together and gently press the 2.7cm (1") cream-coloured circle on top of the spaghetti to make two holes.

11 Roll out 38g (1½oz) of Red Sugar Dough and cut out seven 2.7cm (1") circles, one 1.5cm (5/8") circle and one 9mm (3/8") circle. Use a length of dried spaghetti to make a hole in the centre of each one and make two holes in one of the 2.7cm (1") circles in the same way as for the cream-coloured circle.

12 Stack the 2.7cm (1") red circles on top of the 2.7cm (1") cream circle to make the torso, then push a 5cm (2") length of dried spaghetti through the middle. Stack the 1.5cm (5/8") circle and the 9mm (3/8") circle on top then secure with edible glue.

13 Roll 10g (½oz) of Soft Beige Sugar Dough into an oval shape for the head. Cut away a small amount of paste from the top of the head to make it flat for the hat to sit on. Roll a tiny ball of paste for the nose and attach to the centre of the face using edible glue. Use a Black food colour pen to draw on two dots for the eyes and a small line for the mouth. Push the head onto the body and secure with edible glue.

14 To make the hat, roll out 15g (½oz) of Black Sugar Dough to 3mm (1/8") thick and cut out two 2.2cm (¾") and three 2.7cm

(1") circles. Stack and glue the two smallest circles, then stack the larger three on top, secure in place and shape if necessary. Attach to the flat part of the head with edible glue.

15 Roll out a small amount of Black Sugar Dough thinly and cut out a 2.2cm (¾") circle of paste. Cut into the circle again with the 2.2cm (¾") cutter to create a crescent shape for the peak of the hat. Attach the peak at the base of the hat with edible glue.

16 Stand the legs in the centre of the 10cm (4") cake, then push the dried spaghetti through into the cake so that none is left showing at the top of the legs. Leave to dry overnight.

17 Once dry, pipe a small amount of royal icing onto the top of the legs and attach the body.

18 Roll 4g (pinch) of Red Sugar Dough into a 7.2cm (2¾") long sausage. Cut in half to create two arms and attach to either side of the body with a little edible glue. Roll out a small amount of cream modelling paste thinly and cut out a 1.3cm (½") circle. Cut the circle into quarters, then secure two pieces to the bottom of each arm for the hands.

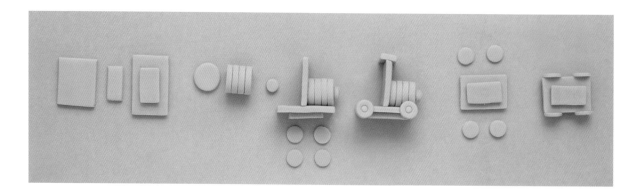

19 Cut two 5mm (¼") wide strips from the cream modelling paste and attach them across the front of the body with a little edible glue. Trim to size at the top and bottom of the body with a craft knife.

Toy train

20 Roll out 100g (3½oz) of Golden Bear Brown Sugar Dough to a 3mm (⅛") thickness. Use a sharp knife and a ruler to cut out six rectangles of paste that are 2.5cm x 1.9cm (1" x ¾") in size. Cut out another rectangle measuring 3.2cm x 1.9cm (1¼" x ¾").

21 Use a 9mm (⅜") round cutter to cut out 25 circles, then use a 1.5cm (⅝") cutter to cut out four more circles. Stack all the 1.5cm (⅝") circles and stick them together with edible glue.

22 Roll out more Golden Bear Brown Sugar Dough and cut out six rectangles that are 2cm x 1cm (¾" x ⅜") and one that is 1cm x 1.9cm (⅜" x ¾") in size.

23 Roll out a small amount of Red Sugar Dough thinly and cut out the letters for the name of your choice with the alphabet cutters. Leave all the cut-out pieces to dry overnight.

24 To make the carriages, place five of the 2.5cm x 1.9cm (1" x ¾") rectangles centrally on top of five 2cm x 1cm (¾" x ⅜") rectangles and secure with a little edible glue. Attach four wheels around each carriage and place them to one side to dry.

top tip

Remember that if you are making this cake for a recipient with a longer name, you can use the same method to make more carriages for the letters.

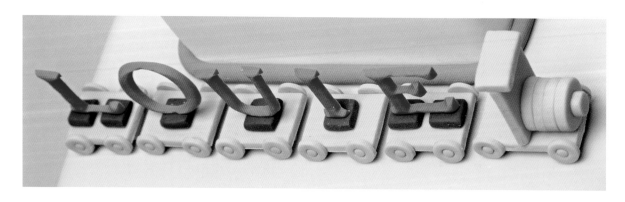

25 For the engine, stick the larger 3.2cm x 1.9cm (1¼" x ¾") rectangle on top of a 2cm x 1cm (¾" x ³⁄₈") rectangle. Secure the stack of circles horizontally on top of the larger rectangle with edible glue and the remaining 9mm (³⁄₈") circle to the front. Stand a 2.5cm x 1.9cm (1" x ¾") rectangle vertically behind the stack. Attach a 1cm x 1.9cm (³⁄₈" x ¾") rectangle on top using edible glue to secure.

26 Roll out a small amount of Blue Sugar Dough and cut out enough 1cm (³⁄₈") squares to hold each of the letters. Push the dried letters into the squares using edible glue to secure them and set to one side to dry. Once dry, attach the letters to each of the train carriages with more edible glue.

Finishing touches

27 Pipe a little royal icing on the bottom of the engine and each of the carriages. Attach the train across the top of the base tier at the front of the cake.

28 Attach the ribbon to the edge of the cake drum with a non-toxic glue stick, being careful that the glue does not come into contact with the cake.

Toy Soldier Cookies

Edibles

20 basic vanilla biscuits (see recipe on page 15)

Apricot glaze (see page 20)

120g (4¼oz) SK Sugarpaste: Vintage Ivory

SK Sugar Dough: 100g (3½oz) Black, 160g (5½oz) Red, 80g (2¾oz) Soft Beige

SK Professional Food Colour Pen: Brown

Equipment

Basic equipment (see pages 6–7)

Cookie sticks

Round cutter: 1.5cm (⅝")

Piping nozzle: no. 2

Templates (see page 121)

Makes 20

1 Make the biscuit dough following the recipe on page 15, cut out 20 toy soldier shapes using a sharp knife and the template and push an ovenproof cookie stick into the centre of each one. Bake according to the recipe instructions then leave to cool.

2 Cut out the templates for the trousers, torso, face and hat from some greaseproof paper. Roll out the Vintage Ivory sugarpaste to a 3mm (⅛") thickness and use the template and a sharp knife to cut out the shape of the trousers.

3 Brush the cookies with boiled, cooled apricot glaze and stick the trousers in position on each of them. Smooth over the edges and use a blade tool to mark a line down the centre of the trousers.

4 Roll out some Red Sugar Dough thinly and cut out the jackets using the template. Stick these to the cookies, smooth over the edges and mark on the arms and cuffs with a blade tool.

5 Roll out some Soft Beige Sugar Dough to a 3mm (⅛") thickness and cut out the faces using the template. Stick these to the cookies and smooth over the sides. Use a no. 2 nozzle to mark a circle onto each for the nose.

6 Roll out the Black Sugar Dough to a 3mm (⅛") thickness and cut out the hats using the template and 20 1.5cm (⅝") circles for the feet. Cut each circle in half then attach two to the bottom of the cookie. Position the hat on the cookie and smooth over the edges.

7 Roll out the remaining Black Sugar Dough slightly more thinly and cut out 10 1.5cm (⅜") circles. Cut each one in half and place a half onto each cookie for the peak of the hat.

8 Roll out the remaining Vintage Ivory sugarpaste thinly and cut out 5mm (¼") wide strips of paste and 10 1.3cm (½") circles. Attach the strip between the red top and the ivory trousers to cover the join, then attach two ivory strips across the body. Trim the paste at the top of the shoulders using a craft knife. Cut the circles into quarters and attach two pieces at the end of each sleeve for the hands.

9 Use a Brown food pen to draw a mouth on each soldier cookie.

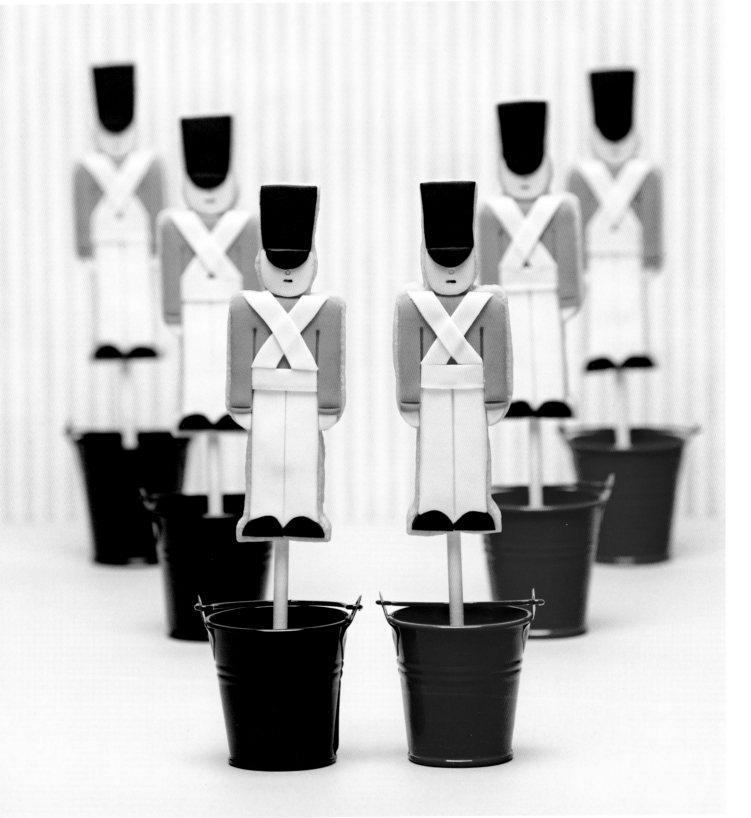

'What a Hoot!' Birthday Cake

The combination of vibrant colours, simple shapes and ever-popular owls make this the perfect party cake. This playful design uses a basic découpage technique where you simply build up the decorations with basic, cut-out shapes to create a striking effect.

Edibles

10cm, 15cm and 20.5cm (4", 6" and 8") sponge cakes, filled and crumb-coated (see page 23)

1.75kg (3lb 8oz) SK Sugarpaste: Bridal White

1 pack each SK Sugar Florist Paste (SFP): Bluebell, Marigold (tangerine), Pale Pink, Poinsettia (red), Violet, White

1 pack SK Sugar Dough: Orange

SK Quality Food Colour (QFC) Pastes: Black, Green, Yellow

Small amount of SK Instant Mix Royal Icing

SK Edible Glue

Equipment

Basic equipment (see pages 6–7)

25.5cm (10") round cake drum (board)

10cm and 15cm (4" and 6") round cake cards

Heart cutter 1: 2.2cm (¾") (FMM)

Small plunger cutters: heart, star (FMM)

8 plastic dowels

Piping nozzle: no. 2

Round cutters: 9mm (³⁄₈"), 1.5cm (⁵⁄₈")

90cm (35") x 15mm (⁵⁄₈") width satin ribbon: orange polka dot

Templates (see page 123)

Cakes and drum

1   Place the 10cm (4") and 15cm (6") cakes on the corresponding cake cards and the 20.5cm (8") cake centrally on the 25.5cm (10") cake drum. Cover all of the cakes and the cake drum with Bridal White sugarpaste (see pages 24–25). Leave the cakes to dry overnight.

2   Insert four dowels into the 20.5cm and 15cm (8" and 6") cakes (see page 26). Dab a little royal icing over the top of each dowelled cake and stack the cakes centrally.

3   Colour 30g (1oz) of White SFP with Yellow paste food colour and mix in 5g (just under ¼oz) of Marigold SFP. Fit a sugar shaper with a medium-sized circle disc, soften half of the yellow paste with a little white vegetable fat and fill the sugar shaper. Extrude a length of paste to fit around the circumference of the base tier. Secure around the base of the cake with edible glue and smooth over the join in the paste with your finger.

4   Repeat step 3 using Bluebell SFP for the second tier and Poinsettia SFP for the top tier.

Bunting

5   Cut a 54cm long x 6cm wide (21" x 2³/₈") strip of parchment paper, wrap it around the 15cm (6") cake to make sure the ends meet and trim to size if necessary. Fold the paper in half and then half again. Use the template to draw a curved line along the top of the paper, making sure the lowest point of the curve is at the fold in the paper. Cut along the line, unfold the template and place it around the 15cm (6") cake. Hold it in place and use a scribing tool to mark out a scalloped line around the cake.

6   Make a template for the 10cm (4") cake in the same way and scribe a scalloped line around the cake.

7   Fit the sugar shaper with the smallest circle disc, mix 15g (½oz) of White SFP with 15g (½oz) of Bridal White sugarpaste and fill the sugar shaper. Use a small paintbrush to paint a thin line of edible glue along the scribed lines on the cake. Extrude lengths of white paste through the sugar shaper and attach them to the glued lines.

8   Roll out a small amount of Marigold SFP thinly and use the template to cut out three bunting flags with a sharp craft knife. Place the triangles on a board and cover with cling film to stop them drying out whilst you are cutting out the other flags. Cut out three triangles from the Pink SFP, four from the Violet SFP and eight from the yellow SFP in the same way.

9   Roll out some more Pink SFP and cut out four hearts with the small heart plunger cutter. Cut a heart out of the centre of four yellow bunting flags and replace them each with a pink heart. Place these under some cling film.

10   To make the stripy paste, roll out 20g (¾oz) of Poinsettia SFP and 20g (¾oz) of White SFP. Cut the White SFP into 3mm

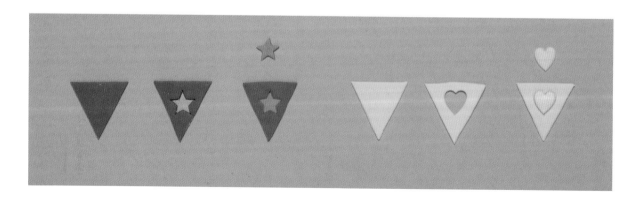

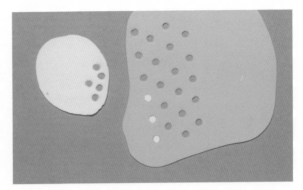

(¹/₈") wide strips and lay them on the red paste so they are equally spaced out. Gently roll over with a small rolling pin to merge the pastes. Using the templates, cut out four bunting flags, two party hats and one of each present shape from the stripy paste.

11   Use Pink SFP and White SFP to make pink stripy paste in the same way, then cut out four bunting flags and one of each present shape.

12   To make the polka dot paste, colour 30g (1oz) of White SFP with Green paste food colour and roll half of it out thinly. Roll a small amount of White SFP out thinly. Use a no. 2 nozzle to cut out an equal number of small circles from the green and white pastes. Replace the circles from the green paste with white circles to make a polka dot pattern. Smooth over the

paste with your hand then cut out four bunting flags and one large present. Keep the green paste in a food-grade plastic bag for the owls, balloons and presents later.

13   Roll out some Bluebell SFP thinly and cut out three bunting flags. Mix a small amount of Bluebell SFP with some White SFP to make a paler shade of blue, then roll it out thinly and cut out three small stars with the plunger cutter. Cut a star shape out of each of the blue flags and replace with pale blue stars.

14   Following the order in the picture, attach the bunting flags just below the string line around the cakes. Brush a little edible glue along the top edge of each flag and secure in place. Lift the point of the flag slightly away from the sugarpaste so it is not flat against the cake.

'What a Hoot' Birthday Cake

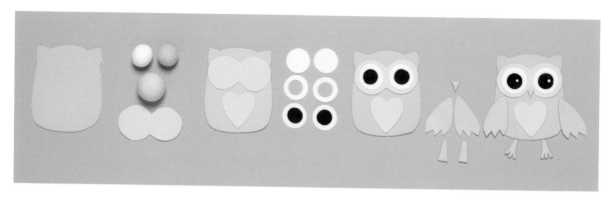

Owls

15 Roll out some Marigold SFP and use the template and a craft knife to cut out an owl shape. Mix some of the Marigold SFP with a little White SFP to lighten it, roll it out again and cut out a set of eyes using the template and a large heart using the cutter. Attach these to the body with edible glue. Roll out a small amount of green paste and cut out one of the wings using the template. Turn the template over and cut out the second wing.

16 Use Violet and Pale Pink SFP to make a purple owl with pink wings in the same way. Make a blue owl with yellow wings using Bluebell and yellow SFP and a red owl with purple wings using Poinsettia and Violet SFP.

17 Roll out some White SFP thinly, cut out eight 1.5cm (⁵⁄₈") circles with a round cutter then cut a 9mm (³⁄₈") circle from the centre of each. Colour a small amount of White SFP with Black paste food colour, roll it out thinly and cut out eight 9mm (³⁄₈") circles. Place these small black circles into the holes in the larger white circles and attach them to the owls with edible glue. Use the end of a no. 2 piping nozzle to cut out eight very small circles of white paste and attach them to the pupils.

18 To make the beaks, roll out some Marigold SFP slightly thicker than the other pastes and cut out four tiny triangles. Secure between each owl's eyes with edible glue.

19 Arrange the red, orange and purple owls around the base tier and secure with edible glue. Secure the blue owl at the front of the top tier so he is at a slight angle. Attach the wings to the sides of each owl using edible glue and bend them out slightly from the cake side. Attach the party hats to the blue and purple owls using a little edible glue.

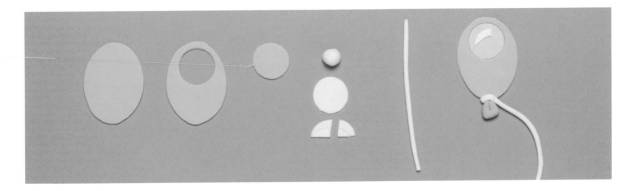

20 For the feet, roll out a little Marigold SFP and cut out eight triangles that are approximately 1cm (³/₈") long. Make two incisions into the bottom of each one with a craft knife. Pull the sections apart to bring out the toes and trim them to size. Attach two legs to the bottom of each owl with edible glue.

Balloons

21 Roll out a small amount of green paste and use the template and a craft knife to cut out a balloon shape. Cut out a circle of paste from the top of the balloon with a 1.5cm (⁵/₈") round cutter. Use half of the paste you have removed to make a small triangle for the tie at the bottom of the balloon. Indent it with a Dresden tool and stick it to the bottom of the balloon with edible glue.

22 Mix a little of the green paste with some White SFP to make a lighter shade of green, then roll out the paste thinly. Cut out a 1.5cm (⁵/₈") circle from the light green paste and place it in the hole in the balloon. Roll out a little White SFP and cut another 1.5cm (⁵/₈") circle. Cut it in half and then use the same round cutter to cut away a section of the paste. Cut away another section of paste from the right of the circle and attach the arc of white paste onto the paler circle on the balloon. Set to one side to dry slightly on a board dusted with icing sugar.

23 Make one blue, one pink, one yellow, one purple and one red balloon in the same way and set aside to dry slightly.

24 Attach one balloon next to each owl on the bottom tier with edible glue, then secure two balloons next to the owl on the top tier. Do not attach the purple balloon to the cake at this stage.

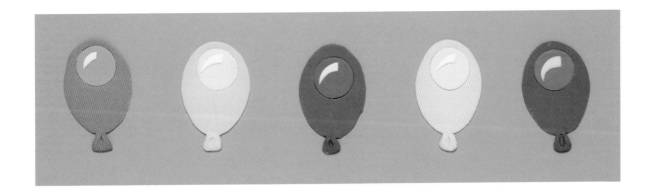

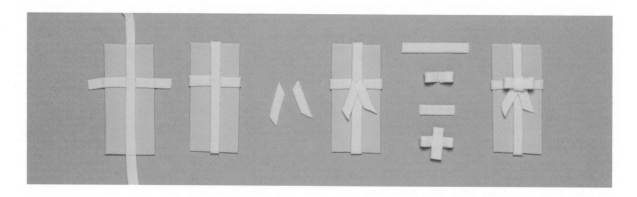

25 Fit the sugar shaper with the smallest circle disc and fill with White SFP. Extrude five lengths of paste for the balloon strings. Attach one end of each string to a balloon and the other end to the owl's wing with edible glue and trim each piece to size.

Presents

26 Use the templates to cut out presents in various sizes from Bluebell, Marigold, Pale Pink and Violet SFP: use the photograph of the main cake as a guide for how many you will need. Attach 5mm (¼") strips of coloured paste across the presents for the ribbon, then secure small stars to some of the presents.

27 To make a small bow, roll out the appropriate colour paste thinly, cut out two 5mm wide x 1.5cm long (¼" x ⅝") strips and cut the ends at an angle. Attach these to the ribbons on the present with edible glue. Cut a 5mm wide x 3cm long (¼" x 1⅛") strip and fold the ends into the centre to make bow loops. Attach a 1cm (⅜") long piece of paste across the middle and attach to the present with edible glue.

28 To make a pompom-style bow, roll out some SFP thinly and cut out five 1.5cm x 5mm (⅝" x ¼") lengths. Fold each one into a loop and attach four of them to the present with edible glue, making sure that they are touching in the middle and equally spaced. Place the last loop in the centre, using edible glue to secure.

29 For the purple rectangular present, use the small heart cutter to cut away three hearts. Roll out a little yellow SFP, cut out three hearts and place them into the holes in the present.

30 Attach the presents around the bottom two tiers of the cake, using edible glue to secure.

Note: Make sure any inedible parts, such as cocktail sticks, are removed before the cake is served.

Number topper

31   Roll out 40g (1½oz) of Orange Sugar Dough to approximately 4mm (³/₁₆") thick. Place the '2' template on the paste and cut around it with a craft knife. Push a length of spaghetti or a cocktail stick into the bottom of the number and leave it to dry completely.

32   Attach the purple balloon to the top of the number using edible glue. Push the number into the top of the cake and secure with a little royal icing along the bottom. Use the sugar shaper to make the balloon string as before and attach to the balloon, trailing it down onto the cake.

Stars

33   Roll out a little of the green, Bluebell, Violet, Poinsettia, yellow and Marigold pastes thinly and cut out around eight to ten stars in each colour using the small star plunger cutter.

34   Use edible glue to attach the stars randomly over the three tiers, but predominantly on the top two tiers. Attach stars to the front and back of the number topper.

Finishing touches

35   Attach the orange polka dot ribbon around the edge of the cake drum with a non-toxic glue stick, being careful that the glue does not come into contact with the cake.

'What a Hoot!' Cupcakes

Edibles

12 cupcakes baked in
SK Star Cupcake Cases:
Amethyst Purple, Emerald
Green, Ruby Red, Sapphire
Blue (see recipe on page 12)

350g (12¼oz) vanilla
buttercream (see page 18)

1 pack each SK Sugar
Florist Paste (SFP): Bluebell,
Marigold (tangerine), Pale
Pink, Poinsettia (red), Violet,
White

SK Quality Food Colour
(QFC) Pastes: Green, Yellow

Equipment

Basic equipment (see
pages 6–7)

Small star plunger cutter
(FMM)

Large piping bag

Large star nozzle

Makes 12

1   Make several coloured stars and twelve presents using
coloured SFP in the same way as for the main cake (see
pages 70–71). Leave to dry slightly on a board dusted lightly
with icing sugar.

2   Fit a large piping bag with a large star nozzle, fill with
vanilla buttercream and start piping around the edge of each
cupcake. Pipe in towards the middle to finish the swirl.

3   Decorate the cupcakes with the stars and presents while
the buttercream is still soft.

'What a Hoot!' Cookies

Edibles

24 basic vanilla biscuits
(see recipe on page 15)

Apricot glaze (see page 20)

SK Sugar Dough: 1 pack
each Black, Blue, Green,
Orange, Red, Violet, Yellow;
2 packs White

Equipment

Basic equipment (see
pages 6–7)

Round cutters: 1.5cm ($^5/_8$"),
2.2cm (¾"), 2.6cm (1")

Balloon cutter (LS)

Owl cutter (LS)

Freesia cutter (SSA)

Heart cutter 3: 3.8cm (1½")
(FMM)

Piping nozzle: no. 4

Small heart plunger cutter
(FMM)

Makes 24

1   Make the biscuit dough following the recipe on page 15 and cut out 12 owls and 12 balloons using the cookie cutters or the enlarged templates. Bake according to the recipe instructions and leave to cool.

Owls

2   Brush four of the owl cookies with cooled, boiled apricot glaze. Roll out the Orange Sugar Dough to a 3mm ($^1/_8$") thickness and cut out four owls using the cookie cutter or template. Place each piece onto a cookie and smooth over the edges.

3   Use a 2.6cm (1") round cutter to mark two circles for the eyes and use a large heart cutter to emboss a heart in the centre of the body.

4   Mix 6g (just under ¼oz) of Orange Sugar Dough with 6g (just under ¼oz) of White Sugar Dough to make a pale orange paste. Roll out the paste thinly and cut out two 2.6cm (1") circles and a heart for each owl. Attach the circles over the marks for the eyes and the heart in the centre and smooth down the edges.

5   Roll out a small amount of White Sugar Dough thinly and cut out two 2.2cm (¾") circles for each owl. Attach these to the eyes and smooth down.

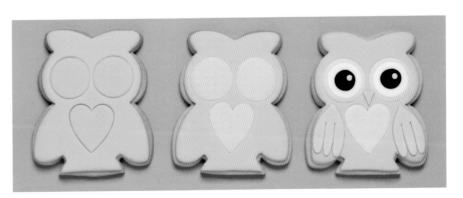

6 Roll out a small amount of Black Sugar Dough thinly and cut out two 1.5cm (⁵/₈") circles for each owl. Attach these to the centre of the eyes and smooth over. Roll out a small amount of White Sugar Dough and cut out tiny circles of paste with the end of a no. 4 nozzle. Attach these to the black pupils.

7 Mix 20g (¾oz) of Green Sugar Dough, 40g (1½oz) of Yellow Sugar Dough and 140g (5oz) of White Sugar Dough to make a light green paste. Roll out a small amount of the paste and cut out two wings for each owl using a freesia cutter or the enlarged template, then attach to the cookie. Roll out a small amount of Orange Sugar Dough and cut small triangles of paste for the beaks. Attach between the eyes with edible glue.

8 Repeat steps 2–7 to make four blue and four red owl cookies, or use colour combinations of your own choice. Use the small heart plunger cutter to add five small hearts to the centre of some of the owls, instead of one in the middle.

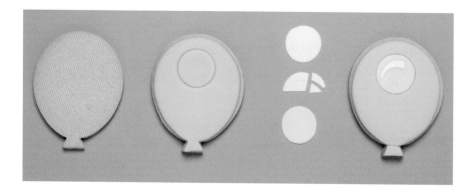

Balloons

9 Brush four of the balloon cookies with cooled, boiled apricot glaze. Roll out some light green Sugar Dough to 3mm (¹/₈") thick and cut out four balloons using the cookie cutter or enlarged template. Place each piece of paste on the cookies and smooth over the edges.

10 Use a 2.6cm (1") round cutter to mark a circle towards the top of each balloon. Mix 6g (just under ¼oz) of light green Sugar Dough with 6g (just under ¼oz) of White Sugar Dough to make a paler green paste. Roll this out and cut out the 2.6cm (1") circles and secure these in place on the balloons, smoothing around the edges. Use a palette knife or Dresden tool to mark a line across the bottom of the balloons.

11 Roll out a little White Sugar Dough and cut out a 2.6cm (1") circle. Cut it in half and then use the same round cutter to cut away a section of the paste. Cut away another section of paste from the right of the circle and attach the arc of white paste onto the paler circle on the balloon.

12 Repeat steps 9–11 to make the yellow and red balloons, or use colour combinations of your own choice.

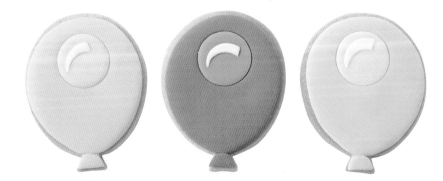

Crafted with Love Valentine's Cake

What better way to win over your Valentine than with a beautifully hand-crafted cake? This heart-shaped design incorporates a range of creative sugarpaste techniques that are simple, quick and guaranteed to make a great impression.

Edibles

20.5cm (8") heart-shaped sponge cake, filled and crumb-coated (see page 23)

SK Sugarpaste: 900g (2lb) Glamour Red, 50g (1¾oz) Lullaby Blue, 100g (3½oz) Vintage Ivory

1 pack each SK Sugar Florist Paste (SFP): Cream, Pale Blue, Poinsettia (red)

1 pack SK Mexican Modelling Paste (MMP): Teddy Bear Brown

SK Quality Food Colour (QFC) Paste: Red

SK Edible Glue

Equipment

Basic equipment (see pages 6–7)

25.5cm (10") heart-shaped cake drum (board)

Quilting embosser (PC)

SK Great Impressions Heart Jewel Mould

Heart cutter set: 2cm (¾"), 2.9cm (1¹/₈"), 3.4cm (1³/₈") (FMM)

Small heart cutter set: 7mm (¼"), 8mm (³/₈") (FMM)

Funky upper case alphabet cutters (FMM)

Heart cookie cutter: 3.2cm (1¼"), from set of 6 (Wilton)

Lace heart cutter set (OP)

Garrett frill cutter (OP)

84cm (33") x 15mm (⁵/₈") width satin ribbon: pale blue

Cake and drum

1   Position the cake centrally on the 25.5cm (10") heart-shaped cake drum and cover both the cake and drum with Glamour Red sugarpaste (see pages 24–25).

Cake top design

2   Mix 50g (1¾oz) of Pale Blue SFP with 50g (1¾oz) of Lullaby Blue sugarpaste to make a light blue modelling paste. Seal half of the paste in a food-grade plastic bag and roll out the rest thinly. Place the quilting embosser on top of the paste and press down gently with an even pressure to transfer the pattern.

3   Arrange the cutters in order so that size 1 is the largest and size 6 the smallest. Cut out two hearts from the embossed paste with the size 1 heart cutter. Cut out another heart using the size 2 cutter and four with the size 3 cutter. Use the alphabet cutters to cut out the letters 'L' and 'V' from the embossed paste, then use a scribing tool to help remove the letters from the cutters. Seal the excess paste in a food-grade plastic bag and leave all the cut-outs to dry on a spare cake drum or board dusted with icing sugar.

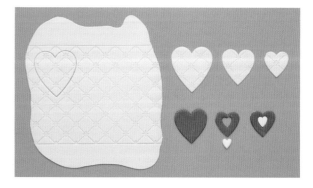

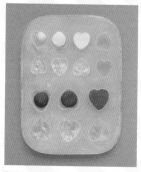

4   Mix 100g (3½oz) of Vintage Ivory sugarpaste with 100g (3½oz) of Cream SFP and place ¾ of it in a food-grade plastic bag. Roll out the remaining paste thinly, cut out two size 1 hearts and run a quilting tool around the edges while the paste is still soft. Cut out six size 5 hearts, four size 4 hearts, three size 3 hearts and one size 6 heart. Set aside to dry.

5   Mix 25g (just over ¾oz) of Poinsettia SFP with 25g (¾oz) of Glamour Red sugarpaste. Add a little Red paste colour and roll out a small amount. Cut out one size 2, one size 3 and one size 5 heart.

6   Take a size 3 red heart and cut out a small heart from the centre using a size 6 cutter. Replace this with a size 6 ivory heart. Repeat using a size 4 cream heart, a size 5 cutter and a size 5 red heart.

7   To make the stripy paste, roll out equal amounts of cream and red paste to an even thickness of approximately 2mm– 3mm (1¹/₁₆"). Cut each colour into 7mm (¼") wide strips then lay five strips next to one another, alternating the colours. Push the strips together gently to create a striped paste then cut out one size 4 and one size 3 heart. Cut the remaining strips in half lengthways to make thinner strips of paste then use them to make more stripy paste. Cut out one size 4 and two size 3 hearts from the thin-striped paste.

8   To make the stripy lettering, roll out a small amount of blue paste and a small amount of red paste. Cut the red paste into 4mm (¼") strips and place them on top of the blue paste, so that the strips are evenly spaced. Gently roll a small rolling pin over the paste to merge them and cut out the letters 'O' and 'E' with the alphabet cutters.

9   Dust the heart jewel mould with a little cornflour, then make two large and two small hearts using the red paste. Trim away any excess paste from the back of the hearts with a palette knife, then turn the mould over and tap it with a rolling pin to release the hearts. Make two more small hearts in the same way using the blue paste.

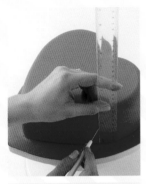

Cake side design

10 Use a scribing tool and a clean ruler to mark a line around the sides of the cake that is approximately 3.8cm (1½") up from the cake drum.

11 Roll out the remaining cream paste to an even thickness and cut out a 70cm long x 10cm wide (27½" x 4") strip. Fit the lace cutter with the lace heart strip cutter in the top row of holes, then fit the straight edge into the middle holes. Press the cutter into the paste and cut it into two lengths that are 70cm (27½") long. Attach the first length along the scribed line, starting at the back of the cake and securing with edible glue. Trim the paste with a sharp knife if necessary. Attach the second length along the top of the first length and trim if necessary.

12 Roll out the remaining pale blue modelling paste into a 70cm (27½") long strip that is at least 4cm (1½") wide and emboss with a quilting embosser. Fit the Garrett frill cutter with the scalloped edge in the last holes and use this to cut a length of scalloped paste to fit around the circumference of the cake. Brush the join between the cream bands with a little edible glue and attach the blue paste around the centre of the cake. Secure at the back of the cake with a little edible glue and trim the paste if necessary. Use a palette knife to mark a line along the centre of the blue strip.

13 Fit the sugar shaper with the smallest circle disc and fill with Teddy Bear Brown MMP. Extrude two 70cm (27½") lengths of paste, wrap them both around the circumference of the cake and use a little edible glue to secure. Extrude another length of Teddy Bear Brown paste, fold it into four loops to make the bow and attach it to the left-hand side of the cake. Secure a red heart jewel to the centre of the bow.

Finishing touches

14 In order to make the large hearts stand out from the top of the cake, turn over all the size 1 hearts and use edible glue to stick a size 3 heart in the corresponding colour to the back of each one. Attach the 'L' and 'V' to the top of the cream hearts and the 'O' and 'E' to the blue hearts.

15 Arrange all the hearts on the top of the cake, making sure the letters spell out the word 'LOVE' from left to right then attach them to the cake with edible glue.

16 Attach the ribbon around the edge of the cake drum with a non-toxic glue stick, being careful that the glue does not come into contact with the cake.

Heart Cookies

Edibles

24 basic vanilla biscuits (see recipe on page 15)

Apricot glaze (see page 20)

SK Sugarpaste: 250g (8¾oz)
Glamour Red, 100g (3½oz)
Lullaby Blue, 100g (3½oz)
Vintage Ivory

SK Edible Glue

Equipment

Basic equipment (see pages 6–7)

Heart cookie cutters: 4.5cm (1¾"), 6.5cm (2½"), 8cm (3⅛"), from set of 6 (Wilton)

Quilting embosser (PC)

Lace heart cutter set (OP)

Garrett frill cutter (OP)

Makes 24

1   Make the biscuit dough following the recipe on page 15. Cut out eight heart shapes using each of the three cookie cutters. Bake according to the recipe instructions then leave to cool.

2   Brush each of the cookies with cooled, boiled apricot glaze. Roll out the Glamour Red sugarpaste to 3mm (⅛") thick and cut out eight larger hearts with the 8cm (3⅛") cookie cutter. Place a piece of paste onto the largest cookies and smooth over the edges.

3   Roll out the Lullaby Blue sugarpaste to 3mm (⅛") thick and use the quilting embosser to emboss the paste. Use the cookie cutter 4.5cm (1¾") to cut out eight heart shapes and stick these onto the smallest cookies.

4   Roll out the remaining Glamour Red sugarpaste and half of the Vintage Ivory sugarpaste to 3mm (⅛") thick. Cut each piece of paste into 1cm (⅜") wide strips using a sharp knife. Alternate the coloured strips of paste and push them together to make a sheet of striped paste. Smooth the paste over with your hand then use the 6.5cm (2½") cutter to cut out eight heart shapes. Attach the hearts to the medium-sized cookies and smooth over the edges.

5   Roll out the remaining Vintage Ivory sugarpaste thinly and use the lace cutter to cut out a strip of paste as explained in the main project on page 79. Use edible glue to attach a lacy strip of paste diagonally across the largest cookies and trim to size with a sharp knife.

6   Roll out the remaining Lullaby Blue sugarpaste thinly and emboss with the quilting embosser. Use the Garrett frill cutter to cut out a 2.5cm (1") wide strip of paste and attach diagonally across each large cookie. Secure with edible glue and trim to size with a sharp knife.

'Hoppy Easter' Cake

Welcome in the spring with this fabulous Easter bunny cake which is sure to brighten everyone's day, whatever the weather. Baking the cake in a tiffin tin avoids having to carve the cake into shape, which means less mess and less waste. The accompanying cookies and cupcakes are also a great way to get little ones baking over the holidays.

Edibles

Sponge cake baked in a tiffin tin, crumb-coated (see page 23)

1.9kg (4lb 6½oz) SK Sugarpaste: Bridal White

SK Quality Food Colour (QFC) Pastes: Black, Dark Green, Orange, Yellow

1 pack SK Sugar Dough: Pink

1 pack SK Sugar Florist Paste (SFP): White

SK Edible Glue

Small amount of SK Instant Mix Royal Icing

Equipment

Basic equipment (see pages 6–7)

2 x 30.5cm (12") round cake drums (boards)

Round cutters: 7mm (¼"), 1.3cm (½"), 2.2cm (¾"), 2.7cm (1"), 10.5cm (4¼")

2 x SK 19cm (7½") Lollipop Sticks

20-gauge floral wires: white

5-petal cutter (OP)

Cupped former, e.g. an apple carton

1m (1yd 3") x 15mm (⅝") width satin ribbon: yellow polka dot

Templates (see page 124)

1   Colour 400g (14oz) of Bridal White sugarpaste with a small amount of Dark Green and a touch of Yellow paste food colours. Roll out the light green paste to 3mm (⅛") thick and cover the cake drum (see page 25).

2   Place the cake on a spare cake drum, roll out 750g (1lb 10½oz) of Bridal White sugarpaste to 5mm (¼") thick and cover the cake (see page 24). Secure the cake to the centre of the covered cake drum with a little royal icing.

3   Roll out 50g (1¾oz) of Pink Sugar Dough very thinly and cut out a circle with a 10.5cm (4") cutter. Attach the circle to the front of the body with edible glue, then use the quilting tool to mark around the edge of the circle. Cut out two 2.7cm (1") and six 1.3cm (½") circles from the pink paste using the round cutters.

4   Divide 180g (6¼oz) of Bridal White sugarpaste into two equal pieces for the back paws. Shape each piece into a ball then flatten it slightly, making one side flatter than the other. Run the quilting tool around the edge of each paw, position them so that the thinner edge is touching the cake drum and attach to the front of the cake with edible glue. Use edible glue to secure one 2.7cm (1") pink circle in the centre of each paw and three smaller pink circles above it.

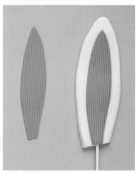

5 For the arm, roll out 100g (3½oz) of Bridal White sugarpaste into a long oval shape that is slightly thinner at one end. Run the quilting tool around the arm and attach it down the side of the cake with edible glue so the thicker end is resting flat on the drum. Make another arm in the same way and attach it down the opposite side of the cake.

6 Mix 125g (4½oz) of Bridal White sugarpaste with 25g (just over ¾oz) of White SFP. Roll out the paste thickly and cut out an ear shape using a craft knife and the template on page 123. Push a lollipop stick right down into the top of the cake to make two deep holes that are approximately 5cm (2") apart. Remove the stick then carefully insert it almost all the way up the middle of the ear.

7 Roll out a small amount of Pink Sugar Dough and cut out the middle of the ear following the template on page 123. Position the paste in the centre of the ear and run a quilting tool around the edges of the Pink paste to secure it in place. Run a quilting tool around the sides of the ear before inserting the stick into one of the holes in the top the cake. Secure the ear in place with edible glue.

8 Make the second ear in the same way, but only push the lollipop stick halfway up the ear so it can still flop over. Push the other end of the stick into the second hole, bend it over and secure the tip to the cake with edible glue.

9 Divide 20g (¾oz) of Bridal White sugarpaste in half. Roll each piece into a ball and flatten slightly for the muzzle. Attach the pieces side-by-side to the front of the cake so the muzzle sits just above the pink tummy. Use a scribing tool or a piece of dried spaghetti to make three whisker holes in each side.

10 Shape 5g (just under ¼oz) of Pink Sugar Dough into an oval for the nose and secure centrally on top of the muzzle with edible glue. Roll a pea-sized ball of Bridal White sugarpaste, flatten it between your finger and thumb and stick it to the top of the nose.

11 Make four small cone shapes from 3g (¹⁄₈oz) of Bridal White sugarpaste for the tufts between the ears. Secure the

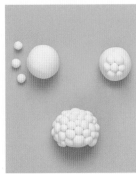

tufts to the top of the head with edible glue and use a Dresden tool to blend the joins.

12   Roll 22g (¾oz) of Bridal White sugarpaste into a ball and attach this to the back of the cake for the tail. Take another 22g (¼oz) of Bridal White sugarpaste and pinch out pea-sized balls from the paste. Cover the tail completely with balls of sugarpaste, using edible glue to secure each one in place.

13   Colour a small amount of White SFP with a little Black paste food colour, then roll out the black paste thinly and cut out two 2.2cm (¾") circles using a round cutter. Model each circle into a slightly more oval shape and attach just above the muzzle with edible glue for the eyes. Roll out a small amount of White SFP thinly, cut out two 7mm (¼") circles of paste and attach them to the black circles to highlight the eyes.

14   Cut two white floral wires into three equal lengths and push them into the sides of the muzzle to make whiskers. Do not push the wires into the cake as they are inedible and should never be inserted into any part that will be eaten. The muzzle and whiskers should be removed before the cake is served.

15   Colour 20g (¾oz) of White SFP with Yellow and a touch of Orange food colours. Roll out the paste thinly and cut out six blossoms using the 5-petal cutter. Roll a small, pea-sized ball of White SFP and attach it to the centre of the blossom with edible glue. Press the centre with a bone or ball tool to make an indent. Leave to dry in a cupped former such as an apple carton.

16   Once dry, secure five blossoms around the cake drum and attach one to the top of the straight ear.

17   Attach the yellow ribbon around the edge of the cake drum using a non-toxic glue stick, being careful that the glue does not come into contact with the cake.

Please note that any inedible items such as floral wires and lollipop sticks must be removed before the cake is served.

'Hoppy Easter' Cupcakes

Edibles

12 cupcakes baked in SK Dotty Cupcake Cases: Pink, Spring Green and Yellow (see recipe on page 12)

Apricot glaze (see page 20)

SK Sugarpaste: 72g (2½oz) Bridal White, 220g (7¾oz) Bridal White coloured with Dark Green and a touch of Yellow paste food colours

20g (¾oz) SK Sugar Dough: Pink

1 pack SK Sugar Florist Paste (SFP): Pale Yellow with a touch of Orange paste food colour

SK Quality Food Colour (QFC) Pastes: Dark Green, Orange, Yellow

SK Edible Glue

Small amount of SK Instant Mix Royal Icing

Equipment

Basic equipment (see pages 6–7)

6cm (2⅜") round cutter

Small blossom cutter

Piping nozzle: no. 1

Makes 12

1 Brush the top of each cupcake with a little cooled, boiled apricot glaze. Roll out the yellow-green sugarpaste to a 3mm (⅛") thickness and cut out twelve 6cm (2⅜") circles of paste. Place these onto the cupcakes and smooth them down with the palm of your hand.

2 Shape 4g (just under ¼oz) of Bridal White sugarpaste into a long teardrop shape for the bunny's ear. Flatten it slightly with the palm of your hand and taper the top of the ear into a point. Roll out a small amount of Pink Sugar Dough and cut out an inner ear shape. Attach it in the centre of the ear with edible glue. Make another ear in the same way but fold it over in the middle. Trim the bottom of each ear straight and use edible glue to attach them to the cupcake. Repeat to make 11 pairs of ears for the remaining cupcakes.

3 Roll out the yellow SFP thinly and cut out 36 little blossoms. Pipe a small dot of royal icing into the centre of each flower using a no. 1 nozzle. Stick one to the straight ear with edible glue. Secure the remaining blossoms over the top of the cupcakes.

Easter Egg Cookies

Edibles

24 basic vanilla biscuits (see recipe on page 15)

Apricot glaze (see page 20)

SK Sugar Dough: 200g (7oz) Pink, 200g (7oz) Yellow

200g (7oz) SK Sugarpaste: Bridal White coloured with Dark Green and a touch of Yellow paste food colours

SK Quality Food Colour (QFC) Pastes: Dark Green, Yellow

SK Quality Food Colour (QFC) Dusts: Orange, Yellow

SK Professional Dust Food Colour: Rose

80g (2¾oz) SK Instant Mix Royal Icing

Equipment

Basic equipment (see pages 6–7)

Easter egg (or oval) cookie cutter

Round cutters: 6mm (¼"), 9mm (³/8"), 1.2cm (½"), 1.5cm (⁵/8")

Piping nozzles: nos. 1.5 x 2

Makes 24

1   Make the biscuit dough following the recipe on page 15, cut out 24 egg shapes using the egg- or oval-shaped cookie cutter and bake according to the recipe instructions. Leave to cool.

2   Brush the biscuits with cooled, boiled apricot glaze. Roll out the green-coloured sugarpaste to 3mm (¹/8") thick and cut out eight egg shapes from the paste. Lay a piece of sugarpaste onto each cookie and smooth down with your hands. Repeat this method with Pink and Yellow Sugar Dough to make eight pink and eight yellow egg cookies.

3   Roll out a small amount of the remaining green sugarpaste thinly and cut out a circle using each of the different-sized round cutters. Attach the green circles randomly over the pink eggs using edible glue.

4   Make up the royal icing according to the packet instructions and divide it into two bowls. Colour one half with Rose dust food colour and the other half with Yellow and a spot of Orange dust food colours.

5   Fit a small piping bag with a no. 1.5 nozzle and fill ²/3 with pink royal icing. Starting from the left and piping one line at a time, pipe a crisscross pattern over the yellow cookies. Pipe loops across the middle of each of the green cookies in pink royal icing.

6   Fit another small piping bag with a no. 1.5 nozzle and fill ²/3 with yellow royal icing. Pipe zigzag lines above and below the pink line on the green cookies.

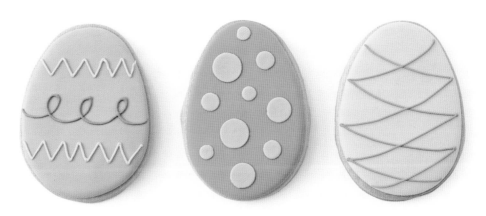

First Pint 18th Birthday Cake

Many an 18th birthday is honoured by a trip to the pub, so this cake is very fitting for the celebration. The crisped rice cereal mix allows you to model large cake top decorations that will still be light enough to sit on the cake.

Edibles

15cm (6") square sponge cake, filled and crumb-coated (see page 23)

One quantity of crisped rice cereal mix (see recipe on page 16)

SK Sugarpaste: 600g (1lb 5¼oz) Iced Mint, 100g (3½oz) Vintage Ivory

1 pack each SK Sugar Dough: Golden Bear Brown, Green, Red, Yellow

1 pack each SK Sugar Florist Paste (SFP): Black, Bulrush, Cream

SK Professional Paste Food Colours: Chestnut (soft beige), Cream

SK Professional Dust Food Colour: Edelweiss (white)

Small amount of SK Instant Mix Royal Icing

White vegetable fat

Clear alcohol, e.g. gin, vodka

SK Edible Glue

Equipment

Basic equipment (see pages 6–7)

25.5cm (10") square cake drum (board)

Half-pint plastic tumbler

Round cutters: 2.2cm (⁷/₈"), 4cm (1½"), 5.3cm (2¼"), 6.5cm (2½")

Piping nozzle: no. 4

Number cutters (PC)

Flat paintbrush (SK)

1.05m (1yd 5") x 15mm (⁵/₈") width satin ribbon: brown

Templates (see page 124)

Cake and cake drum

1 Position the 15cm (6") cake centrally on the 20.5cm (8") cake drum and cover both the cake and drum with Iced Mint sugarpaste (see pages 24–25). Leave to dry overnight.

Pint of beer

2 Make one quantity of the crisped rice cereal mix following the recipe on page 16. When it is cool enough to handle, dust the inside of the half-pint tumbler with icing sugar and push 100g (3½oz) of the cereal mix into it. Compact it down until it is level with the top of the tumbler then squeeze the sides to release the mix. To make it resemble a classic pint glass shape, mould the lower half with your hands then add a little more rice cereal to make the shape more concave. Refrigerate for 30 minutes.

3 Remove the rice cereal pint from the fridge and place it on a spare cake board. Roll out a small amount of Cream SFP to a 3mm (⅛") thickness and place the pint top-down onto the sugarpaste. Trim 5mm (¼") around the edge with a palette knife and push the excess icing up the sides of the pint. This will give the top of the beer a flat surface.

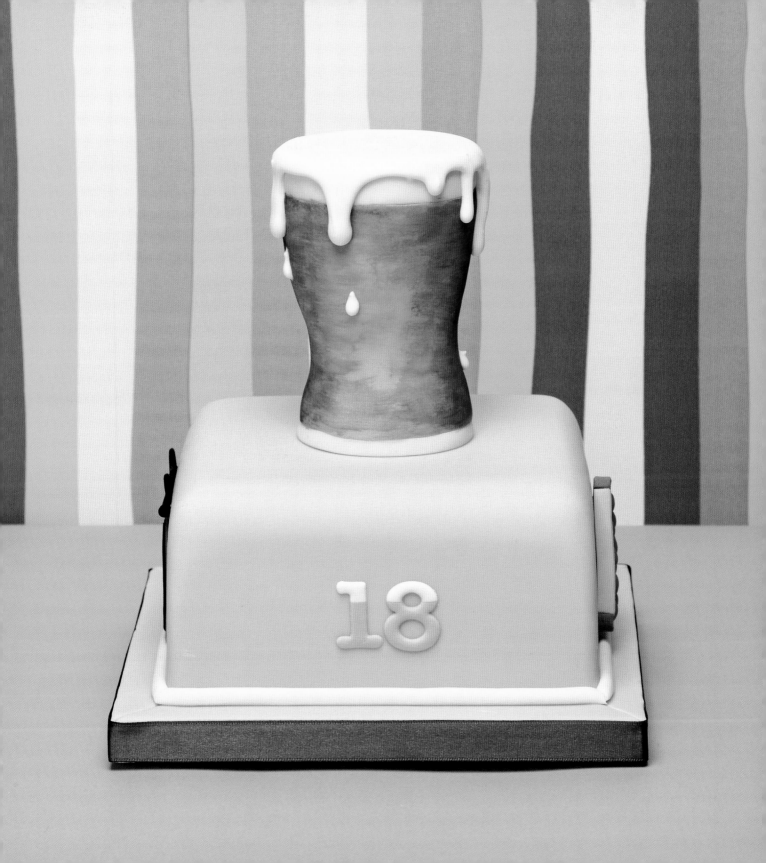

4 Use a palette knife to spread royal icing over the sides of the pint to fill in any gaps. Roll out some Cream SFP to a 3mm (1/8") thickness and cut a 1.5cm (5/8") wide strip of paste to go around the top edge. Wrap it around the top of the pint, trim to size and smooth the join with your fingers.

5 Mix 75g (2½oz) of Yellow Sugar Dough with 75g (2½oz) of Golden Bear Brown Sugar Dough then roll the paste out to a 3mm (1/8") thickness. Measure the height of the pint from the base to the cream band of icing and cut out a rectangle of paste that is large enough to fit around the shape. Wrap the paste around the pint and trim away any excess paste with a palette knife.

6 Roll out a small amount of Vintage Ivory sugarpaste to a 6mm (just over ¼") thickness and cut out a 6.5cm (2½") circle. Stick the paste to the bottom of the pint.

7 Mix some Chestnut paste food colour with a little clear alcohol. Start to paint two opposite sides of the pint with the darker shade, then add more alcohol to dilute the colour as you continue to paint around the glass to create a rounded effect.

8 Make up some royal icing and colour 40g (1½oz) with Cream paste food colour. Let the icing down slightly with a few drops of cold, pre-boiled water to give it a softer consistency, but not so it is runny. Fit a paper piping bag with a no. 4 nozzle and fill 2/3 with the cream-coloured icing. Starting from the middle, pipe in a spiral around the top of the pint. Once the top is covered, start to pipe around the top edge of the pint and let it drip down the sides to make the froth. Use the end of a paintbrush to swirl the froth on top of the beer. Leave to dry.

Snooker triangle

9 Roll out a small amount of Bulrush SFP to a 2mm (1/16") thickness. Use a sharp knife and a ruler to cut out a 6mm (just over ¼") wide strip of paste, then cut the strip into three 1cm (3/8") long pieces. Bend each of the pieces to shape following the template for the triangle, then leave them arranged on the paper template.

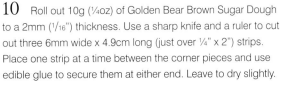

10 Roll out 10g (¼oz) of Golden Bear Brown Sugar Dough to a 2mm (¹⁄₁₆") thickness. Use a sharp knife and a ruler to cut out three 6mm wide x 4.9cm long (just over ¼" x 2") strips. Place one strip at a time between the corner pieces and use edible glue to secure them at either end. Leave to dry slightly.

11 Roll 11g (¼oz) of Red Sugar Dough into a long, thin sausage and cut it into 15 equal-sized pieces. Roll each piece into a small ball and use edible glue to secure the balls inside the triangle, making sure that they are glued to each other so they don't fall out.

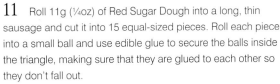

Pub sign

12 Fit the sugar shaper with the 3mm (⅛") circle disc. Soften a small amount of Black SFP with a little white vegetable fat. Place in the sugar shaper and extrude a 5.5cm (2¼") length of paste. Lay it out straight on a spare cake board and attach a small ball of Black SFP to one end.

13 Replace the 3mm (⅛") disc with the smallest circle and then extrude an 8.5cm (3³⁄₈") length of paste. Use the template to bend the paste into the correct shape. Attach to the top of the pole using edible glue and leave to dry.

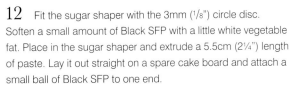

14 Roll out 8g (¼oz) of Bulrush SFP thinly and cut out a 5cm (2") square of paste. Use a blade tool to mark a smaller square 5mm (¼") inside the edge of the paste. Extrude four lengths of Black SFP using the smallest circle in the sugar shaper and attach them to the marked lines with edible glue.

15 Roll out a small amount of Cream SFP thinly and cut out the letters for 'PUB' using the alphabet cutters. Secure the letters to the sign with edible glue.

Number '18'

16 Roll out small amounts of Cream SFP and light brown Sugar Dough. Cut the edges straight with a sharp knife, position the Cream paste above the light brown paste and

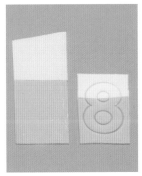

push them together. Roll over the paste gently to stick them together, cut them in half vertically and use the number cutters to cut out '18'.

Dartboard

17 Roll out 25g (just over ¾oz) of Black SFP thinly and cut out two 5.3cm (2¼") circles. Cut a 4cm (1½") circle from the centre of one of the larger black circles. Set the circles aside to dry slightly.

18 Cut the smaller 4cm (1½") circle of paste into quarters, then cut two of these quarters into five equal triangles to make ten altogether.

19 Roll out a small amount of Cream SFP, cut out a 4cm (1½") circle and cut this into sections in the same way to make ten cream triangles.

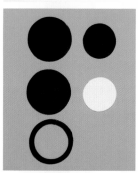

20 Turn over the black ring of paste and arrange the black and cream triangles of paste alternately in the centre. Brush the second 5.3cm (2¼") black circle of paste with a little edible glue. Attach this over the back of the dartboard to secure the pieces in place and flip the dartboard over. Mark the inner ring on the dartboard with a 2.2cm (⁷/₈") round cutter.

21 Make an indent in the very centre of the board with the end of a paintbrush. Roll a tiny ball of Green Sugar Dough, push this into the indent then attach a tiny ball of Red Sugar Dough on top to make the bullseye.

22 Roll out a small amount of Red Sugar Dough and a small amount of Green Sugar Dough thinly and cut them into several 2mm (¹/₁₆") wide strips. Trim the strips to size using a sharp craft knife, attach them around the inner and outer rings on the dartboard and secure with edible glue. Mix a little Edelweiss dust colour with a little clear alcohol and paint the numbers around the dartboard, using the picture as a guide.

Finishing touches

23 Once they are all dry, attach the number 18, dartboard, pub sign and snooker triangle to the sides of the cake using a little edible glue. Place the pint of beer on the top of the cake and secure with royal icing.

24 Attach brown ribbon around the edge of the cake drum with a non-toxic glue stick, being careful that the glue does not come into contact with the cake.

Pint Cookies

Edibles

Basic vanilla biscuits (see recipe on page 15)

Apricot glaze (see page 20)

SK Sugar Dough: 300g (10½oz) Golden Bear Brown, 300g (10½oz) Yellow

SK Professional Paste Food Colours: Bulrush (dark brown), Chestnut (soft beige), Cream

Small amount of SK Instant Mix Royal Icing

Clear alcohol, e.g. gin or vodka

Makes 24

Equipment

Basic equipment (see pages 6–7)

Number cutters (JEM)

Piping nozzle: no. 2

Template (see page 124)

1   Make the biscuit dough following the recipe on page 15, then cut out 24 pint shapes using the template and a sharp knife. Bake according to the recipe instructions then leave to cool.

2   Mix together the Golden Bear Brown and Yellow Sugar Dough. Cut out the middle section of the pint template, roll out the paste to a 3mm (1/8") thickness and use the template and a sharp craft knife to cut out the middle section from the paste. Brush the cookies with cooled, boiled apricot glaze then place the Sugar Dough shape centrally on the cookie and smooth over the edges. While the paste is still soft, push the number cutters into the surface to emboss the number '18'.

3   Mix Chestnut paste food colour with a little clear alcohol and paint the paste in the same way as for the pint topper on the main cake (see page 90). Leave to dry.

4   Colour a small amount of royal icing with a little Cream paste food colour. Fit a paper piping bag with a no. 2 nozzle and fill 2/3 with the icing. Pipe a rectangular outline around the top and bottom of the cookie then leave to dry.

5   Let the royal icing down with a few drops of cooled, boiled water to make a run-out consistency. Fit another piping bag with a no. 2 nozzle and fill 2/3 with the icing. Flood inside the piped outline at the bottom of each cookie, then fill in the top outline and let it dry.

6   Once dry, pipe a little of the icing along the top and down the sides of the cookie to represent dripping froth.

7   Use the Bulrush paste food colour and a flat paintbrush to paint over the number 18, keeping within the embossed outline.

Designer Handbag Cake

Anyone who is fashion-conscious would be thrilled to receive a designer handbag that is both stylish and edible! A great idea for a 21st birthday treat, you can always personalise the cake to suit the recipient's individual style. Cake carving allows you to transform a sponge cake into any shape you want – simply follow the templates provided to achieve a recognisable handbag shape.

Edibles

20.5cm (8") square sponge cake

One quantity of buttercream (see page 18)

SK Sugarpaste: 400g (14oz) Vintage Ivory, 760g (1lb 11oz) Vintage Pink

1 pack SK Sugar Florist Paste (SFP): Cream

SK Designer Metallic Lustre Dust Food Colour: Silver

SK Edible Glue

SK Instant Mix Royal Icing

Clear alcohol, e.g. gin or vodka

top tip

I find that it is always easier to carve a cake the day after it's been made.

Equipment

Basic equipment (see pages 6–7)

25.5cm (10") round cake drum (board)

Piping nozzle: no. 4

Round cutters: 7mm, 1.5cm, 3.5cm (just over $^1/_4$", $^5/_8$", $1^3/_8$")

Large numerals cutter (PC)

1m (1yd 3") x 15mm ($^5/_8$") width satin ribbon: dark pink

Templates (see page 126)

Cake and drum

1 Cover the cake drum with 300g (10½oz) of Vintage Ivory sugarpaste (see page 25).

2 Use a cake leveller to trim off the top of the cake to make it 5cm (2") deep. Cut the sponge into three sections using the bag layer templates and a sharp knife. Start with the largest section at the bottom and stack the sponges, spreading buttercream between each layer.

3 Cut out two of the bag side template from greaseproof paper and use sterilised glass-headed pins to secure the templates to either side of the cake. Using a serrated knife, carve the top of the cake to give the bag a rounded shape. Carefully remove both the pins and the templates.

4 Use the knife to round off all the edges of the cake. Working from the centre, carve from the top and down the sides of the cake to shape the bag. Place the cake on a spare cake drum and spread with a thin layer of buttercream to prepare it for covering.

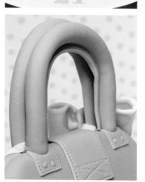

5   Roll out 550g (1lb 3½oz) of Vintage Pink sugarpaste to a thickness of 5mm (¼"), place the paste over the top of the cake and smooth it down. Trim away the excess paste and smooth over the surface of the cake with your hands.

6   Use a ruler and a scribing tool to mark a zip line along the centre of the cake and down the sides of the bag. Mark a horizontal line all the way around the cake, approximately 2.5cm (1") up from the base.

7   Mix 50g (1¾oz) of Vintage Pink sugarpaste with 50g (1¾oz) of Vintage Ivory sugarpaste to make a pale pink modelling paste. Roll the paste out to an even thickness and cut out two strips of paste that are 2.5cm wide x 27cm long (1" x 10½"). Brush the back of each strip with edible glue and wrap them around the base of the cake to make the trim, smoothing the paste along the top edge as you go. Place the cake in the centre of the covered cake drum.

Handles

8   Mix 26g (just under 1oz) of Cream SFP with the same amount of Vintage Ivory sugarpaste to make an ivory modelling paste. Split the paste equally into two pieces and roll each one into a sausage that is 21cm (8") long. Push a 10cm (4") length of dried spaghetti into each end of the sausage, leaving approximately 6.5cm (2½") sticking out at either end.

9   Roll out 50g (1¾oz) of Vintage Pink sugarpaste into a long strip and cut out a piece that is 25cm long x 5cm wide (10" x 2"). Place the ivory part of the handle on top of the Vintage Pink paste and wrap the paste around it. Secure the join with edible glue and trim the paste to create a neat, straight edge. Run a quilting tool along the join then bend the handle into shape, making sure that the distance between each piece of spaghetti is 8cm (3⅛") wide. Repeat to make a second handle and leave them to dry overnight.

10   Push the spaghetti directly into the cake, so one handle sits either side of the zip line and secure with edible glue. Roll out a small amount of Vintage Pink sugarpaste thinly and use a

craft knife and a ruler to cut out three 2cm (¾") squares. Cut away a semicircle of paste from the top of each square using a 15mm (⅝") round cutter. Run a quilting tool around the edges and attach to the cake around the base of the handles to cover the joins. You will need two squares for the back of the bag and one for the front right handle: the other will be covered by the bow.

11 Use the end of a no. 4 nozzle to mark two circles on each piece of paste. Roll out a small amount of Cream SFP and cut out six small circles using the no. 4 nozzle. Attach the circles over the marks and paint them using a little Silver lustre dust mixed with clear alcohol.

Flap

12 Roll out 40g (1½oz) of Vintage Pink sugarpaste thinly and cut out a 4cm x 11cm (1½" x 4½") rectangle of paste. Cut one end with a 3.5cm (1⅜") round cutter to make it curved, then run a quilting tool around the whole piece of paste.

13 At the square end of the flap, use a quilting tool to draw a line across the paste that is approximately 1.5cm (⅝") up from the straight edge. Within the lines, draw a cross from corner to corner. Attach the flap over the cake between the handles with edible glue.

Clasp

14 Roll out a small amount of Cream SFP and use a ruler and a craft knife to cut out a 1.5cm x 2.5cm (⅝" x 1") rectangle. Use a 1.5cm (⅝") round cutter to round off the ends of the rectangle. Make two holes in the centre with a no. 4 piping nozzle, then cut two lines between the holes and remove this small section of paste. Make a small ball from the excess paste and push this into the middle of the hole. Use a no. 4 nozzle to make two indents in either end of the paste.

15 Shape a small piece of Cream SFP into a cylinder that is approximately 1cm x 3mm (⅜" x ⅛") in size and dust with Silver lustre dust. Attach the clasp to the flap and the catch on top of the clasp with a little edible glue.

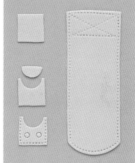

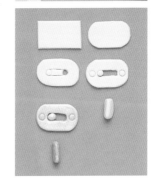

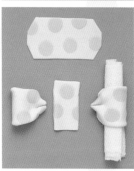

Bow

16 Mix 27g (1oz) of Vintage Ivory sugarpaste with the same amount of Cream SFP and roll out thinly until the paste measures approximately 20cm x 14cm (7¾" x 5½") in size. Roll out the leftover pale pink modelling paste thinly and cut out 28 1.5cm (⅝") circles of paste with a round cutter. Arrange the pink circles in several rows on the cream paste, then roll the rolling pin gently over the paste to merge the spots.

17 Use a sharp knife to cut the spotty paste into two 20cm x 5cm (7¾" x 2") lengths. Make a diagonal cut across the middle of the first strip to cut it in two. Cut away the corners on the opposite ends to make the bow tails. Gather the tails at one end and secure them to the side of the bag using edible glue.

18 Cut out a thin strip of spotty paste that is 2cm (¾") long and attach it around the bag handle so it meets the bow tails at the front of the cake. Cut another length of paste and attach it around the other side of the handle.

19 For the bow loops, take the remaining 20cm x 5cm (7¾" x 2") length of paste, cut it in half and cut all four corners away at an angle. Fold the ends together to make the loops and roll along the edges slightly to soften them.

20 Cut a 3cm x 6cm (1⅛" x 2⅜") rectangle of paste and tuck the long sides under to give a neat edge. Wrap this around the centre of the bow loops to join the two pieces together and use edible glue to secure it in place. Attach the finished bow to the bag.

Fabric flower

21 Mix 14g (½oz) of Vintage Ivory sugarpaste with 14g (½oz) of Cream SFP to make a pale ivory modelling paste. Roll out the paste to make a 30.5cm (12") long strip of paste

widest point. Hold the end of the strip and start rolling the paste up, pinching the paste as you wrap it around. Turn over and twist off the excess paste from the back.

22 Leave to dry for an hour, then push a 4cm (1½") length of spaghetti into the back of the flower. Brush a little edible glue over the back of the flower and push it into the cake on the opposite side to the bow.

Tag

23 Roll out the remaining Vintage Pink sugarpaste to approximately 2mm–3mm ($^1/_{16}$"–$^1/_8$") thick and cut out a 6cm x 3cm (2$^3/_8$"x 1$^1/_8$") rectangle. Use the 3.5cm (1$^3/_8$") round cutter to make one end of the tag rounded then run the quilting tool around the edge. Use a 7mm (just over ¼") round cutter to remove a circle of paste from the end of the tag, then leave to dry slightly.

24 Roll out 8g (¼oz) of Cream SFP into a very narrow, long strip that is 23cm x 1cm (9" x $^3/_8$") in size. Fold the paste in half lengthways and run the quilting tool along either side. Thread this through the hole in the tag and secure with a little edible glue at the top. Hang the tag around the handle, use edible glue to secure it in place and cut away any excess paste with a craft knife.

Finishing touches

25 Roll out a small amount of Vintage Pink sugarpaste thinly and cut out the numerals using the cutters. Use a scribing tool to remove the numbers from the cutter. Attach to the front of the covered cake drum with edible glue.

26 Attach the ribbon around the edge of the cake drum using a non-toxic glue stick, being careful that the glue does not come into contact with the cake.

Designer Handbag Cake

Fabric Flower Cupcakes

Edibles

12 cupcakes baked in SK Soft
Grey Rose cupcake cases
(see recipe on page 12)

Apricot glaze (see page 20)

SK Sugarpaste: 150g (5¼oz)
Vintage Ivory, 220g (7¾oz)
Vintage Pink

1 pack SK Sugar Florist Paste
(SFP): Cream

SK Edible Glue

Equipment

Basic equipment (see
pages 6–7)

5.5cm (2¼") round cutter

Makes 12

1   Brush the top of each cupcake with a little
cooled, boiled apricot glaze. Roll out the Vintage
Pink sugarpaste to 3mm (⅛") thick and cut out 12
5.5cm (2¼") circles of paste. Place these onto the
cupcakes and smooth down with the palm of your hand.

2   Roll out 14g (½oz) of Vintage Ivory sugarpaste for
each fabric flower and follow the instructions on pages
100–101. These flowers should be slightly smaller than
the one on the main cake.

3   Attach one flower to the top of each cupcake with a
little edible glue.

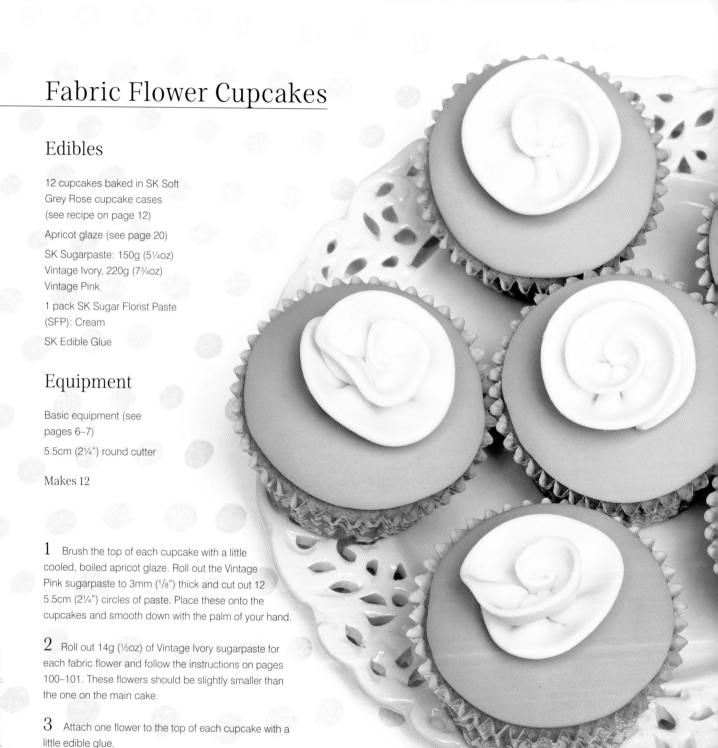

Pompom Wedding Cake

Pretty pompoms and lace leaves add a delicate touch to this vibrant pink and lime wedding cake. Pompoms make great girly decorations and the technique for making them can be adapted easily to create other pretty frill effects.

Edibles

10cm, 15cm, 20.5cm and 25.5cm (4", 6", 8" and 10") square cakes, filled and crumb-coated (see page 23)

SK Sugarpaste: 900g (2lb) Bridal Rose, 2.5kg (5lb 8¼oz) Bridal White coloured with Vine and Yellow Paste Food Colours

SK Professional Paste Food Colour: Vine

SK Quality Food Colour (QFC) Paste: Yellow

SK Sugar Florist Paste (SFP): Pale Pink, White

SK Edible Glue

80g (2¾oz) SK Instant Mix Royal Icing

Equipment

Basic equipment (see pages 6–7)

30.5cm (12") square cake drum (board)

10cm, 15cm and 20.5cm (4", 6" and 8") square cake cards

8 plastic dowels

Round cutters: 2cm, 2.5cm, 4cm (¾", 1", 1½")

Lace leaf cutters: nos. 3, 4 (OP)

Piping nozzle: no. 2

3.6m (4yd) x 6mm (¼") width grosgrain ribbon: pink

1.5m (1yd 23") x 15mm (⅝") width grosgrain ribbon: pink

Cakes and cake drum

1   Colour the Bridal White sugarpaste with a little Vine and Yellow paste food colours to make a lime green colour. Pick up the paste colour with on a cocktail stick and touch it to the sugarpaste. Knead in the colour well until it is evenly mixed.

2   Position the 10cm, 15cm and 20.5cm (4", 6" and 8") cakes on the corresponding cake cards and the 25.5cm (10") cake onto the 30.5cm (12") cake drum. Cover the 20.5cm (8") cake with Bridal Rose sugarpaste (see page 25). Cover the 25.5cm, 10cm and 15cm (10", 4" and 6") cakes and the cake drum with lime green sugarpaste (see pages 24–25). Leave cakes to dry overnight.

3   Dowel the first, second and third (base and two middle) tiers then stack the cakes on top of one another, securing each tier in place with a little royal icing (see page 26).

Pompoms

4   Roll out a small amount of Pale Pink SFP thinly and cut out one 2.5cm (1") circle and seven 4cm (1½") circles with the round cutters. Roll a cocktail stick around the

edges of each circle to frill the paste. Fold each of the 4cm (1½") circles in half and then into three to make a cone shape. Arrange all seven triangles on the 2.5cm (1") base circle, secure with a little edible glue and set to one side.

5   Roll out another piece of Pale Pink SFP thinly and cut out six more 4cm (1½") circles. Repeat as before, frilling the edges of each and folding them into cone shapes. Attach five cones on top of the first layer of the pompom and push the final piece into the centre. Fluff up the frills with your fingers then leave to dry.

6   To make a smaller pompom, use the 2cm (¾") cutter for the base circle and the 2.5cm (1") cutter for the folded sections. You will need one 2cm (¾") circle and 12 x 2.5cm (1") circles: six for the bottom layer, five for the second layer and one on top.

7   Make one large and one small pompom from White SFP. Mix 5g (just under ¼oz) of Pale Pink SFP with 5g (just under ¼oz) of White SFP to make a lighter pink, then make one large and one small pompom from the paste. Leave all the pompoms to dry.

Lace leaves

8   Mix 10g (¼oz) of the remaining green sugarpaste with 10g (¼oz) of White SFP. Roll out thinly and cut out one leaf using each of the lace leaf cutters and leave to dry.

9   Roll out a small amount of Pale Pink SFP and some pale green paste very thinly. Cut each piece of paste into 3mm (⅛") wide strips using a ruler and a craft knife then set to one side.

10   Roll out a 10g (¼oz) piece of White SFP thinly then arrange the pink and green strips alternately on the paste. Gently roll the rolling pin over the paste to secure the strips in place. Use the lace leaf cutters to cut out a striped leaf shape in each size. Leave to dry.

Finishing touches

11 Fit a small paper piping bag with a no. 2 nozzle and fill ²/₃ with royal icing. Trim the base of each tier with 6mm (¼") ribbon and secure at the back of the cake with a small dot of royal icing.

12 Arrange two large pompoms and one small pompom in a cluster towards the left of the bottom tier and attach to the cake with small dots of royal icing. Secure two lace leaves either side of the smallest pompom.

13 Secure one large pompom and two smaller pompoms in the same way towards the right of the third tier. Attach two lace leaves either side of the highest pompom.

14 Tie two bows from the remaining 6mm (¼") ribbon and attach one bow at the base of the top tier and one at the base of the second tier.

15 Attach the 15mm (⁵/₈") ribbon around the cake drum using a non-toxic glue stick, being careful that the glue does not come into contact with the cake.

Macaroon Favours

Edibles

SK Instant Macaroon Mix

SK Quality Food Colour
(QFC) Dusts: Green, Pink,
Yellow

Vanilla buttercream (see
page 18)

Makes 18

1   Make the macaroons
following the recipe on page
17. Add Pink QFC dust food
colour to half the mix to make
pink-coloured macaroons,
and a mixture of Green and
Yellow QFC dust food colours
to make the lime-coloured
macaroons. Bake following
the recipe and allow to cool.

2   Sandwich the macaroon
halves together with a layer of
vanilla buttercream coloured
with Pink or Green and Yellow
dust food colours to match.

Pompom Wedding Cake

Ruby Anniversary Cake

Quilling is a popular paper craft technique that can be easily adapted for use in cake design. This anniversary cake incorporates the quilling technique to build up a flowing, elegant design – simply change the colour scheme to personalise this romantic cake for any wedding anniversary.

Edibles

20.5cm (8") hexagonal sponge cake, filled and crumb-coated (see page 23)

1kg (2lb 3¼oz) SK Sugarpaste: Vintage Ivory

SK Quality Food Colour (QFC) Pastes: Black, Red

1 pack each SK Sugar Florist Paste (SFP): Cream, Poinsettia (Red)

SK Edible Glue

White vegetable fat

Small amount of SK Instant Mix Royal Icing

Equipment

Basic equipment (see pages 6–7)

30.5cm (12") round cake drum (board)

Piping nozzle: no. 1.5

98.5cm (1yd 3") x 15mm (⅝") width satin ribbon: champagne

Templates (see page 125)

1   Position the hexagonal cake centrally on the 25.5cm (10") round cake drum and cover the cake and drum with Vintage Ivory sugarpaste (see pages 24–25). Leave to dry overnight.

2   Place the top design template on the surface of the cake, then press gently along the outline of the letter 'A' and the scroll design below with a scribing tool to mark out the sugarpaste.

3   Fit the sugar shaper with a 6mm (¼") ribbon disc. Soften a small amount of Poinsettia SFP with a little white vegetable fat: this will make the paste easier to push through the sugar shaper. Extrude the paste from the shaper and cut each ribbon to size using small scissors and the 'A' template as a guide.

4   Once the paste is the right length, use a little edible glue to stick the narrow edge of the sugar ribbon to the sugarpaste: the paste should stand proud from the top of the cake to create a 3D-effect. Continue cutting and sticking the ribbons of paste until the outline of the 'A' is complete. Leave to dry slightly.

5   Make 10g (¼oz) of Poinsettia SFP a little darker by adding some Red paste food colour and a spot of Black food colour. Extrude ribbons of the Red, dark red and Cream SFP to complete the scroll design below the letter 'A'. Use the template

as a guide to get the shape of the ribbon right before placing it on the cake. To curl the paste, wrap a piece of sugar ribbon gently around the end of a paintbrush and release. Make all the pieces of the same colour, shape and leave to dry slightly before attaching to the cake and moving on to the next colour. Following the marks on the cake, attach all the pieces using edible glue.

6   Make the quilled decoration inside the 'A' frame in the same way as described in steps 3 and 4, using a paintbrush to curl the paste more tightly. Use the template to adjust the ribbon to the correct shape and size, then brush the edge of each ribbon with a little edible glue and stick it into the frame.

7   Place the cake onto a turntable and tilt it away from you as far as it will go. Use the 6mm (¼") ribbon disc again and fill the sugar shaper with softened Poinsettia SFP. Extrude six lengths of paste for the border around the base of the cake. Trim to size and attach along the base of each side with edible glue.

8   Hold the side design template up against each of the six sides in turn and mark the design onto the cake with a scribing tool, as before. Use the sugar shaper to extrude ribbons of Red, dark red and Cream SFP and shape as before. To make it easier to attach the ribbons to the side of the cake, brush the outline of the side design with edible glue and then stick the quilled paste to the glued area.

9   Use the template and a scriber to mark out the inscription on the top of the cake. Fit a small paper piping bag with a no 1.5 nozzle. Colour a small amount of royal icing dark red with Red paste food colour and a spot of Black paste colour. Fill the bag ²/₃ with the icing and carefully pipe the inscription onto the cake.

10   Attach the ribbon around the edge of the cake drum using a non-toxic glue stick, being careful that the glue does not come into contact with the cake.

top tip

I find it easiest to fill the sugar shaper with the first colour of paste and make all the pieces required in that colour, then wash the sugar shaper and repeat for the other colours of paste one-by-one.

Heart Cupcakes

Edibles

12 cupcakes, baked in plain cupcake cases (see recipe on page 12)

350g (12¼oz) vanilla buttercream (see page 18)

300g (10½oz) SK Sugarpaste: Vintage Ivory

1 pack SK Sugar Florist Paste (SFP): Poinsettia (red), half coloured with Red and Black QFC Pastes (see page 110)

Equipment

Basic equipment (see pages 6–7)

Large piping bag

Large star nozzle

Small heart cookie cutter

5cm (2") fluted round cutter

Red heart cupcake wrappers

Makes 12

1 Roll out some Vintage Ivory sugarpaste to a 3mm (⅛") thickness and cut out 12 fluted circles from the paste. Place the circles on a spare cake board dusted with icing sugar. While the paste is still soft, gently press the heart cutter into the paste to emboss an outline for the quilled heart.

2 Fit the sugar shaper with the 6mm (¼") ribbon disc and extrude 9cm (3½") lengths of Poinsettia and dark red paste for each cupcake, following the instructions for the main cake (see pages 110–111). Brush edible glue along the embossed heart outline and attach the quilled lengths to the glued area. Leave these to dry.

3 Use a palette knife to cover the top of the cupcake with vanilla buttercream, spreading it level across the cake. Fit a large piping bag with a large star nozzle, fill with buttercream and pipe a small swirl in the centre of the cupcake.

4 Once the sugarpaste decoration is dry, place it on top of the buttercream swirl and place the cupcake into a red wrapper.

Red-nosed Reindeer Christmas Cake

This festive cake design would make a fantastically fun centrepiece for any Christmas table. Modelled from just a few basic shapes, the reindeer figurines are much easier to make than you might think and you can get all the family involved in making cookies and truffles to match.

Edibles

20.5cm (8") round fruit cake, prepared for covering (see page 20)

1kg (2lb 3oz) SK Sugarpaste: Bridal White

1 pack SK Mexican Modelling Paste (MMP): Teddy Bear Brown

1 pack each SK Sugar Florist Paste (SFP): Bulrush, Poinsettia (red), White

SK Professional Food Colour Pens: Black, Brown

SK Designer Fairy Sparkles Dust Food Colour: Ice White

SK Designer Metallic Lustre Dust Food Colour: Classic Gold

SK Quality Food Colour (QFC) Dust: Red

SK Gildesol

SK Edible Glue

Equipment

Basic equipment (see pages 6–7)

25.5cm (10") round cake drum (board)

Large upper case alphabet cutters (PC)

Daisy leaf cutter (JEM)

80cm (31½") x 15mm (⁵/₈") width satin ribbon: brown

90cm (35½") x 15mm (⁵/₈") width grosgrain ribbon: red stitched

Cake and drum

1   Position the cake centrally on the drum and cover both the cake and drum with Bridal White sugarpaste (see pages 24–25).

2   Wrap the brown satin ribbon around the base of the cake and secure with a little edible glue.

Reindeer

3   Roll out a small amount of Bulrush SFP thinly and use the daisy leaf cutter to cut out six antlers. Cut away the small pieces from the bottom of the shape and leave to dry on a flat surface dusted with cornflour.

4   Shape a 20g (¾oz) ball of Teddy Bear Brown MMP into a cone. Place the cone in the centre of the cake and secure with a little edible glue. Push a 6cm (2³/₈") length of dried spaghetti into the body, leaving 2cm (¾") sticking out of the top.

5   Shape a small pinch of Bulrush SFP into a thick disc, then run the stitching tool around the top and bottom edges. Push this

down onto the top of the body for the collar and secure with a little edible glue.

6   To make the bell, roll a pinch of Bridal White sugarpaste into a pea-sized ball, make small holes on either side with a Dresden tool then mark a line that joins the holes. Rub some Gildesol in the palm of your hand, roll the ball in your hand to coat it then use a paintbrush to dust with Classic Gold lustre dust.

7   For the head, roll 25g (just over ¾oz) of Teddy Bear Brown MMP into an oval shape. Pinch the oval at one end to make it slightly thinner and round off the snout at the other end. Push the head down onto the neck and secure with edible glue. Use a craft knife to make two slits in the top of the head that are large enough to hold the antlers.

8   For the left reindeer, shape a 17g (just over ½oz) ball of Teddy Bear Brown MMP into the body as for the first reindeer and flatten it slightly. Position the body belly-down on the cake to the left of the first reindeer and secure with edible glue. Make another collar and head in the same way as before and attach to the front of the body.

9   Shape 10g (¼oz) of Teddy Bear Brown MMP into the shape of a snout and attach it to the cake on the right of the central reindeer using edible glue.

10   Split 4g (a pinch) of Poinsettia SFP into three pieces and roll them into balls for the noses. Rub a small amount of Gildesol into the palm of your hand, roll the red noses in your palm one at a time to coat them and then roll in a mixture of Red dust food colour and Ice White lustre dust. Attach the noses to the end of the reindeers' snouts with edible glue, then attach a small, flat dot of White SFP to each nose.

11   Cut pieces of dried spaghetti into eight 3.7cm (1⅜") lengths and split 8g (¼oz) of Teddy Bear Brown MMP into four equal pieces for the legs. Roll each piece of paste to 5cm (2") in length, cut them in half to give you eight lengths and insert a piece of dried spaghetti into each one.

12   To make the hooves, roll a small, pea-sized ball of Bulrush SFP and make a small indent in one end with a Dresden tool. Attach the hoof to the end of one of the legs with edible glue. Repeat to add hooves to the other seven legs. Push the legs into the bodies of the right-hand and central reindeer and the remaining four into the cake for the left-hand reindeer.

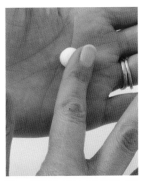

13   Shape a pea-sized piece of Teddy Bear Brown paste into a long, oval shape. Taper each end to a point and then cut the paste in half. Mark the centre of each ear with a Dresden tool and attach to the head just behind each cut for the antlers.

14   Divide a small pinch of White SFP into four small balls, then pinch them lightly between your finger and thumb to flatten each ball slightly. Attach the eyes to the faces of the central and left reindeer with edible glue. Once they have dried, draw on the pupils with a Black food pen and the mouths with a Brown food pen.

15   For the central and left reindeer, push the dried antlers directly into their heads and stick the third pair of antlers into the cake just above the third reindeer's head.

16   Rub a tiny amount of Gildesol onto a non-stick board and roll out a small piece of Poinsettia SFP into a thin sheet coated with the Gildesol. Lift the paste and turn it over then use a flat dusting brush to dust the surface of the paste with Ice White lustre dust. Use the large alphabet cutters to cut out each of the letters for 'CHRISTMAS' and set these to one side to dry.

Snowballs

17   Roll several small balls of paste from 100g (3½oz) of White SFP and place into a food-grade plastic bag. Add ½tsp of Ice White lustre dust to the bag and shake it to cover the balls in dust colour, ensuring to hold the top of the bag closed. Empty the balls into a sieve to remove any excess dust.

18   Arrange the snowballs around the reindeer and place a few around the bottom of the cake using edible glue to secure them in place.

Finishing touches

19 Attach the letters to the legs and antlers using edible glue to spell the word 'Christmas'.

20 Attach the red ribbon around the edge of the cake drum using a non-toxic glue stick, being careful not to come into contact with the cake.

Rudolf Tree Decorations

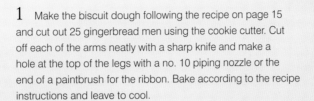

Edibles

25 gingerbread biscuits (see recipe on page 15)

550g (1lb 3½oz) SK Instant Mix Royal Icing

SK Quality Food Colour (QFC) Dust: Red

SK Professional Dust Food Colour: Bulrush (dark brown)

SK Professional Food Colour Pen: Black

SK Designer Scintillo Piping Sparkles: Red

Equipment

Basic equipment (see pages 6–7)

Piping nozzles: nos. 2, 4, 10 (optional)

SK Gingerbread Man Cookie Cutter

7mm (just over ¼") width ribbon: red

Makes 25

1 Make the biscuit dough following the recipe on page 15 and cut out 25 gingerbread men using the cookie cutter. Cut off each of the arms neatly with a sharp knife and make a hole at the top of the legs with a no. 10 piping nozzle or the end of a paintbrush for the ribbon. Bake according to the recipe instructions and leave to cool.

2 Make up 250g (8¾oz) of royal icing and colour it with Bulrush dust food colour. Fit a paper piping bag with a no. 2 nozzle and fill ⅔ with the brown icing. Turn the cookies upside down, so the gingerbread men's legs make the antlers. Pipe a teardrop shape to outline the face, then pipe the outline of the ears separately. Repeat for all the cookies and then leave the icing to dry.

3 Let down the remaining brown royal icing with a few drops of cooled, boiled water to make a runny consistency suitable for run-outs. Put this icing into a small piping bag and cut the very tip off the piping bag. Flood the face with the run-out icing, starting around the outline and working in towards the middle. Once the face has dried slightly, fill in the ears.

4 Add a little more Bulrush dust colour to 80g (2¾oz) of royal icing to make it a darker brown colour. Fit a paper piping bag with a no. 2 nozzle and fill ⅔ with the dark brown icing. Pipe thin lines for the antlers and leave to dry.

5 Once the face is dry, colour 120g (4¼oz) of royal icing with Red dust food colour. Fit a paper piping bag with a no. 2 nozzle and fill ⅔ with red icing. Pipe an oval for the nose in the centre of the face, leave the outline to dry before adding a few drops of cooled, boiled water and flooding it with run-out consistency red icing.

6 Let down 100g (3½oz) of white royal icing slightly with a few drops of cooled, boiled water. Fit a paper piping bag with a no. 4 nozzle and fill ⅔ with white royal icing. Pipe on two eyes and a tiny white dot on the noses.

7 When all of the royal icing is dry, draw on the mouth with a Black food colour pen and add black dots in the centre of the eyes. Fill a small paper piping bag with Red piping sparkles and snip the tip off the end of the bag. Pipe over the red nose with the piping sparkles to make it shiny. Leave to dry completely.

Red-nosed Reindeer Christmas Cake

Red Nose Truffles

Edibles

Chocolate truffles (see recipe on page 16)

Red vermicelli

Small amount of SK Instant Mix Royal Icing

Equipment

Basic equipment (see pages 6–7)

SK Spotty Miniature Cupcake Cases: Brown

Piping nozzle: no. 2

1   Use your hands to roll the truffle mixture into small balls. Place the red vermicelli in a small bowl and roll the truffles in the vermicelli until they are completely covered. Place each truffle into a miniature cupcake case.

2   Fit a paper piping bag with a no. 2 nozzle and fill $^2/_3$ with white royal icing. Pipe a small white dot slightly off-centre on the top of each truffle.

Templates

Rub-a-Dub-Dub Baby
Shower Cake, pages 32–37

'Bright as a Button'
Birthday Cake, pages 42–48

Pitter Patter Christening Cake, pages 38–41

Toy Soldier Birthday Cake, pages 56–63

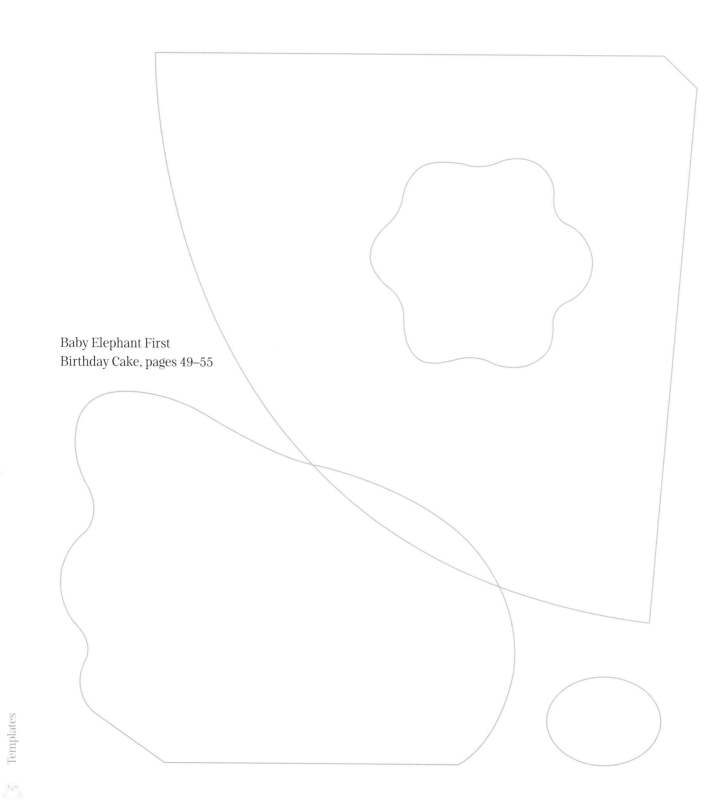

Baby Elephant First
Birthday Cake, pages 49–55

'What a Hoot!' Birthday Cake,
pages 64–75

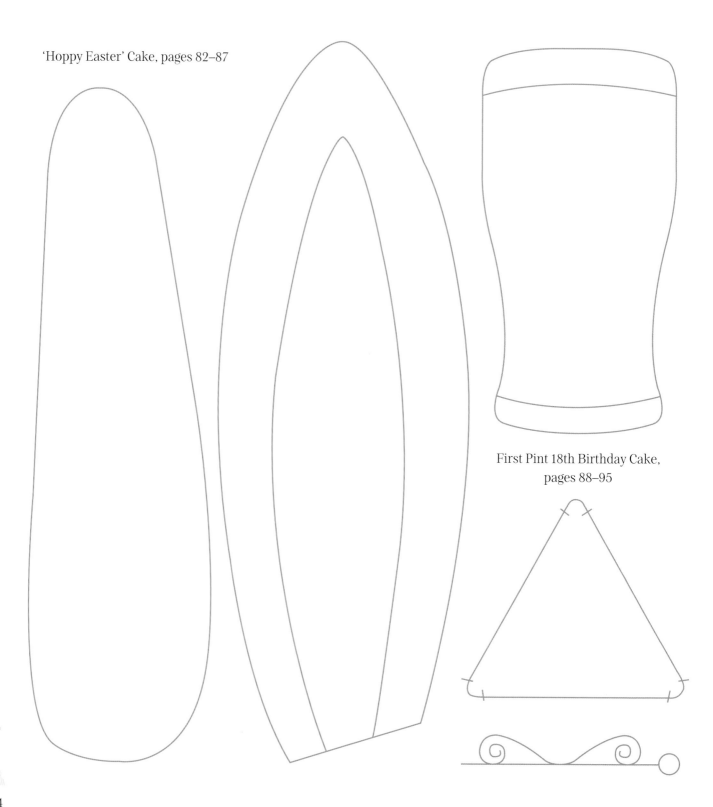

'Hoppy Easter' Cake, pages 82–87

First Pint 18th Birthday Cake,
pages 88–95

Ruby Anniversary Cake,
pages 110–113

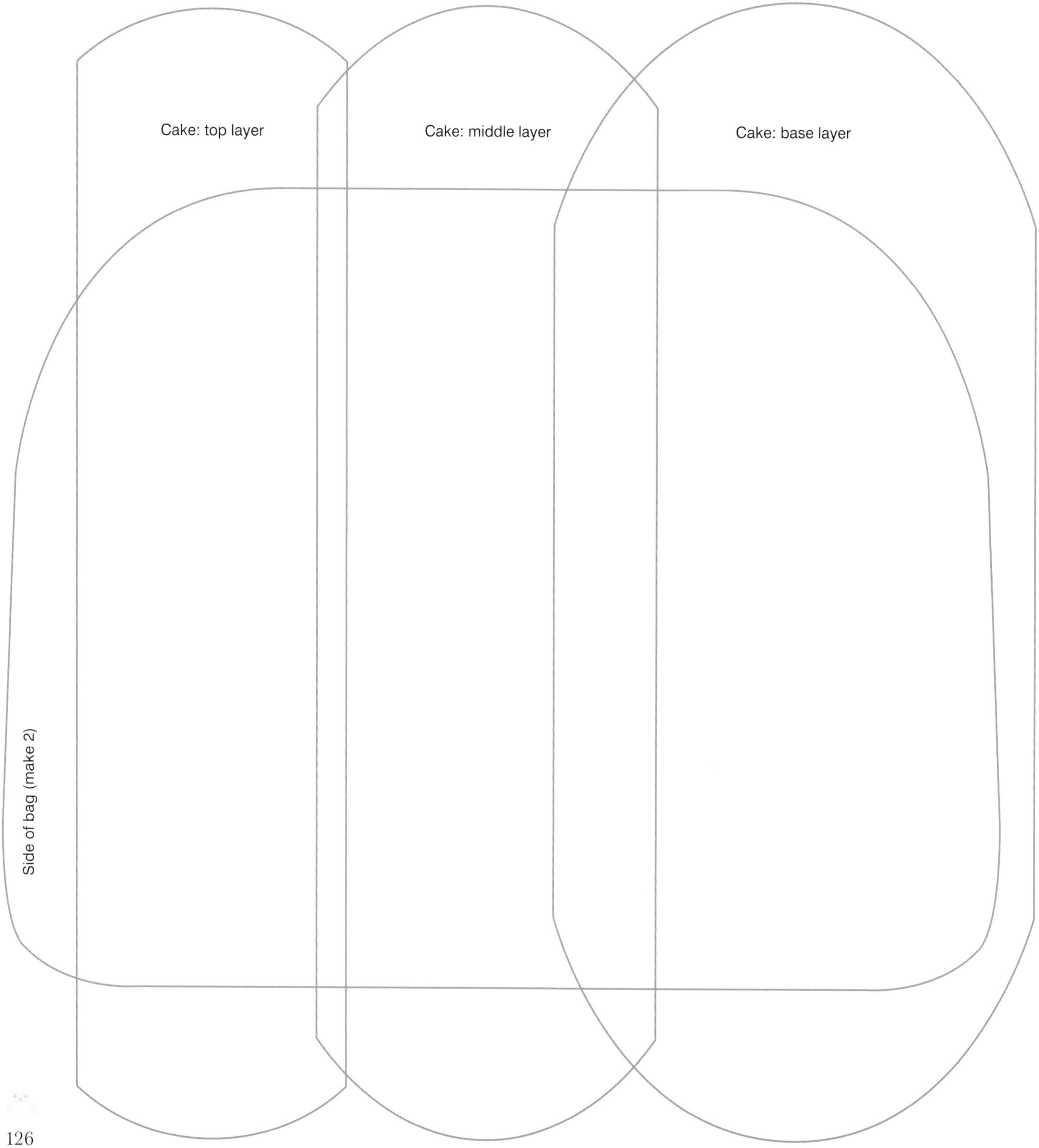

Cake: top layer

Cake: middle layer

Cake: base layer

Side of bag (make 2)

Project Gallery

Karen Taylor has been a regular contributor to Cakes & Sugarcraft and Wedding Cakes – A Design Source magazines since 2007. She has created over 40 step-by-step celebration cake projects, a small selection of which are shown here. For stockists of these magazines, turn to the Suppliers list on page 128.

Drummer Boy Christening Cake (Cakes & Sugarcraft issue 110)

Double Decker Bus (Cakes & Sugarcraft issue 113)

I Love London (Cakes & Sugarcraft issue 117)

Pretty Pinwheels (Cakes & Sugarcraft issue 122)

Owl I Want for Christmas (Cakes & Sugarcraft issue 123)

Retro Oven (Cakes & Sugarcraft issue 124)

Contemporary Heart Wedding Cake (Wedding Cakes issue 31)

Macaroon Wedding Cake (Wedding Cakes issue 41)

Suppliers

Squires Kitchen, UK
3 Waverley Lane
Farnham
Surrey
GU9 8BB
0845 61 71 810
+44 (0) 1252 260 260
www.squires-shop.com

Squires Kitchen International School
The Grange
Hones Yard
Farnham
Surrey
GU9 8BB
0845 61 71 810
+44 (0) 1252 260 260
www.squires-school.co.uk

Squires Kitchen, France
+33 (0) 1 82 88 01 66
clientele@squires-shop.fr
www.squires-shop.fr

Squires Kitchen, Spain
+34 93 180 7382
cliente@squires-shop.es
www.squires-shop.es

Squires Kitchen, Italy
cliente@squires-shop.it
www.squires-shop.it

Squires Kitchen, Germany
kunde@squires-shop.de
www.squires-shop.de

Distributors

UK
Culpitt Ltd.
Northumberland
www.culpitt.com

Guy, Paul & Co. Ltd.
Buckinghamshire
www.guypaul.co.uk

Squires Kitchen
Surrey
www.squires-shop.com

For your nearest sugarcraft supplier, please contact your local distributor.

Europe
Cake Supplies
Netherlands
www.cakesupplies.nl

Dom Konditera LLC
Belarus
www.domkonditera.com

Sugar World – Aliprantis Ltd.
Greece
www.sugarworld.gr

Tårtdecor
Küngalv
www.tartdecor.se

ACKNOWLEDGEMENTS

I would like to thank Beverley Dutton and Jennifer Kelly for giving me this wonderful opportunity, and to everyone at Squires Kitchen for all their hard work. Thank you also to Alister Thorpe for all the wonderful photography.

A huge thank you to all my family and friends for their continued support and encouragement while putting this book together.

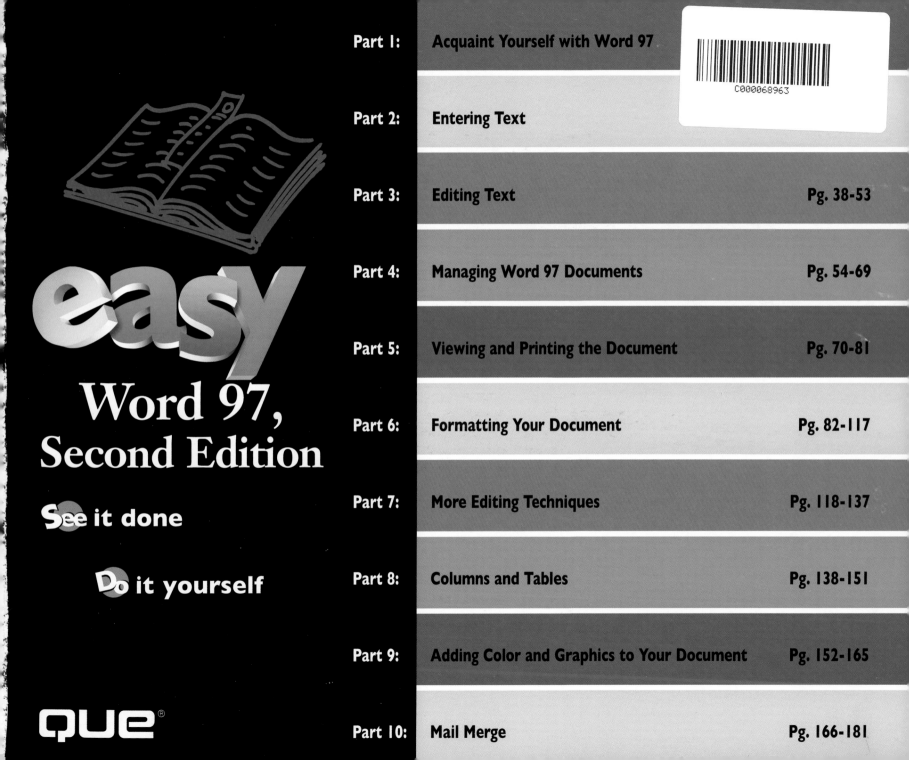

easy

Word 97,
Second Edition

See it done

Do it yourself

que ®

Part 1:	Acquaint Yourself with Word 97	
Part 2:	Entering Text	
Part 3:	Editing Text	Pg. 38-53
Part 4:	Managing Word 97 Documents	Pg. 54-69
Part 5:	Viewing and Printing the Document	Pg. 70-81
Part 6:	Formatting Your Document	Pg. 82-117
Part 7:	More Editing Techniques	Pg. 118-137
Part 8:	Columns and Tables	Pg. 138-151
Part 9:	Adding Color and Graphics to Your Document	Pg. 152-165
Part 10:	Mail Merge	Pg. 166-181

C000068963

Part **2: Entering Text**

1 — Typing Text
2 — Moving Around the Document with the Mouse
3 — Moving Around the Document with the Keyboard
4 — Going to a Specific Page
5 — Inserting Text
6 — Combining and Splitting Paragraphs

Part **1: Acquaint Yourself with Word 97**

1 — Starting Word 97
2 — Exiting Word 97
3 — Working with the Word 97 Window
4 — Using Pull-down Menus
5 — Using Context Menus
6 — Hiding the Ruler
7 — Working with Dialog Boxes
8 — Working with Toolbars
9 — Asking the Office Assistant for Help
10 — Getting Help from the Help Menu

Part **3: Editing Text**

1 — Selecting Text with the Mouse
2 — Selecting Text with the Keyboard
3 — Deleting Text
4 — Copying Text
5 — Moving Text
6 — Inserting a Tab
7 — Using the Show/Hide Button
8 — Using Undo

Part ▶ 4: **Managing Word 97 Documents**

1 — Saving a Document
2 — Closing a Document
3 — Opening a Document
4 — Creating a New Document
5 — Using a Template
6 — Using a Wizard
7 — Finding a Document

Part ▶ 5: **Viewing and Printing the Document**

1 — Displaying a Document in Page Layout View
2 — Zooming a Document
3 — Previewing a Document
4 — Printing a Document
5 — Printing an Envelope
6 — Printing Labels

Part ▶ 6: **Formatting Your Document**

1 — Making Text Bold, Italic, and Underlined
2 — Changing the Font and Font Size
3 — Changing Paragraph Alignment
4 — Changing Line Spacing
5 — Adding Indents
6 — Creating Bulleted and Numbered Lists
7 — Setting a Custom Left or Right Tab
8 — Setting a Custom Center or Decimal Tab
9 — Moving and Deleting a Custom Tab
10 — Changing Margins
11 — Inserting a Page Break
12 — Adding a Border to a Paragraph
13 — Shading a Paragraph
14 — Centering a Page Vertically
15 — Numbering Pages
16 — Creating Headers and Footers
17 — Using the Header and Footer Toolbar

Part **7:** More Editing Techniques

1 — Searching for Text
2 — Finding and Replacing Text
3 — Using Automatic Spell Checking
4 — Checking Your Spelling with the Spell Checker
5 — Using the Thesaurus
6 — Inserting a Special Character
7 — Inserting the Date
8 — Using AutoCorrect
9 — Using AutoText

Part **8:** Columns and Tables

1 — Creating Columns
2 — Formatting Columns
3 — Creating a Table
4 — Entering Text in a Table
5 — Changing the Structure of a Table
6 — Formatting a Table

 Part **9:** Adding Color and Graphics to Your Document

1 — Adding Color to Your Text
2 — Inserting a Graphic in Your Document
3 — Moving and Sizing a Graphic
4 — Formatting a Graphic
5 — Adding Shapes
6 — Creating WordArt

Part **10:** Mail Merge

1 — Starting the Main Document
2 — Creating and Saving the Data Source
3 — Entering Records into the Data Source
4 — Typing and Saving the Main Document
5 — Merging the Documents
6 — Merging Envelopes
7 — Merging Labels

Easy Word 97, Second Edition

Copyright© 1998 by Que® Corporation

Library of Congress Catalog No.: 98-84856

ISBN: 0-7897-1691-7

99 98   6 5 4 3 2 1

Interpretation of the printing code: the rightmost double-digit number is the year of the book's printing; the rightmost single-digit number, the number of the book's printing. For example, a printing code of 98-1 shows that the first printing of the book occurred in 1998.

Screen reproductions in this book were created using Collage Plus from Inner Media, Inc., Hollis, NH.

This book was produced digitally by Macmillan Computer Publishing and manufactured using computer-to-plate technology (a film-less process) by GAC/Shepard Poorman, Indianapolis, Indiana.

About the Author

Heidi Steele is a freelance writer and computer trainer. She specializes in demystifying computer concepts and making programs such as Word 97 accessible to home users and professionals alike. Heidi Steele is also the author of *How to Use the Internet* and *How to Use Word 97 for Windows*. She lives in Port Orchard, Washington.

Executive Editor
Karen Reinisch

Acquisitions Editor
Don Essig

Development Editor
Melanie Palaisa

Technical Editor
Bill Bruns

Managing Editor
Thomas F. Hayes

Project Editor
Heather E. Butler

Copy Editors
Julie McNamee
Sean Medlock

Indexer
Tim Tate

Book Designer
Jean Bisesi

Cover Designer
Anne Jones

Production Team
Chris Livengood
Trina Wurst

How to Use This Book

It's as Easy as 1-2-3

Each part of this book is made up of a series of short, instructional lessons, designed to help you understand basic information that you need to get the most out of your computer hardware and software.

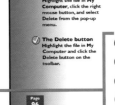 Each step is fully illustrated to show you how it looks onscreen.

 Click: Click the left mouse button once.

 Double-click: Click the left mouse button twice in rapid succession.

 Tips and ! Warnings give you a heads-up for any extra information you may need while working through the task.

 Right-click: Click the right mouse button once.

2 Each task includes a series of quick, easy steps designed to guide you through the procedure.

 Pointer Arrow: Highlights an item on the screen you need to point to or focus on in the step or task.

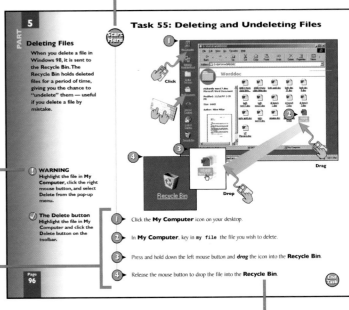

Task 55: Deleting and Undeleting Files

Selection: Highlights the area onscreen discussed in the step or task.

3 Items that you select or click in menus, dialog boxes, tabs, and windows are shown in **Bold**. Information you type is in a `special font`. Terms that you will find in the glossary are shown in ***Bold italic***.

 Click & Type: Click once where indicated and begin typing to enter your text or data.

 How to Drag: Point to the starting place or object. Hold down the mouse button (right or left per instructions), move the mouse to the new location, then release the button.

Next Step: If you see this symbol, it means the task you're working on continues on the next page.

 End Task: Task is complete.

Easy Word 97

Learning to use Word 97 doesn't have to be an agonizing, drawn-out process. *Easy Word 97, Second Edition* distills the key skills for you and presents them in colorful, visual steps. This book assumes that you view Word 97 as a tool for getting your work done—no more, no less. You don't see learning a software program as an end in itself. Consequently, this book won't lead you into every nook and cranny of the program. You won't learn five ways of doing the same thing. You will, however, learn the fastest, most straightforward techniques, and you will certainly learn the shortcuts that are truly helpful.

Easy Word 97, Second Edition is a book for beginners. It doesn't assume that you have ever used a word processing program such as Word before, or that you are familiar with Windows. You can use this book regardless of whether you're using Windows 95 or Windows 98. Word 97 behaves exactly the same way with both versions of Windows.

The foundation for *Easy Word 97, Second Edition* is many years "on the front lines" teaching Word classes to beginners. The explanations in this book have been refined in the classroom on thousands of people like you, who want to get up and running in Word without making it a lifetime project. This book does not merely provide stock explanations of how the program is *supposed* to work, but rather explains how it actually behaves from your viewpoint. If a particular nuance of Word behavior is confusing to most people in the classroom, it's explained here as well, on the assumption that it might be perplexing to you too.

Easy Word 97, Second Edition is intended to be both a tutorial and a reference. Feel free to flip to the exact task that you need to learn about at the moment. Of course, if you have the time, you can certainly work through the tasks sequentially, but it's not necessary to do so. You don't have to take time out from your day for "study sessions," but can instead apply the instructions in this book to your own documents, dipping into the various tasks as needed.

Word 97 is an intuitive, powerful program, and learning to use it can (and should) be fun. Enjoy!

PART I

Acquaint Yourself with Word 97

Learning a new program is a bit like driving into a new town. You can guess where to find some things right away, and others you may have to putter around awhile to locate. In this part, we help you with this process by taking you on a tour of the Word environment. You'll get a sense of where the various tools are and how to use them. After you know the general contours of the program, you'll be all set to delve into the specific skills required to create documents.

Tasks

Task #		Page #
1	Starting Word 97	10
2	Exiting Word 97	11
3	Working with the Word 97 Window	12
4	Using Pull-down Menus	14
5	Using Context Menus	16
6	Hiding the Ruler	17
7	Working with Dialog Boxes	18
8	Working with Toolbars	20
9	Asking the Office Assistant for Help	22
10	Getting Help from the Help Menu	24

Task 1: Starting Word 97

Starting Word 97

When you want to use Word 97, you have to ask Windows to start it for you. After you've started Word, you can work on as many documents as you like, for as long as you like. You know when Word is open, even if it's hidden behind other windows, because a button labeled Microsoft Word appears on the *taskbar* at the bottom of your screen. When you are finished using Word, you need to exit the program. See the next task to find out how.

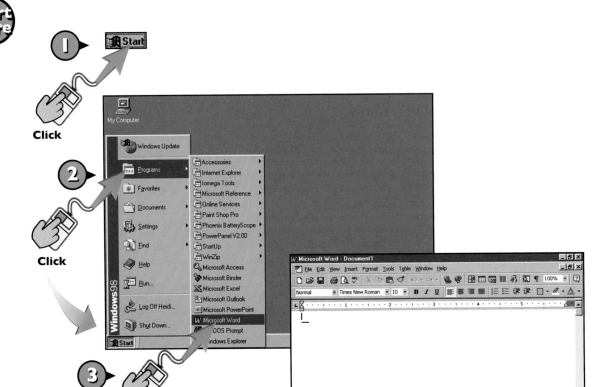

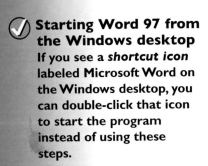

✓ **Starting Word 97 from the Windows desktop**
If you see a *shortcut icon* labeled Microsoft Word on the Windows desktop, you can double-click that icon to start the program instead of using these steps.

① ▶ Click the **Start** button.

② ▶ Point to **Programs** in the Start menu.

③ ▶ Click **Microsoft Word**.

④ ▶ The Word window opens and the Microsoft Word button appears on the taskbar.

Task 2: Exiting Word 97

Start Here

Click

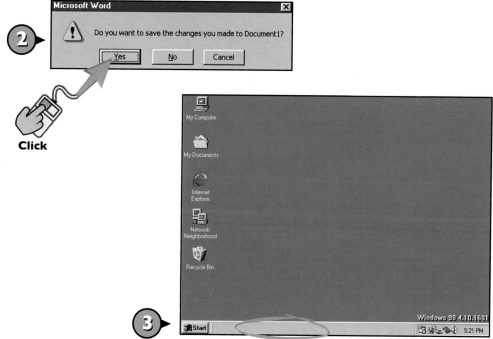

Click

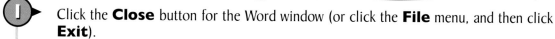

Exiting Word 97

When you are finished working with Word, you need to exit the program. When you issue the command to exit, Word checks to see if you are working on a document that has unsaved changes. If you are, it gives you a chance to save the document before closing it. As soon as you exit Word, the Microsoft Word button disappears from the taskbar to tell you that the program is no longer running.

1. Click the **Close** button for the Word window (or click the **File** menu, and then click **Exit**).

2. If Word asks whether to save changes to your document, click **Yes** or **No**. (See "Saving Your Documents" in Part 4.)

3. The Word window closes, and the Microsoft Word button is no longer on the taskbar.

End Task

Resizing and Moving a Word 97 Window

You can change the appearance of the Word window in a variety of ways. You can make it fill up the screen to give you more room to work, restore it back to a smaller size, or make it disappear temporarily so that you can see what's behind it on the Windows desktop. You can also move the Word window around on your desktop, or adjust its size.

✓ **Closing the Word window or closing the document window?**
The set of Minimize, Restore/Maximize, and Close buttons that you use in this task control the entire Word window. The three buttons directly beneath them control the document. The only one of these lower three buttons that you'll need to use frequently is the Close button (see "Closing a Document" in Part 4).

Task 3: Working with the Word 97 Window

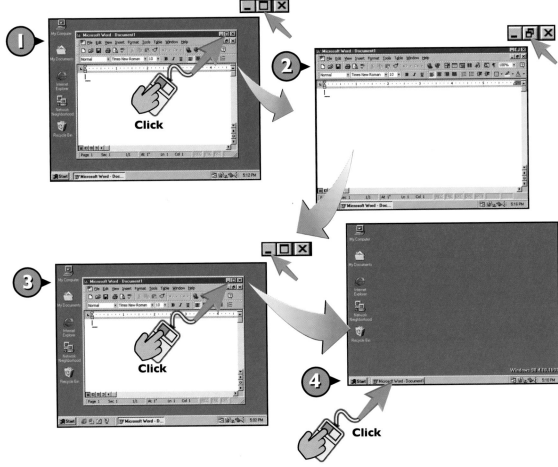

Click

Click

Click

1 ▸ Click the Word window's **Maximize** button to make the window fill up the screen.

2 ▸ The Maximize button is now a **Restore** button. Click it to return (restore) the window to its previous size.

3 ▸ Click the Word window's **Minimize** button to temporarily hide the window.

4 ▸ Click the **Taskbar** button to bring the window back.

Next Step ▸

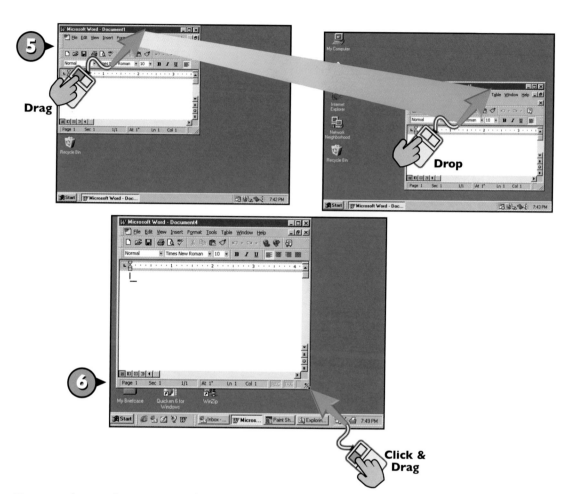

Drag

Drop

Click & Drag

To move the window, point to the **title bar**, drag the window to a different location onscreen, and release the mouse button.

To resize the Word window, point to the lower-right corner of the window; the mouse pointer becomes a diagonal black arrow. Drag in the desired direction to enlarge or shrink the window.

Task 4: Using Pull-down Menus

Using Pull-down Menus

The menu bar contains nine pull-down menus— File, Edit, View, and so on— that contain commands for executing Word tasks. Many of these commands have equivalent buttons on the toolbars, and in most cases, it's more convenient to use the toolbar buttons than the menus. However, if you accidentally hide a toolbar or if you don't like using the mouse, you can always rely on the menus instead.

✓ **Use the keyboard instead of the mouse**
If you want to use the keyboard to issue a menu command, press the **Alt** key and the letter that's underlined in the menu name. For example, press **Alt+V** to pull down the View menu. After the menu is displayed, press the underlined letter in the command you want to issue.

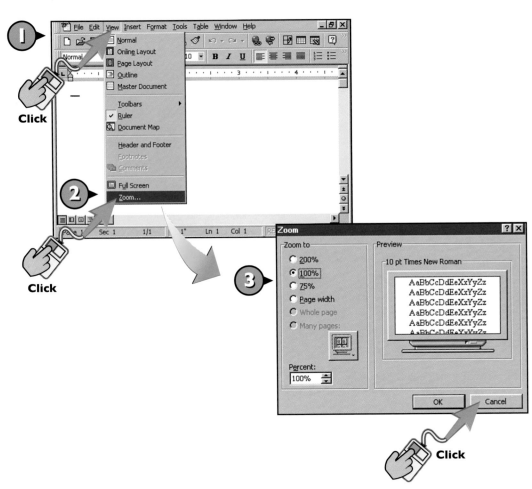

Start Here

Click

Click

Click

1 ▶ Click the **View** menu to pull it down.

2 ▶ Look at the **Zoom** command. It's followed by three dots (...) to show you that it leads to a dialog box. Click the command.

3 ▶ The Zoom dialog box appears. Click the **Cancel** button to close it.

Page
14

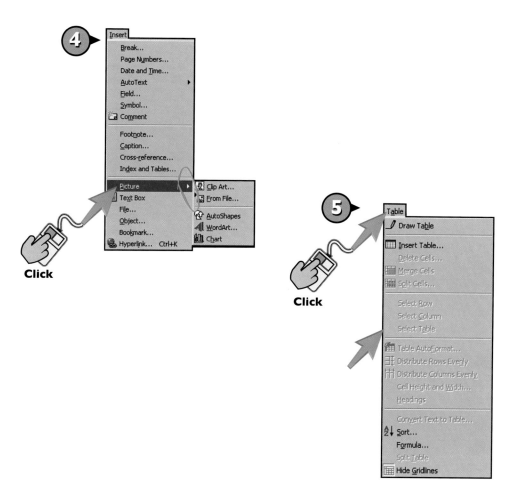

Insert

Break...
Page Numbers...
Date and Time...
AutoText ▶
Field...
Symbol...
Comment

Footnote...
Caption...
Cross-reference...
Index and Tables...

Picture ▶
Text Box
File...
Object...
Bookmark...
Hyperlink... Ctrl+K

Clip Art...
From File...
AutoShapes
WordArt...
Chart

Click

Table

Draw Table

Insert Table...
Delete Cells...
Merge Cells
Split Cells...

Select Row
Select Column
Select Table

Table AutoFormat...
Distribute Rows Evenly
Distribute Columns Evenly
Cell Height and Width...
Headings

Convert Text to Table...
Sort...
Formula...
Split Table
Hide Gridlines

Click

 Click the **Insert** command, and then point to **Picture**. The small triangle on the right tells you that a submenu will appear. Click outside the Insert menu to hide it.

 Click the **Table** command. The dim commands are not currently active. Click outside the menu to hide it.

Using Context Menus

In addition to using the pull-down menus at the top of the Word window, you can also use *context menus*. These are small menus that you display by clicking the right mouse button. The commands in a context menu vary depending on where you right-click. For example, if you right-click text, you get commands for editing and formatting text, and if you right-click a toolbar, you get a list of toolbars that you can display or hide (see "Working with Toolbars" later in this part for more about toolbars). To choose a command in a context menu, left-click.

Task 5: Using Context Menus

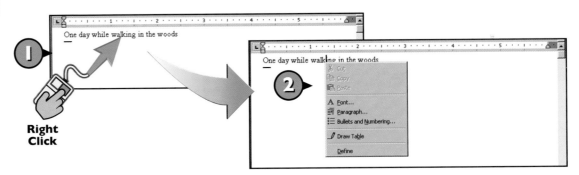

Right Click

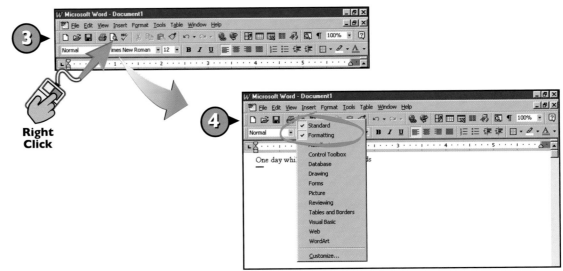

Right Click

1. Type a few words in your document, and then right-click anywhere on the text.

2. A context menu appears with commands for working with text. Click outside the menu to hide it.

3. Right-click one of the toolbars.

4. This time, the context menu lists your available toolbars. Click outside the menu to hide it.

Task 6: Hiding the Ruler

Start Here

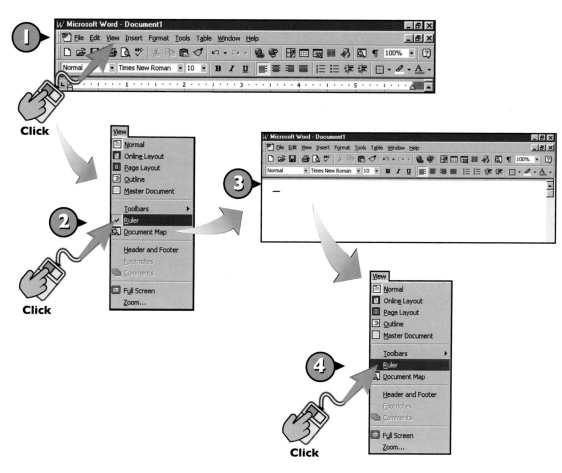

Click

Click

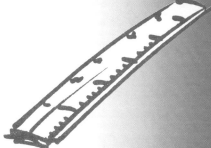

Click

Hiding the Ruler

By default, the ruler appears underneath the toolbars. You can use the ruler to quickly adjust tabs, indents, and margins (you'll learn about these formatting techniques in Part 6 of this book). However, you might want to hide the ruler so that you can see more of your document. You can easily display the ruler again whenever you like.

1. ▶ Click **View** in the menu bar.

2. ▶ The check mark next to the Ruler command tells you that the ruler is currently displayed. Click the **Ruler** command.

3. ▶ The ruler is now hidden.

4. ▶ Choose **View**, **Ruler** again to bring the ruler back.

End Task

Task 7: Working with Dialog Boxes

How Dialog Boxes Work

All of Word's menu commands that are followed by ellipses (...) lead to a *dialog box*. Some dialog boxes give you options for specifying exactly what you want to do before Word actually issues the command. After you've made your selections in a dialog box, you click the **OK** button to tell Word to carry out the command. If you decide not to go ahead with a command, you can back out of the dialog box by clicking the **Cancel** button. Here you take a quick look at the elements commonly found in dialog boxes, using the Print dialog box as an example.

✓ Selecting options

If you see a group of option buttons in a dialog box, you can only select one of them. In contrast, if you see a group of check boxes, you can select as many of them as you like.

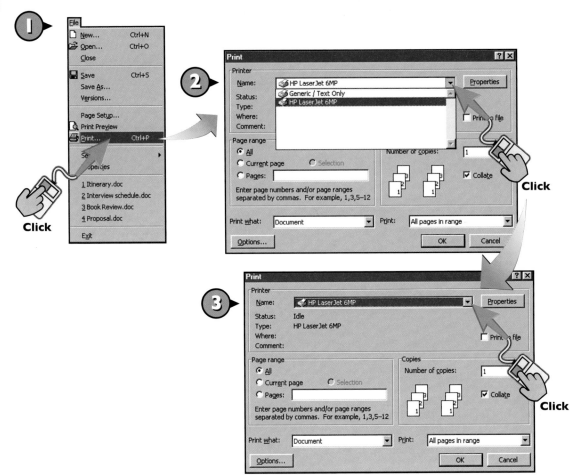

Start Here

Click

Click

Click

1 Choose **File**, **Print** to display the Print dialog box.

2 Click the **down arrow** to the right of the **Name** drop-down list.

3 Click the **down arrow** again to hide the list without making a selection.

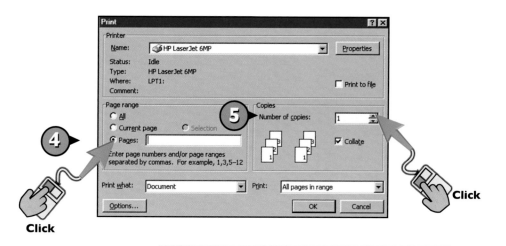

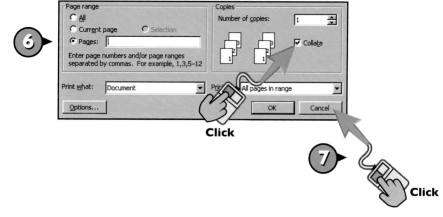

4 ▸ Click the **Pages *option button*** to select it. The ***text box*** to its right lets you type the page numbers that you want to print.

5 ▸ Click the up and down ***spinner arrows*** to the right of the **Number of copies** box to increase and decrease the number.

6 ▸ Click the **Collate *check box*** twice to clear the check box and then mark it again.

7 ▸ Click the **Cancel** button to close the Print dialog box without printing your document.

Task 8: Working with Toolbars

Using Word 97 Toolbars

Word's toolbars contain buttons you can use to issue commonly used commands. Most people find clicking toolbar buttons more convenient than accessing commands in the pull-down menus. However, you can use any combination of toolbar buttons and menu commands that you choose. Word comes with 13 toolbars. By default, it displays the Standard and Formatting toolbars. You can easily hide or display any of the toolbars to suit your preferences.

Start Here

Click

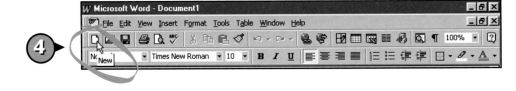

The Standard toolbar contains buttons for creating, saving, and opening documents, as well as for common editing tasks.

The Formatting toolbar contains buttons for formatting your text.

Point to the leftmost toolbar button in the Standard toolbar.

A **ToolTip** appears to tell you the name of the button (in this case, **New**). All the buttons have ToolTips.

Next Step

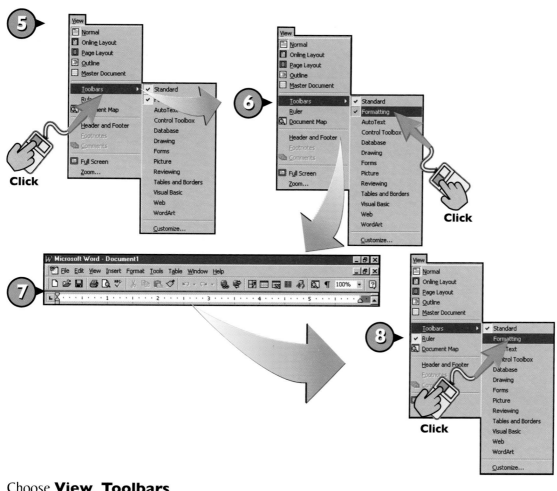

5 ▸ Choose **View**, **Toolbars**.

6 ▸ Notice that Standard and Formatting toolbars have check marks next to them. Click **Formatting**.

7 ▸ The Formatting toolbar is now hidden.

8 ▸ Choose **View**, **Toolbars**, and click **Formatting** again to bring the toolbar back.

Using the Office Assistant

Thoughtful, friendly, and well informed, the Office Assistant offers tips on how to type and format your documents more efficiently, helps you search Word's online help system, and provides alerts about events that require your attention, all with amusing sound effects and animation.

✓ **The Office Assistant keeps an eye on you**
As you're working in Word, the Office Assistant observes your actions and offers assistance that relates to what you're doing. For example, if you type something like "Dear Jenny," the Office Assistant will likely ask if you need help writing a letter.

Task 9: Asking the Office Assistant for Help

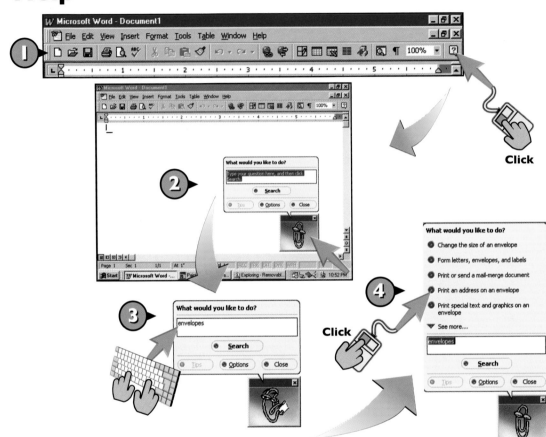

Start Here

Click

Click

1. Click the **Office Assistant** button on the Standard toolbar.

2. The Office Assistant (most likely a paper-clip figure) appears with a yellow bubble attached to it.

3. Type **envelopes** in the yellow bubble and click the **Search** button.

4. In the list of topics that appears, click **Print an address on an envelope**.

Next Step

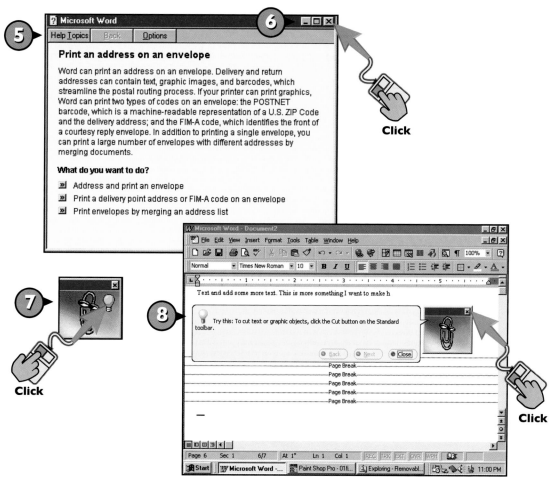

Print an address on an envelope

Word can print an address on an envelope. Delivery and return addresses can contain text, graphic images, and barcodes, which streamline the postal routing process. If your printer can print graphics, Word can print two types of codes on an envelope: the POSTNET barcode, which is a machine-readable representation of a U.S. ZIP Code and the delivery address; and the FIM-A code, which identifies the front of a courtesy reply envelope. In addition to printing a single envelope, you can print a large number of envelopes with different addresses by merging documents.

What do you want to do?

- Address and print an envelope
- Print a delivery point address or FIM-A code on an envelope
- Print envelopes by merging an address list

Click

Text and add some more text. This is more something I want to make h

Try this: To cut text or graphic objects, click the Cut button on the Standard toolbar.

Click

Click

5 ▸ The Office Assistant displays the information from the help system.

6 ▸ Click the **Close** button in the upper-right corner of the help window.

7 ▸ If you see a lightbulb in the Office Assistant window, click it to display a tip.

8 ▸ When you're finished reading the tip, click the **Close** button.

Using the Help Menu

Although the Office Assistant (described in the previous task) provides the speediest access to help, at times you might want to investigate a topic in depth by delving into the help system directly via the Help menu.

Task 10: Getting Help from the Help Menu

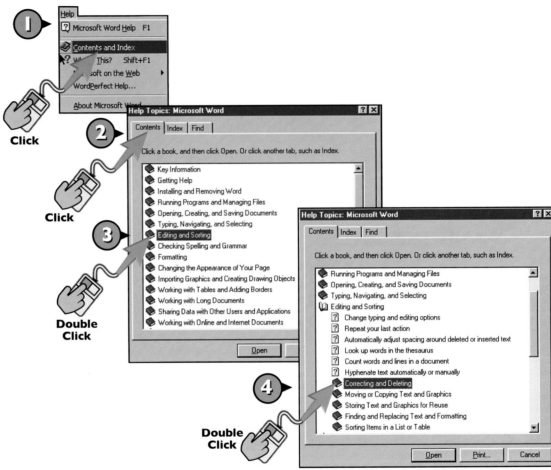

Start Here

Click

Click

Double Click

Double Click

✓ **Printing a help topic**
To print a help topic, click the **Options** button at the top of the Help dialog box, choose **Print Topics**, and click **OK** in the Print dialog box that appears.

 Choose **Help**, **Contents and Index**.

2 ▶ Click the **Contents** tab if it isn't already in front.

3 ▶ Double-click the **Editing and Sorting** book icon.

4 ▶ Double-click the **Correcting and Deleting** book icon.

Next Step

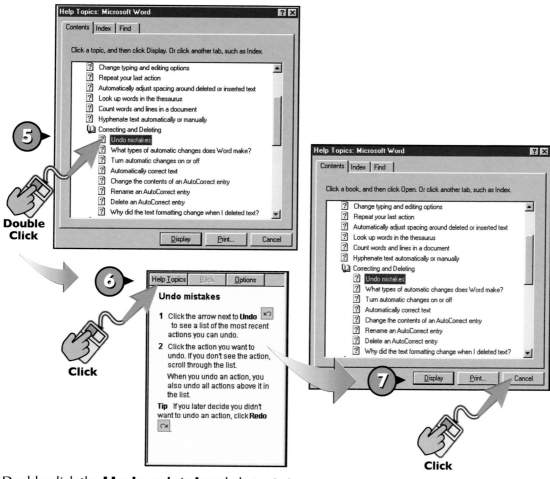

5 Double-click the **Undo mistakes** help topic icon.

6 Click the **Help Topics** button to return to the main help window.

7 Click the **Cancel** button.

PART 2

Entering Text

Even if you have never used a word processing program before, you'll feel comfortable typing text in Word in no time. In this part, you learn typing basics such as when to press Enter and how to move around the document. You also find out how to insert new text into text that you've already typed, and how to track down a document that you've misplaced.

Tasks

Task #   Page #

1   Entering Text   28

2   Moving Around the Document with the Mouse   30

3   Moving Around the Document with the Keyboard   32

4   Going to a Specific Page   34

5   Inserting Text   36

6   Combining and Splitting Paragraphs   37

Task 1: Entering Text

Entering Text

Typing text in a Word document is simple. As soon as you start Word, you can begin typing in the blank document that appears. You don't have to worry about leaving room for margins. Word assumes that you're typing on 8 1/2-by 11-inch paper, with 1-inch margins on the top and bottom and 1 1/4-inch margins on the left and right. If you're typing a paragraph more than one line long, do not press Enter at the end of the lines. Word wraps the text from line to line for you.

✅ **The mouse pointer and the insertion point**
The mouse pointer, called the *I-beam*, is often confused with the insertion point. The insertion point shows you where your text will appear when you type. The I-beam just lets you move the insertion point around the document (see the next task).

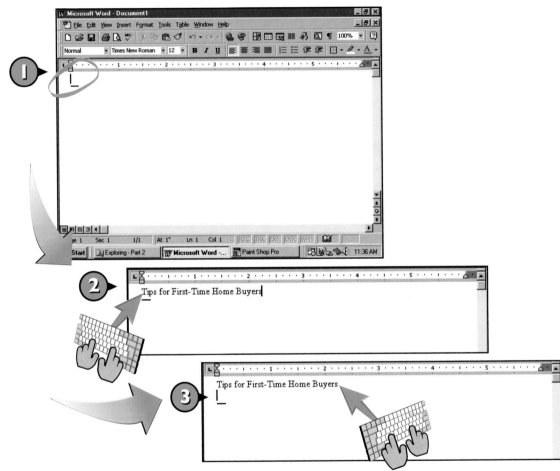

1 Start Word. The flashing vertical bar you see in the blank document is called the ***insertion point***.

2 Type **Tips for First-Time Home Buyers**.

3 Press **Enter** to end the paragraph and move the insertion point to the next line.

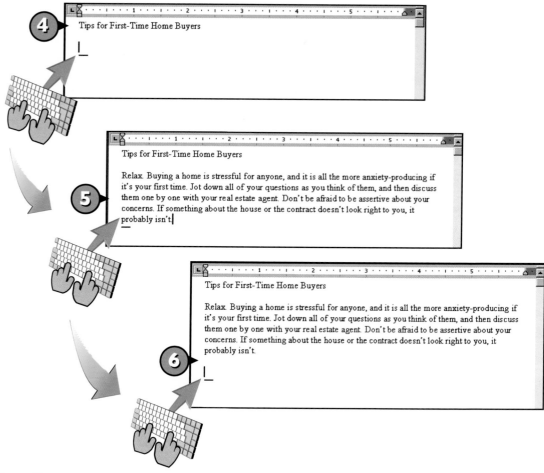

4 Tips for First-Time Home Buyers

5 Tips for First-Time Home Buyers

Relax. Buying a home is stressful for anyone, and it is all the more anxiety-producing if it's your first time. Jot down all of your questions as you think of them, and then discuss them one by one with your real estate agent. Don't be afraid to be assertive about your concerns. If something about the house or the contract doesn't look right to you, it probably isn't.

6 Tips for First-Time Home Buyers

Relax. Buying a home is stressful for anyone, and it is all the more anxiety-producing if it's your first time. Jot down all of your questions as you think of them, and then discuss them one by one with your real estate agent. Don't be afraid to be assertive about your concerns. If something about the house or the contract doesn't look right to you, it probably isn't.

4 ▶ Press **Enter** again. Pressing Enter on a new line creates a blank line.

5 ▶ Type the paragraph shown here. *Do not* press Enter at the end of the lines.

6 ▶ Press **Enter** twice to both end the paragraph and create a blank line.

End Task

Task 2: Moving Around the Document with the Mouse

Using the Mouse to Move Around

As soon as you've typed some text in a blank document, you need to know how to move the insertion point around within the text to make editing changes. You can move the insertion point by clicking the mouse or by pressing keys on the keyboard. Here you learn how to navigate with the mouse. In the next task, you learn how to navigate with the keyboard. Experiment a little to see which method you like the best.

Start Here

I.   Introduction
It is ironic the large emphasis that is placed on the "personal interview" when arriving at selection decisions within organizations, despite its low reliability and low accuracy in predicting future job performance. These interviews are usually relatively unstructured, and many recent literature reviews suggest that its low validity is often due to judgmental errors made by the interviewer and also the numerous errors and biases associated with the processing of the applicant information. Since the workforce is the primary asset in most organizations, one might assume that the most effective selection strategy would be chosen to maximize productivity.

I.   Introduction
It is ironic the large emphasis that is placed on the "personal interview" when arriving at selection decisions within organizations, despite its low reliability and low accuracy in predicting future job performance. These interviews are usually relatively unstructured, and many recent literature reviews suggest that its low validity is often due to judgmental errors made by the interviewer and also the numerous errors and biases associated with the processing of the applicant information. Since the workforce is the primary asset in most organizations, one might assume that the most effective selection strategy would be chosen to maximize productivity.

Click

strategy would be chosen to maximize productivity.
Personal interviewing continues to be the most widely used method for selecting employees and is often used in conjunction with other techniques such as reference checking, weighted application blanks, skill tests, and psychological testing. There are obviously good reasons for the popularity of the employment interview despite the controversy regarding its validity.
This paper analyzes the validity of the interview - the measure of the degree to

Click

1 ▶ To move to a place that's visible onscreen, first position the I-beam at the desired location.

2 ▶ Then click. The insertion point moves to the new location.

3 ▶ Click the down scroll arrow on the *scrollbar* to bring the lower part of a long document into view.

Next Step ▶

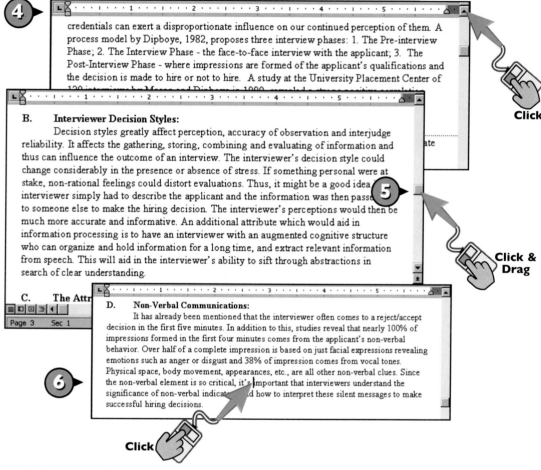

credentials can exert a disproportionate influence on our continued perception of them. A process model by Dipboye, 1982, proposes three interview phases: 1. The Pre-interview Phase; 2. The Interview Phase - the face-to-face interview with the applicant; 3. The Post-Interview Phase - where impressions are formed of the applicant's qualifications and the decision is made to hire or not to hire. A study at the University Placement Center of

Click

B. **Interviewer Decision Styles:**

Decision styles greatly affect perception, accuracy of observation and interjudge reliability. It affects the gathering, storing, combining and evaluating of information and thus can influence the outcome of an interview. The interviewer's decision style could change considerably in the presence or absence of stress. If something personal were at stake, non-rational feelings could distort evaluations. Thus, it might be a good idea interviewer simply had to describe the applicant and the information was then passe to someone else to make the hiring decision. The interviewer's perceptions would then be much more accurate and informative. An additional attribute which would aid in information processing is to have an interviewer with an augmented cognitive structure who can organize and hold information for a long time, and extract relevant information from speech. This will aid in the interviewer's ability to sift through abstractions in search of clear understanding.

Click & Drag

C. **The Attr**

Page 3   Sec 1

D. **Non-Verbal Communications:**

It has already been mentioned that the interviewer often comes to a reject/accept decision in the first five minutes. In addition to this, studies reveal that nearly 100% of impressions formed in the first four minutes comes from the applicant's non-verbal behavior. Over half of a complete impression is based on just facial expressions revealing emotions such as anger or disgust and 38% of impression comes from vocal tones. Physical space, body movement, appearances, etc., are all other non-verbal clues. Since the non-verbal element is so critical, it's important that interviewers understand the significance of non-verbal indicat   d how to interpret these silent messages to make successful hiring decisions.

Click

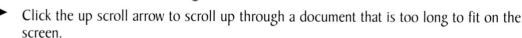

④ Click the up scroll arrow to scroll up through a document that is too long to fit on the screen.

⑤ Point to the **scroll box** and drag it up or down the scrollbar to move quickly through a long document.

⑥ After you've scrolled the document, remember to click to move the insertion point before you start typing.

Task 3: Moving Around the Document with the Keyboard

Using the Keyboard to Move Around

Most people find it faster to navigate with the keyboard than the mouse, because you don't have to take your hands away from the keyboard to grab the mouse. When you navigate with the keyboard, the insertion point moves as you press the keys. You don't have to click once before you start typing to move the insertion point, as you do if you navigate with the mouse.

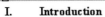

✓ **The end mark**
You can always tell when you're at the end of your document because you'll see a short horizontal bar on the far left edge of the document window. This bar is called the *end mark* (see the figure for step 7 of this task).

1 ▶ Press the **Left-** and **Right-arrow** keys to move one character to the left or to the right.

2 ▶ Press the **Up-** and **Down-arrow** keys to move one line up or down.

3 ▶ Press **Ctrl+Left arrow** (hold down the Ctrl key as you press the Left-arrow key) and **Ctrl+Right arrow** to move one word to the left or to the right.

4 ▶ Press **Ctrl+Up arrow** and **Ctrl+Down arrow** to move one paragraph up or down.

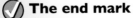

Next Step

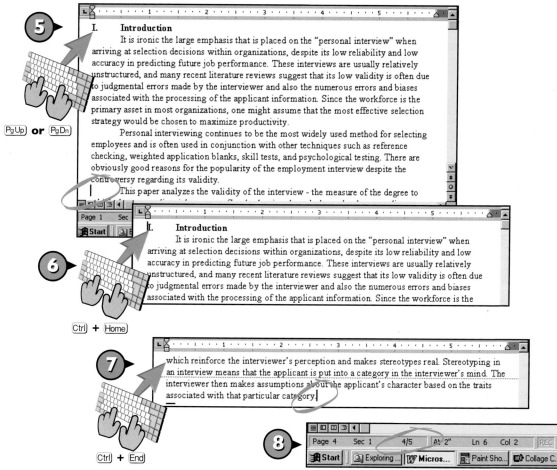

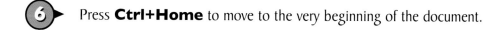

5 ▶ Press **Page Down** and **Page Up** to move one screenful of text down or up.

6 ▶ Press **Ctrl+Home** to move to the very beginning of the document.

7 ▶ Press **Ctrl+End** to move to the very end of the document.

8 ▶ You can always tell what page you're on by looking at the **status bar**. Here, the insertion point is on page 4 of a 5-page document.

Task 4: Going to a Specific Page

Finding a Specific Page

When you're editing a long document, you often need to go to a particular page to make a change. You can, of course, navigate to that page using the standard mouse and keyboard techniques described in the previous two tasks. However, it's often faster to use Word's Go To feature, which lets you jump directly to any page in your document.

✅ **Using Go To to make changes**

You can use the Go To feature to make editing changes on several pages. Jump to the first page, click outside the dialog box to deactivate it, and make the change in the text. Then click the title bar of the dialog box to reactivate it and jump to the next page, and so on.

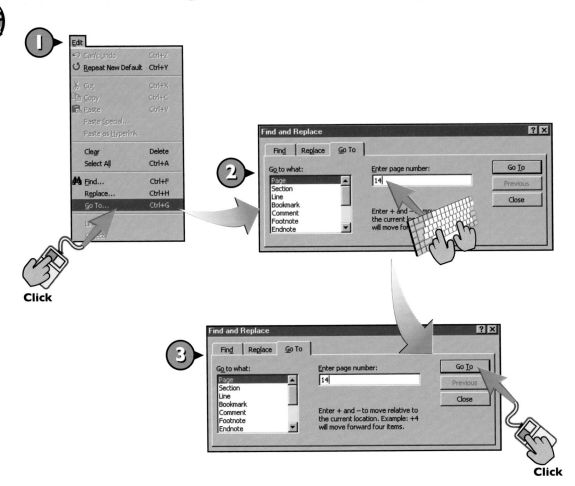

Click

Click

① Choose **Edit**, **Go To** to display the **Go To** tab of the Find and Replace dialog box.

② Type the number of the page in the **Enter page number** text box.

③ Click the **Go To** button.

Next Step

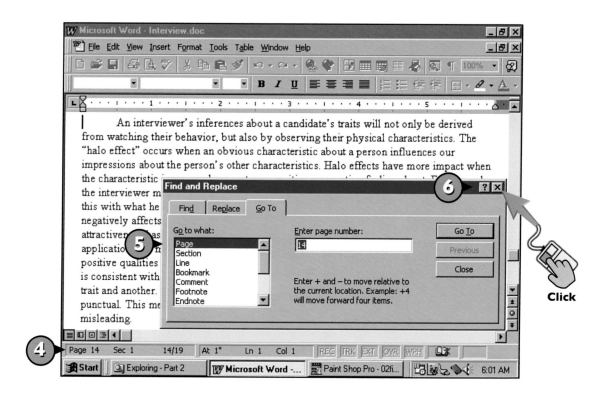

Find and Replace

Find | Replace | Go To

Go to what:

Page
Section
Line
Bookmark
Comment
Footnote
Endnote

Enter page number:

14

Enter + and − to move relative to the current location. Example: +4 will move forward four items.

Go To
Previous
Close

Click

Page 14   Sec 1   14/19   At 1"   Ln 1   Col 1   REC TRK EXT OVR WPH

Start | Exploring - Part 2 | Microsoft Word -... | Paint Shop Pro - 02fi...   6:01 AM

(4) Word jumps to that page. (Check the page number in the status bar.)

(5) The dialog box remains onscreen so you can go to another page.

(6) When you're finished using Go To, click the **Close** button.

End Task

Task 5: Inserting Text

Inserting Text

Inserting Text

As you're typing a document, you'll no doubt need to go back and add some text here and there. Inserting text is extremely straightforward. When you type new text, Word pushes the existing text out of the way to make room for it. Depending on the exact location of the insertion point when you start typing, you will either need to add a space at the beginning of the insertion or at the end.

Start Here

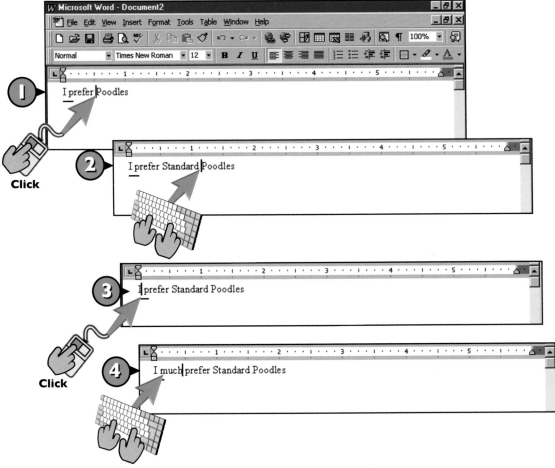

Click

Click

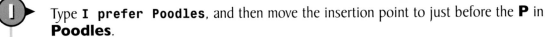

✓ **Replacing a block of text**

If you want to *replace* a block of text with new text, you can quickly *select* (highlight) the existing text first and then type over it with the new text. See "Deleting Text" in Part 3 for more information.

I ► Type **I prefer Poodles**, and then move the insertion point to just before the **P** in **Poodles**.

2 ► Type **Standard** and press the **Spacebar**.

3 ► Move the insertion point to just after the **I** at the beginning of the sentence.

4 ► This time, press the **Spacebar** first, and then type **much**.

End Task

Task 6: Combining and Splitting Paragraphs

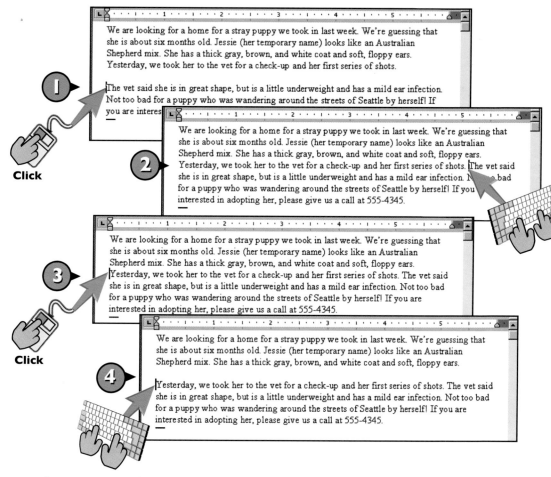

Combining and Splitting Paragraphs

When you're composing a new document, you'll most often revise the paragraph structure as you go. You may need to combine shorter paragraphs into one longer one, or break up a long paragraph into two or more shorter ones. You can adjust the breaks between paragraphs by using only the Enter and the Backspace keys.

1 Type the two paragraphs shown here, and then place the insertion point at the beginning of the second paragraph.

2 Press **Backspace** twice to join the paragraphs.

3 Move the insertion point just before the **Y** in **Yesterday**.

4 Press **Enter** twice to split the paragraph into two paragraphs.

PART 3

Editing Text

Word processing programs would be worthless if we couldn't use them to revise text. Indeed, the most valuable aspect of using Word is probably that you can quickly and painlessly edit text that you've already typed. The skills you learn here—selecting (highlighting) text, deleting text, cutting and pasting text, undoing actions, and so on—form the foundation for everything else you'll do in Word.

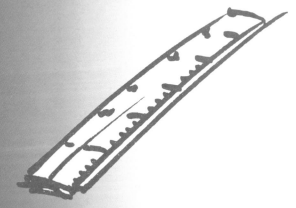

Tasks

Task #		Page #
1	Selecting Text with the Mouse	40
2	Selecting Text with the Keyboard	42
3	Deleting Text	44
4	Moving Text	46
5	Copying Text	48
6	Inserting a Tab	50
7	Using the Show/Hide Button	51
8	Using Undo	52

Task 1: Selecting Text with the Mouse

Use the Mouse to Select Text

Selecting (or highlighting) text is an essential word-processing skill. In many cases, you have to select text before issuing a command so Word knows what text you want to affect. For example, you have to select text before cutting and pasting or applying many kinds of formatting. In this task, you learn how to select text using the mouse (the next task teaches you how to select with the keyboard). Steps 1 through 3 show you the most basic way of selecting text. Steps 4 through 7 illustrate some shortcuts for selecting specific amounts of text.

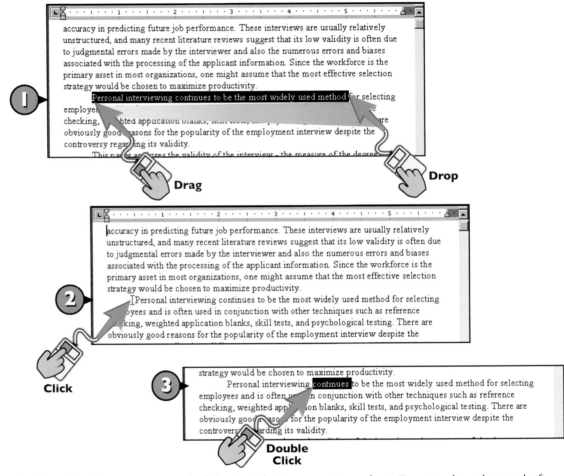

Drag

Drop

Click

Double Click

1. Position the I-beam at one end of the text that you want to select. Drag to the other end of the text, and then release the mouse button.

2. If you selected the wrong amount of text, deselect it by clicking anywhere in the document.

3. To select an individual word, double-click it.

Next Step

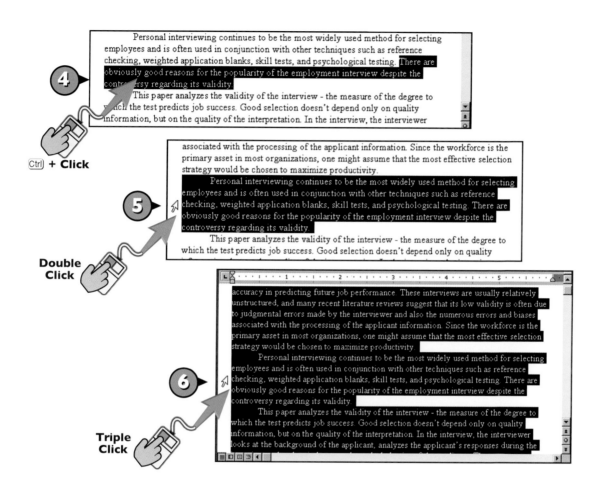

Ctrl + Click

Double Click

Triple Click

End Task

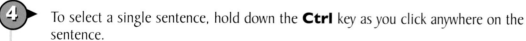

④ To select a single sentence, hold down the **Ctrl** key as you click anywhere on the sentence.

⑤ To select a paragraph, move the mouse pointer to the left of the paragraph and double-click.

⑥ To select the entire document, move the mouse pointer to the left of the text and triple-click.

ⓘ WARNING
If you have released the mouse button after selecting a block of text, you can't adjust the amount of text that's selected by pointing to it and dragging. If you try to do this, you'll end up *moving* the text instead. You can, however, adjust the selection by using the keyboard (see the next task).

ⓘ WARNING
As you'll see in "Deleting Text" in Task 3, when text is selected, any text you type *replaces* the selected text. If you don't want this to happen, deselect the text before typing.

Task 2: Selecting Text with the Keyboard

Use the Keyboard to Select Text

Although you'll probably use the mouse to select most of the time, you may want to use the keyboard once in awhile. If you only want to select a couple of characters, it's usually easiest to use the keyboard. You can also use the keyboard to adjust the size of a selection that you initially made with the mouse. (As mentioned in the preceding task, you can't adjust a selection with the mouse after you've released the mouse button.) The first five steps describe "keyboard-only" techniques. The last step shows you a method that uses the keyboard and the mouse together.

Start Here

Tips for the First-Time Home Buyer

1 Relax. Buying a home is stressful for anyone, and it is all the more anxiety-producing if it's your first time. Jot down all of your questions as you think of them, and then discuss them one by one with your real estate agent. Don't be afraid to be assertive about your concerns. If something about the house or the contract doesn't look right to you, it probably isn't.

⬆Shift + →

Tips for the First-Time Home Buyer

2 Relax. Buying a home is stressful for anyone, and it is all the more anxiety-producing if it's your first time. Jot down all of your questions as you think of them, and then discuss them one by one with your real estate agent. Don't be afraid to be assertive about your concerns. If something about the house or the contract doesn't look right to you, it probably isn't.

⬆Shift + Ctrl + →

Tips for the First-Time Home Buyer

3 Relax. Buying a home is stressful for anyone, and it is all the more anxiety-producing if it's your first time. Jot down all of your questions as you think of them, and then discuss them one by one with your real estate agent. Don't be afraid to be assertive about your concerns. If something about the house or the contract doesn't look right to you, it probably isn't.

⬆Shift + Ctrl + ↓

1 ▶ Press **Shift+Right arrow** to select character by character to the right, or **Shift+Left arrow** to select to the left.

2 ▶ Press **Shift+Ctrl+Right arrow** to select word by word to the right, or **Shift+Ctrl+Left arrow** to select to the left.

3 ▶ Press **Shift+Ctrl+Down arrow** to select down paragraph by paragraph, or **Shift+Ctrl+Up arrow** to select up.

Next Step

Relax. Buying a home is stressful for anyone, and it is all the more anxiety-producing if it's your first time. Jot down all of your questions as you think of them, and then discuss them one by one with your real estate agent.

Don't be afraid to be assertive about your concerns. If something about the house or the contract doesn't look right, it probably isn't.

④

Shift + End

Relax. Buying a home is stressful for anyone, and it is all the more anxiety-producing if it's your first time. Jot down all of your questions as you think of them, and then discuss them one by with your real estate agent.

Don't be afraid to be assertive about your concerns. If something about the house or the contract doesn't right to you, it probably isn't.

⑤

Shift + Ctrl + End

Relax. Buying a home is stressful for anyone, and it is all the more anxiety-producing if it's your first time. Jot down all of your questions as you think of them, and then discuss them one by with your real estate agent.

Don't be afraid to be assertive about your concerns. If something about the house or the contract doesn't look right to you, it probably

⑥

Click

Shift + **Click**

④ Press **Shift+End** to select to the end of the line, or **Shift+Home** to select to the beginning of the line.

⑤ Press **Shift+Ctrl+End** to select to the end of the document, or **Shift+Ctrl+Home** to select to the beginning of the document.

⑥ To select any amount of text, click at the beginning of the block of text, and then **Shift+click** at the end of it.

✓ **Multiple key combinations**
With the keyboard methods that involve pressing the Shift and/or Ctrl key with one of the arrow keys, just keep the Shift and/or Ctrl key held down as you press the arrow keys repeatedly to continue selecting character by character, word by word, and so on.

End Task

Task 3: Deleting Text

Deleting Text

It's as important to know how to delete text as to insert it. In this task, you learn techniques for deleting text that you'll use every time you edit a document.

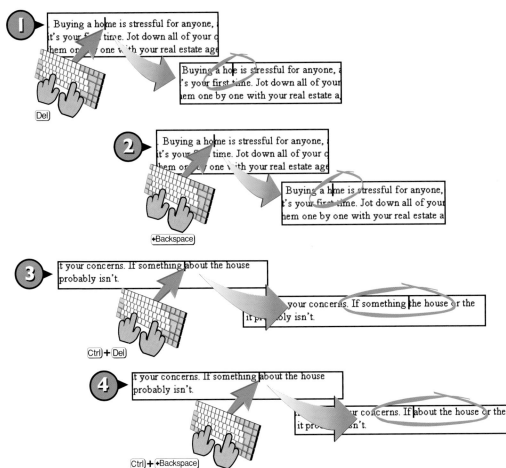

Deleting several words simultaneously
To delete several words at once, just keep the **Ctrl** key held down as you press the **Delete** or **Backspace** key repeatedly.

1 Press the **Delete** key to delete the character to the right of the insertion point.

2 Press the **Backspace** key to delete the character to the left.

3 Press **Ctrl+Delete** to delete the word to the right of the insertion point

4 Press **Ctrl+Backspace** to delete the word to the left.

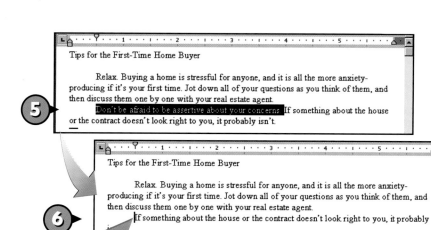

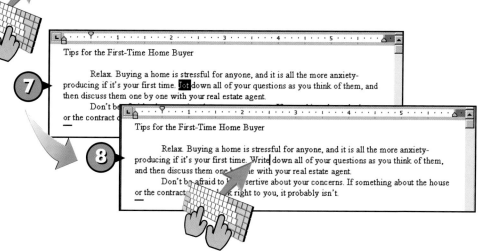

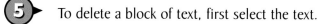

5 To delete a block of text, first select the text.

6 Then press the **Delete** key.

7 To replace existing text with text you type, first select the existing text.

8 Then type the new text.

Task 4: Moving Text

Moving Text

What most people appreciate most about writing with a word-processing program is the ability to *cut and paste* text from one place in your document to another. In this task, you learn how to *cut* (move) text. When you perform a cut, you remove the text from one location and paste it into another. In the next task, you learn how to *copy* text. Copying leaves the text in its current location and places a duplicate somewhere else.

Start Here

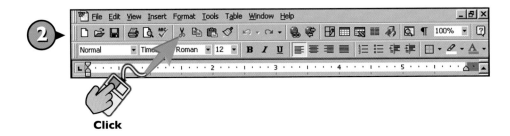

Click

1 Select the text that you want to cut.

2 Click the **Cut** button on the Standard toolbar.

3 The text disappears from the document.

Next Step

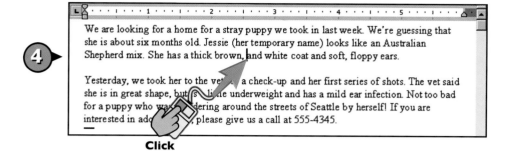

Click

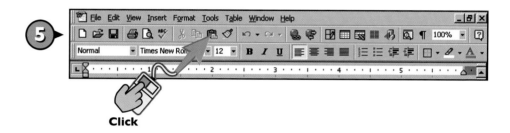

Click

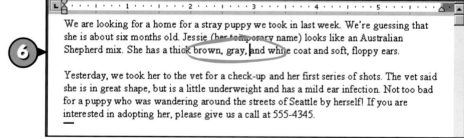

④ ▸ Move the insertion point to the place where you want to move the text.

⑤ ▸ Click the **Paste** button on the Standard toolbar.

⑥ ▸ The text is moved to the new location.

Copying Text

Copying text can save you a lot of typing time. If you have a block of text in one place in your document that you want to use somewhere else, it's much faster to copy it than to type it again. The steps here show you how to copy text from one location to another within the same document.

✓ **Copy text from one document to another**

If you want to copy text into another document, open the document that contains the text (the source) and the one to which you want to copy the text (the target). (See "Opening a Document" in Part 4.) Follow the steps shown here, with one variation: In step 4, click the **Window** menu, and then click the name of the target document at the bottom of the menu to switch to it. Move the insertion point to the desired location in that document, and continue with the remaining steps.

Task 5: Copying Text

Start Here

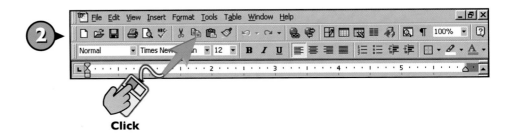

 We are looking for a home for a stray puppy we took in last week. We're guessing that he is about six months old. Max (his temporary name) looks like a German Shepherd mix. He has a thick brown coat and soft, floppy ears.

Last week, we noticed our ten-month-old puppy Max was limping, so we took him to the vet. It turns out that he has Eosinophilic Panosteitis ("growing pains"). is a disease of puppies between five and twelve months of age.

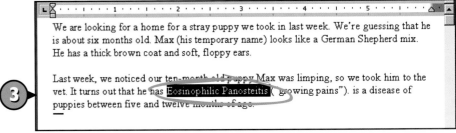

Click

 We are looking for a home for a stray puppy we took in last week. We're guessing that he is about six months old. Max (his temporary name) looks like a German Shepherd mix. He has a thick brown coat and soft, floppy ears.

Last week, we noticed our ten-month-old puppy Max was limping, so we took him to the vet. It turns out that he has Eosinophilic Panosteitis ("growing pains"). is a disease of puppies between five and twelve months of age.

 Select the text that you want to copy.

 Click the **Copy** button on the Standard toolbar.

3 The selected text remains in its current location because you're copying it, not moving it.

Next Step

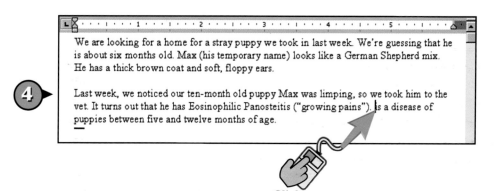

Click

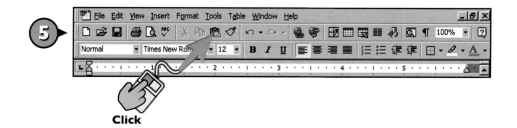

Click

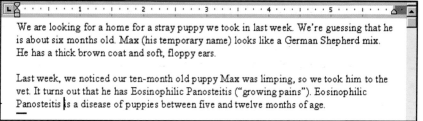

4 Move the insertion point to the place you want to copy the text.

5 Click the **Paste** button on the Standard toolbar.

6 The text is copied to the new location.

Using Tabs

Word's *default tabs* are set every half inch across the page. When you press the Tab key, Word pushes the text to the right of the insertion point out to the next tab stop. The default tabs are all that you need if you just want to indent the first line of your paragraphs. If you want to use tabs to align text more precisely, however, you need to create *custom tabs* (see "Setting a Custom Left or Right Tab," and "Moving and Deleting a Custom Tab," in Part 6).

✓ **What's a first-line indent?**

Depending on how Word is set up on your computer, when you press the Tab key at the beginning of a paragraph, Word 97 may actually set a *first-line indent* for the paragraph instead of inserting a tab. (See "Adding Indents" in Part 6.) The paragraph will look the same either way, and you can remove a first-line indent with the Backspace key.

Task 6: Inserting a Tab

Click

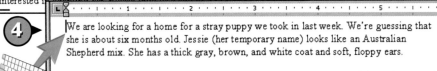

 The faint gray tick marks spaced every half inch along the lower edge of the ruler represent Word's default tab stops.

 Move the insertion point to the location where you want to insert the tab.

 Press the **Tab** key. Word pushes the text out to the next default tab stop.

 To remove a tab, make sure that your insertion point is just to the right of the tab, and press the **Backspace** key.

Task 7: Using the Show/Hide Button

Start Here

Click

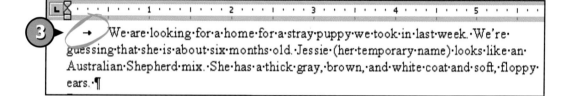

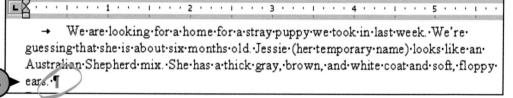

1 Click the **Show/Hide** button on the Standard toolbar.

2 Word uses a dot to show where you pressed the Spacebar.

3 Word uses an arrow to indicate where you pressed the Tab key.

4 Word uses the ***paragraph mark*** symbol (¶) to indicate where you pressed Enter to end a paragraph.

Hiding and Displaying Hidden Symbols

The Show/Hide button is an extremely handy tool. It displays (nonprinting) symbols onscreen to show you where you pressed the Spacebar, the Enter key, and the Tab key. You might, for example, use this button to check whether you typed an extra space between two words, to see how many blank lines are between two paragraphs, or to confirm that you inserted only one tab at the beginning of a paragraph.

✓ **A word about the Show/Hide button**
The Show/Hide button is a ***toggle*** button. You click it once to turn it on, and again to turn it off. You can turn the Show/Hide button on and off whenever you choose.

End Task

Task 8: Using Undo

Undoing Mistakes

Word lets you undo most actions, including typing, deleting, moving, copying, and formatting text. One of the best aspects of Word's Undo feature is that it lets you undo multiple actions, not just your most recent one. As you experiment with Undo, keep in mind that Word cannot undo a few actions, such as opening, saving, or printing a document.

Start Here

1

Buying a home is stressful for anyone, and it is all the more anxiety-producing if it's your first time. Jot down all of your questions as you think of them, and then discuss them one by one with your real estate agent. Don't be afraid to be assertive about your concerns. If something about the house or the contract doesn't look right to you, it probably isn't.

2

Buying a home is stressful for anyone, and it is all the more anxiety-producing if it's your first time. Jot down all of your questions as you think of them, and then discuss them one by one with your real estate agent. Don't be afraid to be assertive about your concerns. If something about the house or the contract doesn't look right to you, it probably isn't.

3

Buying a home is stressful for anyone, and it is all the more anxiety-producing if it's your first time. Don't be afraid to be assertive about your concerns. If something about the house or the contract doesn't look right to you, it probably isn't.

4

Click

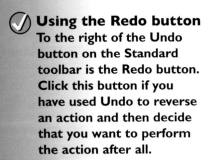

✓ Using the Redo button

To the right of the Undo button on the Standard toolbar is the Redo button. Click this button if you have used Undo to reverse an action and then decide that you want to perform the action after all.

1 To practice using Undo, type the paragraph shown here.

2 Select the second sentence.

3 Press **Delete** to remove it.

4 Click the **Undo** button on the Standard toolbar. (Click the button itself, not the down arrow to its right.)

Next Step

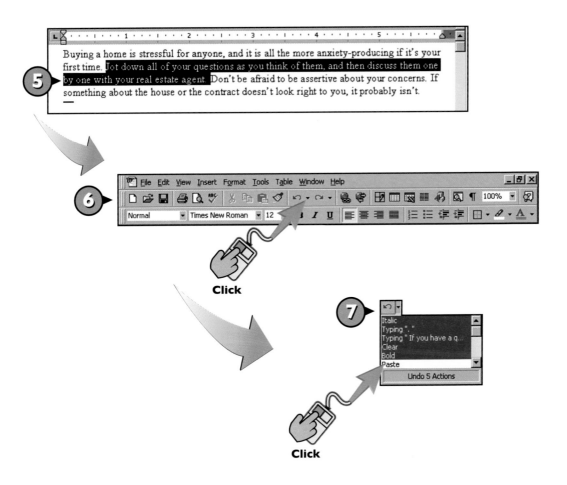

Buying a home is stressful for anyone, and it is all the more anxiety-producing if it's your first time. Jot down all of your questions as you think of them, and then discuss them one by one with your real estate agent. Don't be afraid to be assertive about your concerns. If something about the house or the contract doesn't look right to you, it probably isn't.

Click

Click

Undo 5 Actions

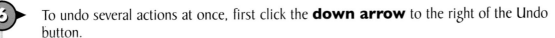
⑤ Word restores the deleted text. If you keep clicking the **Undo** button, Word reverses previous actions one by one.

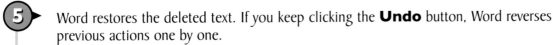
⑥ To undo several actions at once, first click the **down arrow** to the right of the Undo button.

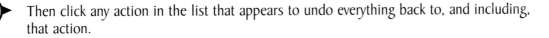
⑦ Then click any action in the list that appears to undo everything back to, and including, that action.

Managing Word 97 Documents

Just as a filing cabinet would be of no use if you weren't able to get files in to and out of the drawers, you have to understand how to access and store Word documents on your computer system to use the program effectively. In this part, you learn elementary yet essential skills, including saving, closing, and opening documents, and starting new ones.

Tasks

Task #		Page #
1	Saving a Document	56
2	Closing a Document	58
3	Opening a Document	60
4	Creating a New Document	62
5	Using a Template	64
6	Using a Wizard	66
7	Finding a Document	68

Task 1: Saving a Document

Saving a Document

A document you are typing exists only in your computer's *memory* until you save it, so you need to save if there's any chance that you'll want to come back to your document later. After saving a document, you can continue working on it or close it.

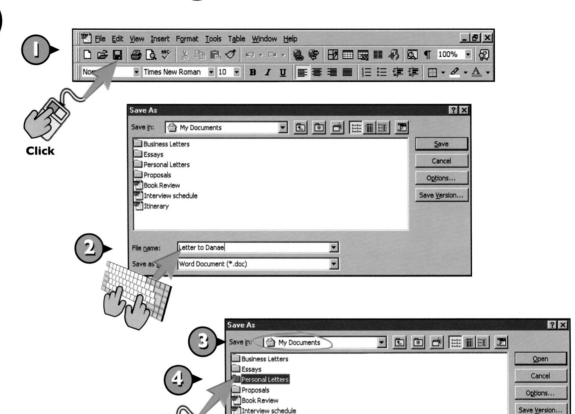

Click

✅ **Saving your document**
After you've saved a document for the first time, you still need to save every time you revise it. When you click the **Save** button these subsequent times, Word assumes you want to keep the same file name and location, so it saves immediately without displaying the Save As dialog box. To save the document with a different name or location, choose **File, Save As** instead.

Double
Click

1 Click the **Save** button in the Standard toolbar to display the Save As dialog box.

2 Type a name for the document in the **File name** text box. (You can include spaces.)

3 Look in the **Save in** box. If you want to save your file in the folder (or drive) listed here, skip to step 7.

4 If you want to save in a subfolder of the location in the **Save in** box, double-click the folder and, if necessary, one of its subfolders.

Next
Step

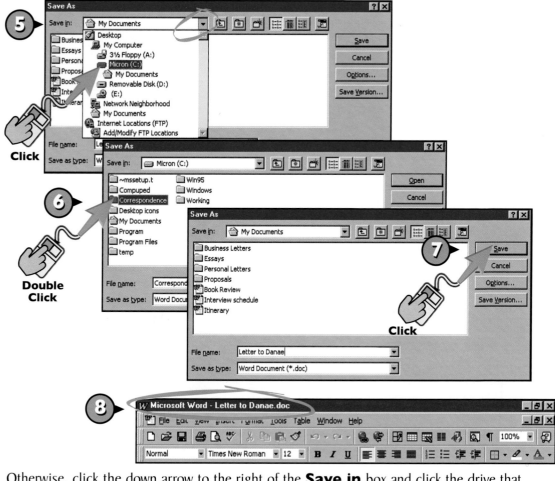

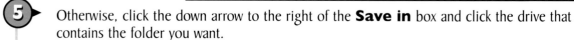

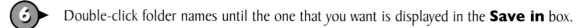

5 ▶ Otherwise, click the down arrow to the right of the **Save in** box and click the drive that contains the folder you want.

6 ▶ Double-click folder names until the one that you want is displayed in the **Save in** box.

7 ▶ Click the **Save** button.

8 ▶ The document's name now appears in the title bar of the Word window.

Closing a Document

When you are finished editing and saving a document, it's a good idea to close it. If you use the steps shown here, the Word window stays open so you can work on other documents. When you're ready to close Word itself, follow the steps in "Exiting Word 97" in Part I.

Task 2: Closing a Document

Click

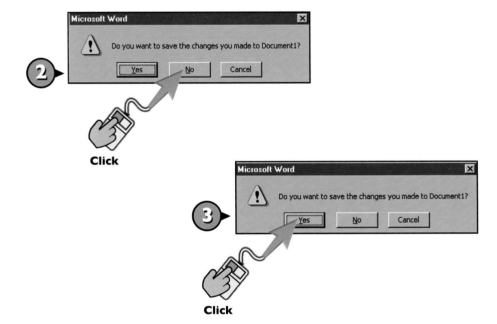

Click

Click

✓ **Another way to close your document**
If you like, you can choose **File, Close** in step I instead of clicking the **Close** button for the document window. The result is the same.

1. ▶ Click the **Close** button in the upper-right corner of the document window (the lower of the two Close buttons). If you don't have any unsaved changes, Word closes the document immediately.

2. ▶ If you have unsaved changes, Word asks if you want to save. If you don't want to save, click the **No** button and skip to step 5.

3. ▶ If you want to save, click the **Yes** button. (Click the **Cancel** button if you decide not to close your document after all.)

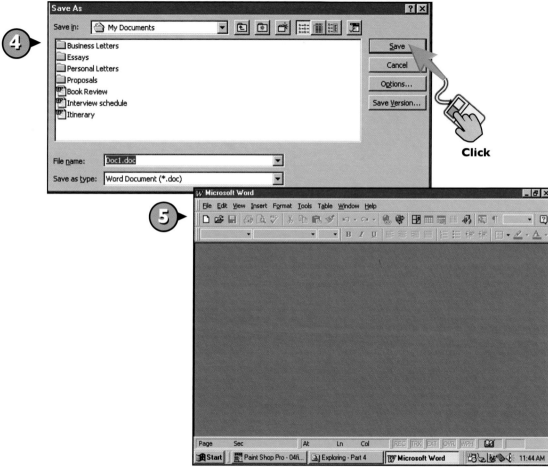

④ If you're saving the document for the first time, Word displays the Save As dialog box. Choose a name and location for the file (see Task 1), and then click the **Save** button.

⑤ The document closes, but the Word window remains open to let you start a new document or open an existing one.

Task 3: Opening a Document

Opening a Document

When you want to revise a
document that you've
previously saved to disk,
follow these steps to open it
again. Word lets you have
more than one document
open at a time and switch
back and forth between
them.

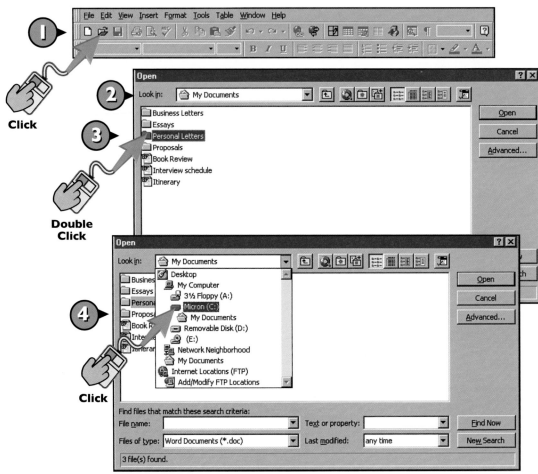

Click

Double
Click

Click

Word lists the four
documents that you've
opened most recently at
the bottom of the **File**
menu. If your document is
on this list, you can just
click it to open it instead of
following these steps.

1 Click the **Open** button in the Standard toolbar to display the Open dialog box.

2 Look at the **Look in** box. If the folder (or drive) listed here is the one that contains your document, skip to step 7.

3 If the folder you want is a subfolder of the location in the **Look in** box, double-click the folder, and, if necessary, one of its subfolders.

4 Otherwise, click the **down arrow** to the right of the **Look in** list. Click the drive that contains the folder you want.

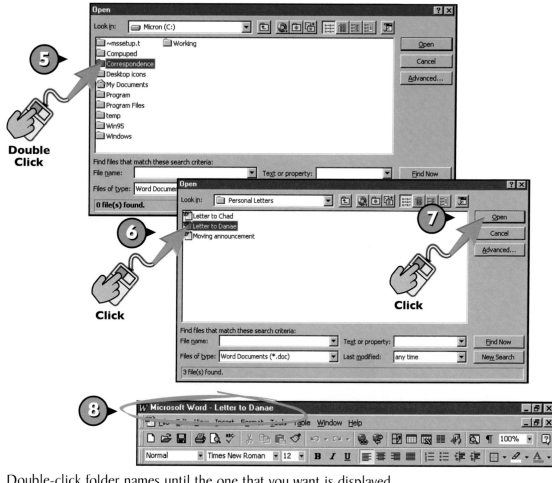

Double Click

Click

Click

5 ▶ Double-click folder names until the one that you want is displayed.

6 ▶ Click the document name.

7 ▶ Click the **Open** button.

8 ▶ Word opens the document for you.

Task 4: Creating a New Document

Creating a New Document

Each time you start Word 97, you get a new blank document that has the temporary name Document1 (which you replace the first time you save). However, at times you may want to start a second or third document in the same Word session. Word lets you keep multiple documents open at once, so you don't have to close the currently active document before beginning another one. At the end of this task, you learn how to switch back and forth between open documents.

✓ **New document names**
When you start a new document, its name may be Document2, Document3, or higher. The number in the name does not mean that you have that number of documents currently *open*. It just means that you *started* that many documents in the current Word session.

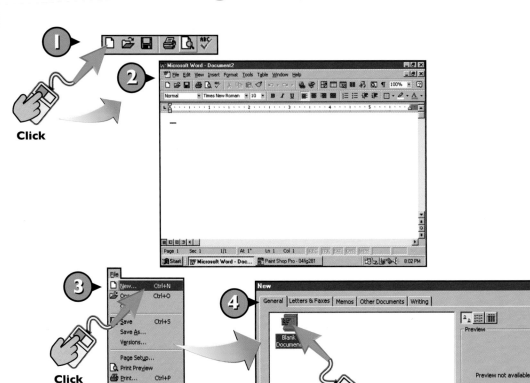

Click

Click

Click

Click

Start Here

1. Click the **New** button in the Standard toolbar.

2. A new blank document opens.

3. Create another new document. This time, choose **File**, **New** instead of clicking the New button to display the New dialog box.

4. Click the **General** tab and select the **Blank Document** icon, and then click the **OK** button.

Next Step

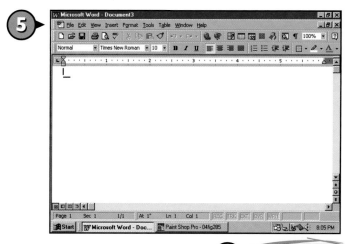

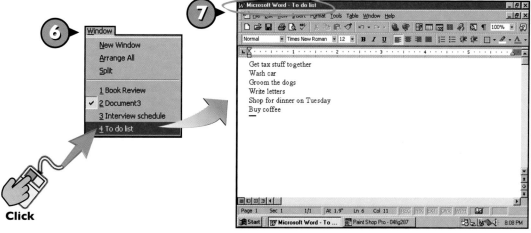

Click

Word displays a new document, just as if you had clicked the New button. (See the next task to find out when the **File**, **New** command is useful.)

To switch among open documents, click the **Window** menu, and then click the file name in the list at the bottom of the menu.

Word displays the document that you chose.

Task 5: Using a Template

Using a Template

You can type and format all of your documents from scratch, but you don't have to. Word's *templates* can help you create a variety of documents, from memos and letters to fax cover sheets. A template is a rough blueprint for a document that usually includes some combination of text and formatting. When you use the New toolbar button to start a document, Word assumes that you want to use the Normal template, which starts you off with a "plain vanilla" document. Here you learn to use other templates that contain text and more complex formatting.

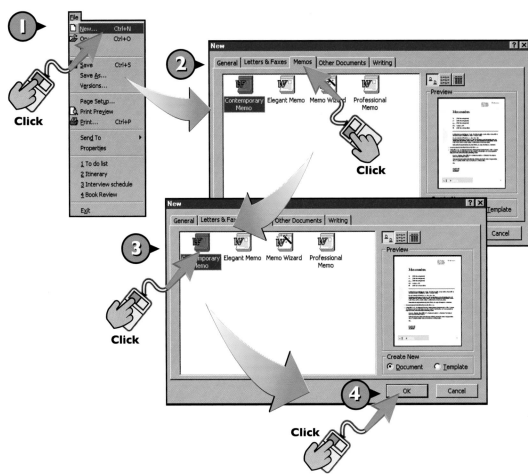

1 Choose **File**, **New** to display the New dialog box.

2 Click the **Memos** tab. (Your tabs may differ from the ones shown here.)

3 Select the **Contemporary Memo** template.

4 Click the **OK** button.

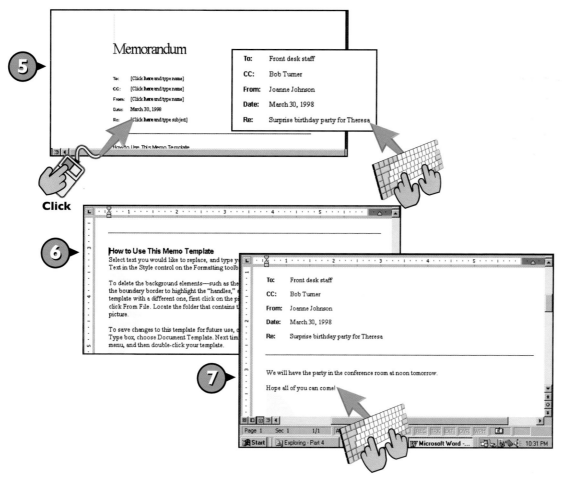

5 ▸ Word creates a new document based on the Contemporary Memo template. Click the **[Click here and type name]** instructions and type over them with the text shown here.

6 ▸ Read the instructions on using the template.

7 ▸ Select the instructions and then type the text shown here. (Your text replaces the selected instructions.) Close the document without saving your changes.

Using a Wizard

If you'd appreciate a bit more hand-holding than you get with standard templates, try using a *wizard*. Wizards, like other templates, give you "blueprint" text and formatting. But they also ask you questions about what you want to include in the document, and then create just what you asked for. Wizard-generated documents look exactly like documents based on standard templates, complete with "click here" instructions to help you fill in the text.

Task 6: Using a Wizard

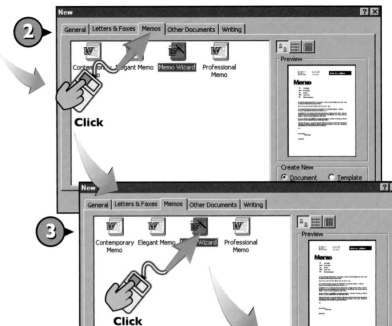

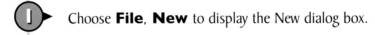

Choose **File**, **New** to display the New dialog box.

Click the **Memos** tab.

Select the **Memo Wizard** template.

Click **OK** to start the wizard.

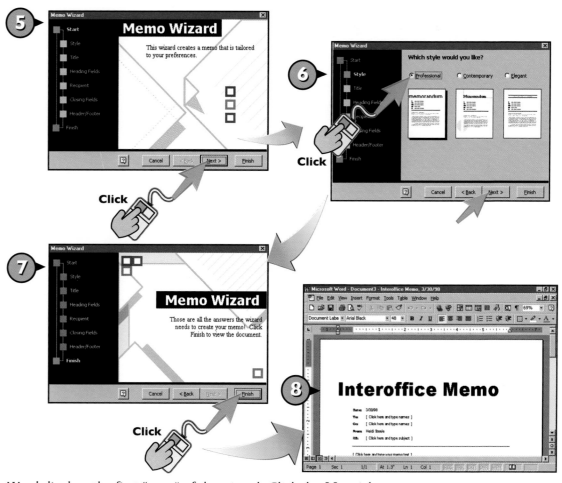

5 Word displays the first "page" of the wizard. Click the **Next** button.

6 The wizard presents its first question. Mark one of the three option buttons, and click **Next** again.

7 Continue answering the wizard's questions. When you reach the Finish page, click the **Finish** button.

8 In a moment, the document appears. Close it without saving it.

End Task

Task 7: Finding a Document

Finding a Document

If you have trouble finding a document that you know you saved, you can use Word's **Find** feature to search it out. This feature is especially useful if you can't remember what you named the document, because you can search for a word or phrase that the document contains. The Find options are conveniently located in the Open dialog box, so they're right there when you need them.

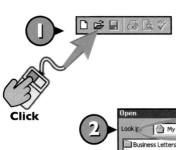

Click

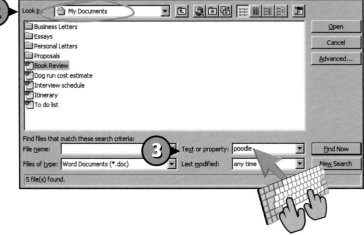

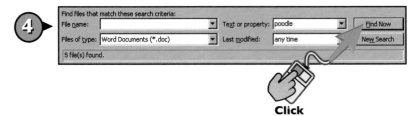

Click

✓ **Searching in subfolders for a document**

If you want Word to search in subfolders of the folder in the **Look in** box, enter your search criteria as described in these steps, click the **Commands and Settings** button at the top of the Open dialog box (it's at the far right), and click **Search Subfolders.**

1 ▶ Click the **Open** button in the Standard toolbar.

2 ▶ Display the folder that you want to search in the **Look in** box. (See "Opening a Document" if you need help.)

3 ▶ Type the word or phrase that your document contains in the **Text or property** box. (Enclose phrases in quotation marks.)

4 ▶ Click the **Find Now** button.

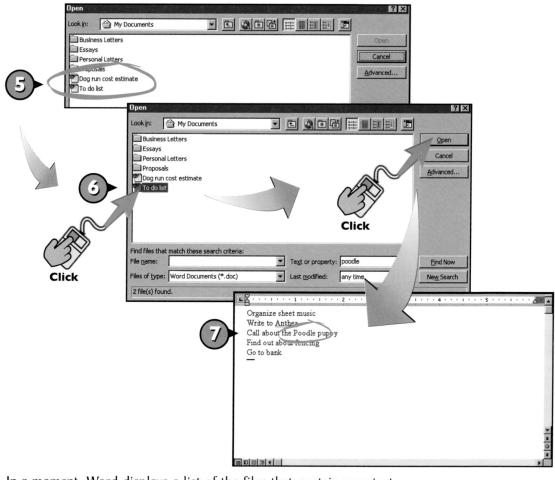

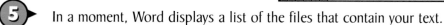

5 In a moment, Word displays a list of the files that contain your text.

6 To open one of the files, just select it and click the **Open** button. (If you don't want to open any of the files that Word found, click the **Cancel** button.)

7 Word opens the document for you.

Viewing and Printing the Document

You can create such a wide variety of documents in Word (from standard letters, memos, and reports to sophisticated flyers and newsletters) that Word has to give you a broad set of choices for viewing documents onscreen and printing them. The first three tasks in this part discuss viewing options; the last three teach you basic printing techniques.

Tasks

Task #   Page #

1   Displaying a Document in Page Layout View   72

2   Zooming a Document   73

3   Previewing a Document   74

4   Printing a Document   76

5   Printing an Envelope   78

6   Printing Labels   80

Using Page Layout View

Word provides several different *views* that you can use to work with your documents. *Normal view*, the one you'll use most of the time, doesn't show the margin areas of your document. If you want to see margin elements, such as page numbers and headers and footers, you need to use *Page Layout view*. You also need to use Page Layout view to work with columns and graphics, among other things.

Task 1: Displaying a Document in Page Layout View

Click

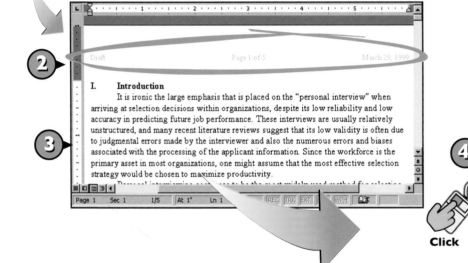

Click

 Choose **View**, **Page Layout** to switch to Page Layout view.

 Now the text in the header of this document is visible, and you can see the top edge of the page.

 Page Layout view gives you a vertical ruler as well as the horizontal one.

 Choose **View**, **Normal** to switch back to Normal view.

Task 2: Zooming a Document

Start Here

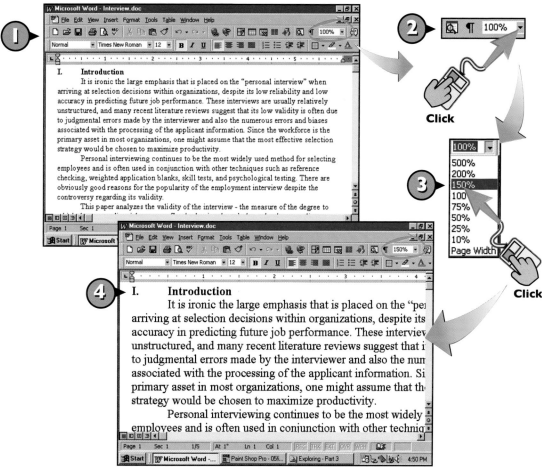

Zooming a Document

Depending on the resolution of your monitor and the size of your text, you might want to *zoom* in on your text to enlarge it, or zoom out to shrink it. Zooming doesn't affect the size of the text when it prints; it only affects its appearance on your screen.

✓ Changing the Zoom setting

If the zoom setting you want (85%, perhaps) isn't one of the options in the Zoom Control list, just click the current entry in the Zoom Control box to select it, type a new number (you don't need to type the percent sign), and press **Enter**.

✓ Using the Page Width setting

One handy option in the Zoom Control list is Page Width, which lets you see the full width of your page onscreen, regardless of your paper size, margin width, font size, and so on.

① Note the setting in the Zoom Control box. By default, Word displays documents at 100% magnification.

② Click the **down arrow** to the right of the Zoom Control box at the right end of the Standard toolbar.

③ Click the magnification percentage that you want to use.

④ Word applies the setting you chose.

End Task

Task 3: Previewing a Document

Using Print Preview

Word lets you see what the printed document will look like before you actually send it to the printer. Using Print Preview is a great way to avoid wasting paper, because you can spot problems in your document before you print.

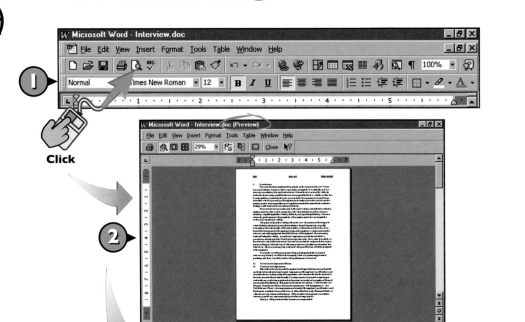

Click

Click

Click & Drag

✓ Fit your document on one page

If your document is spilling over onto two pages and you'd like to get it to fit on one page, you can click the **Shrink to Fit** button on the Print Preview toolbar (the fourth button from the right) to make the text fit on a single page.

 Click the **Print Preview** button in the Standard toolbar.

 Word switches to Print Preview. (The title bar now contains **[Preview]**.) Press the **Page Up** and **Page Down** keys to bring different parts of the document into view.

 To view several pages at the same time, click the **Multiple Pages** button.

 Drag through the number of pages you want to view in the grid that drops down.

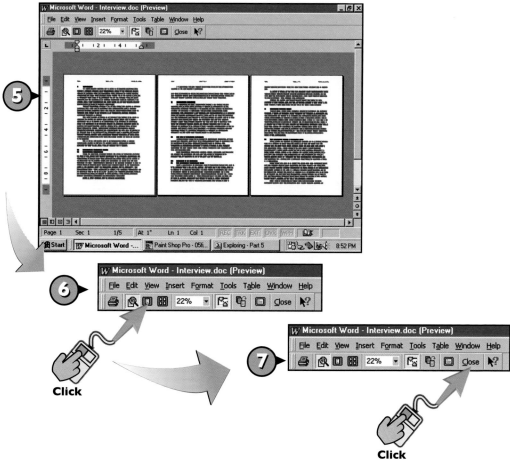

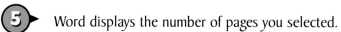
Click

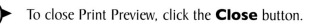
Click

5 Word displays the number of pages you selected.

6 To return to viewing one page, click the **One Page** button.

7 To close Print Preview, click the **Close** button.

End Task

Printing a Document

Word assumes that you will frequently want to print one complete copy of your document, so it provides a toolbar button to let you do just that. If you need to customize your printing at all, you'll find all the options you need in the Print dialog box. Before you follow these steps, make sure that your printer is turned on.

Task 4: Printing a Document

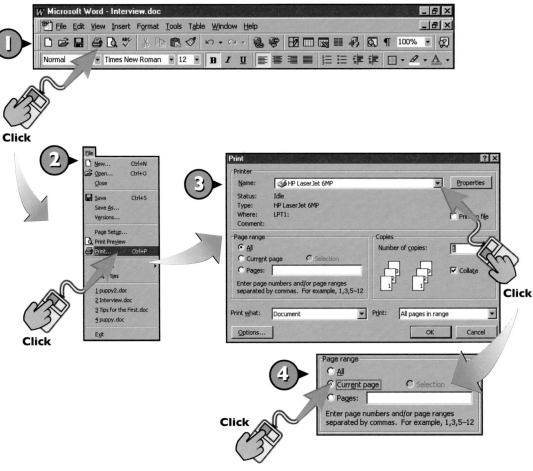

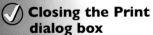

✓ **Closing the Print dialog box**
If you display the Print dialog box but then decide that you're not ready to print yet, make sure to click the Cancel button instead of the OK button to close the dialog box without printing.

1. To print one copy of your document, click the **Print** button on the Standard toolbar.

2. For other printing options, choose **File**, **Print** to display the Print dialog box.

3. If you have more than one printer, select the one you want to use in the **Name** drop-down list.

4. To print only the page that the insertion point is on, click the **Current page** option button.

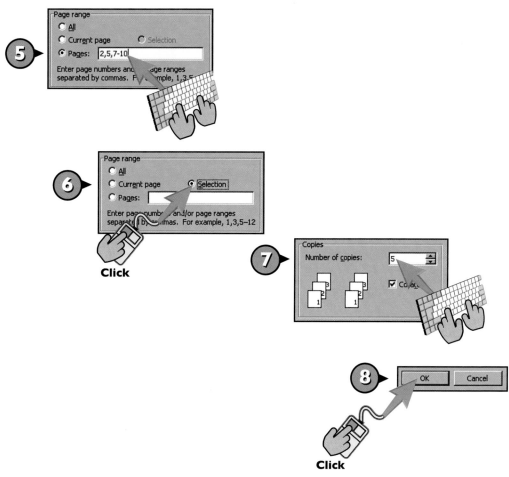

Click

Click

5 ▶ To print a range of pages, type the page numbers in the **Pages** text box.

6 ▶ To print only a block of text, select the text before displaying the Print dialog box, and then mark the **Selection** option button.

7 ▶ To print multiple copies, type the desired number in the **Number of copies** text box.

8 ▶ When you've made your choices, click the **OK** button.

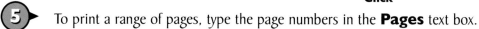

Task 5: Printing an Envelope

Printing an Envelope

Printing an envelope in Word is simple: You make sure that the address is right, put the envelope in the printer, and issue the command to print. Word assumes that you want to print on a standard business-size envelope, but you can choose a different envelope size if necessary. Check your printer's documentation to find out how to load the envelope. This varies from printer to printer.

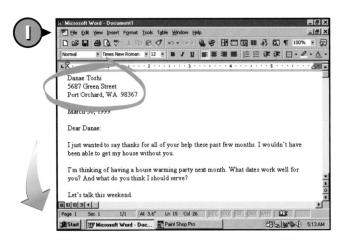

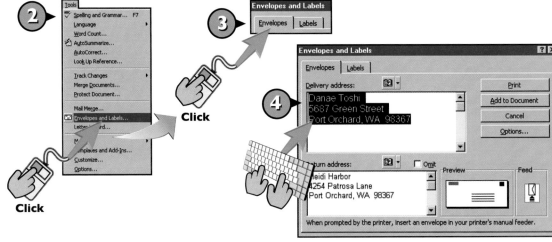

Click

Click

(✓) **Delivery address**

You can follow the steps here even if you don't have a document that contains the recipient's address onscreen. You just have to take the extra step of typing the delivery address in step 4.

1 If you used Word to type the letter addressed to the recipient, open it now.

2 Choose **Tools**, **Envelopes and Labels**.

3 Click the **Envelopes** tab in the Envelopes and Labels dialog box.

4 Word finds the address in the document you have open onscreen. Edit it in the **Delivery address** box if needed.

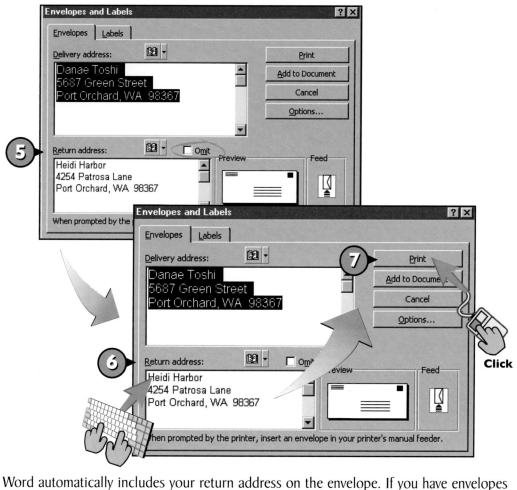

5 Word automatically includes your return address on the envelope. If you have envelopes with a preprinted return address, mark the **Omit** check box.

6 If you want to print a return address, check the address in the **Return address** box and edit it if necessary.

7 Put the envelope in your printer and click the **Print** button.

✓ **Your return address**
Word finds your return address in the User Information tab of the Options dialog box. To change it, choose **Tools, Options,** click the **User Information** tab, edit the address in the **Mailing address** box, and click **OK.**

Task 6: Printing Labels

Printing Labels

The steps for printing labels are similar to those described in the previous task for printing envelopes. The one difference is that you'll likely need to choose another label type because labels come in such a wide variety of sizes.

Start Here

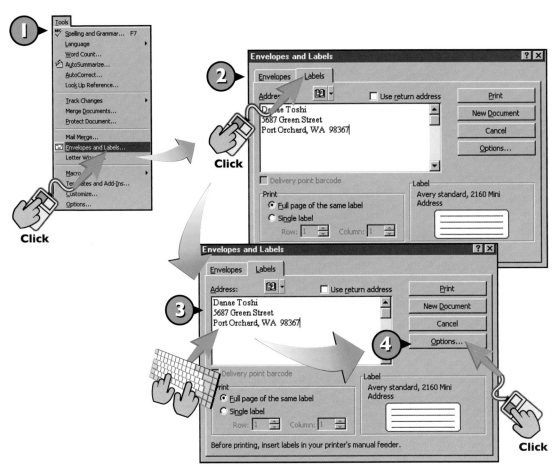

1 Choose **Tools**, **Envelopes and Labels**.

2 Click the **Labels** tab.

3 Type the address in the **Address** box. (If you want to print your return address instead, mark the **Use return address** check box.)

4 Click the **Options** button to display the Label Options dialog box.

Next Step

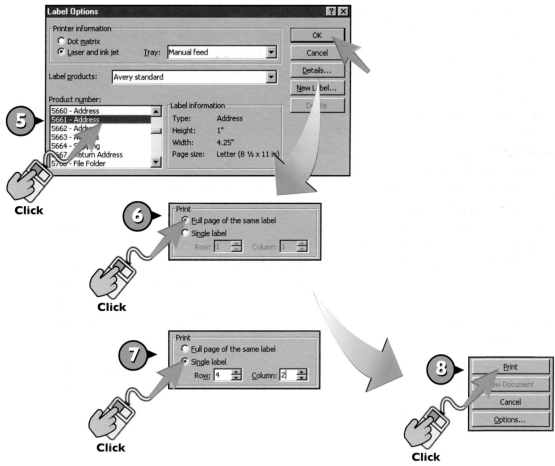

5 Select the product number for your labels in the **Product number** list, and click **OK**. (If you don't have standard Avery labels, choose a different label from the **Label products** drop-down list.)

6 Mark the **Full page of the same label** check box if you want a whole page of labels with the same address on each one.

7 If you want a single label, mark the **Single label** option button, and then enter the label's row and column number.

8 Put the sheet of labels in your printer, and click the **Print** button.

End Task

Formatting Your Document

Formatting a document (improving its appearance) can be a lot of fun, but it can also leave you rather befuddled if you don't understand how the formatting commands work. This part gives you an organized introduction to the techniques you'll use every day. You start with formatting that affects individual characters, such as changing fonts, applying bold, italic, and underline, and so on. Then you learn formatting that affects paragraphs, such as setting alignment, adding indents, and working with custom tabs. Finally, you learn two formatting features that affect entire pages: changing margins and inserting page breaks.

Tasks

Task #		Page #
1	Making Text Bold, Italic, and Underlined	84
2	Changing the Font and Font Size	86
3	Changing Paragraph Alignment	88
4	Changing Line Spacing	90
5	Adding Indents	92
6	Creating Bulleted and Numbered Lists	94
7	Setting a Custom Left or Right Tab	96
8	Setting a Custom Center or Decimal Tab	98
9	Moving and Deleting a Custom Tab	100
10	Changing Margins	102
11	Inserting a Page Break	104
12	Adding a Border to a Paragraph	106
13	Shading a Paragraph	108
14	Centering a Page Vertically	110
15	Numbering Pages	112
16	Creating Headers and Footers	114
17	Using the Header and Footer Toolbar	116

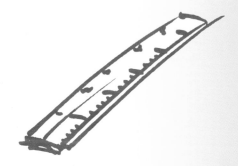

Adding Emphasis to Text

Applying a little **bold**, *italic*, or <u>underlining</u> here and there can add just the right emphasis to your text. You can also apply more than one of these three formats to the same text. A word that has all three formats applied looks like *<u>this</u>*.

Task 1: Making Text Bold, Italic, and Underlined

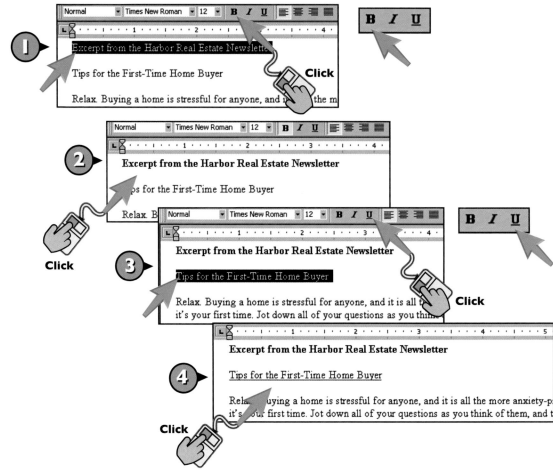

✓ **Shortcut Keys**
Instead of clicking the Bold, Italic, and Underline toolbar buttons after selecting your text, you can press **Ctrl+B** for bold, **Ctrl+I** for italic, and **Ctrl+U** for underlining.

1 To make text bold, select the text and click the **Bold** button on the Formatting toolbar.

2 Click anywhere to deselect the text so that you can see the bold formatting more easily.

3 To underline text, select the text and click the **Underline** button on the Formatting toolbar.

4 Click anywhere to deselect the text so that you can see the underlining.

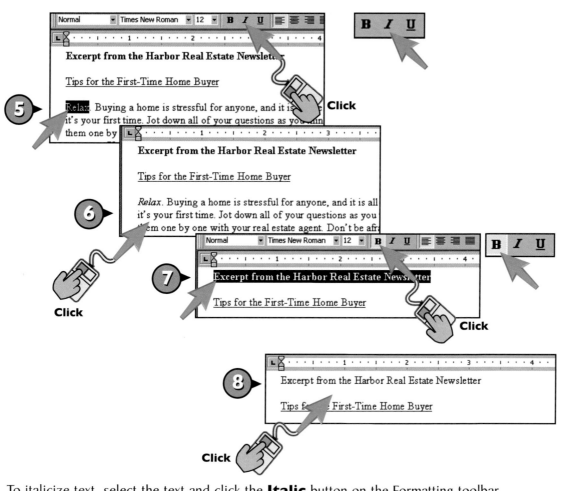

5 To italicize text, select the text and click the **Italic** button on the Formatting toolbar.

6 Click anywhere to deselect the text so that you can view your italic.

7 To turn off bold, italic, or underlining, select the text first; then click the appropriate button. (In this example, bold is turned on.)

8 Click anywhere to deselect the text. The formatting is turned off.

Task 2: Changing the Font and Font Size

Changing the Font and Font Size

One of the things that people like most about word processing is that you can quickly change the *font* (typeface) and font size of your text. Font size is measured in *points*. (A 10–12-point font is commonly used for body text.) Word assumes that you want to use a Times New Roman, 10-point font, but as you'll see here, you can change these settings with just a couple of mouse clicks.

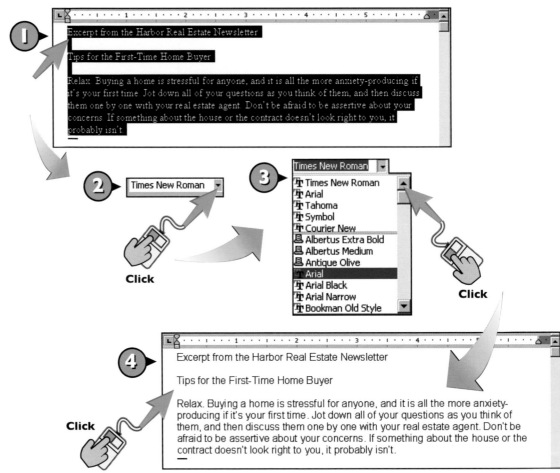

✓ **Frequently used fonts**
The fonts you use the most frequently appear above the horizontal double line in the Font list (see the figure for step 3) so you can get to them easily. Below the double line is an alphabetical list of all your fonts.

1 ▶ Select the text whose font you want to change.

2 ▶ Click the **down arrow** to the right of the **Font** list in the Formatting toolbar.

3 ▶ Use the scrollbar on the right edge of the list to move through the list, and click the font that you want to use.

4 ▶ Click anywhere to deselect the text so that you can see the new font.

Next Step

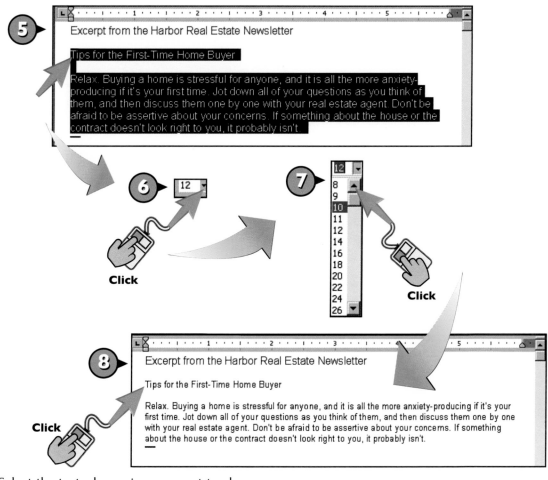

Excerpt from the Harbor Real Estate Newsletter

Tips for the First-Time Home Buyer

Relax. Buying a home is stressful for anyone, and it is all the more anxiety-producing if it's your first time. Jot down all of your questions as you think of them, and then discuss them one by one with your real estate agent. Don't be afraid to be assertive about your concerns. If something about the house or the contract doesn't look right to you, it probably isn't.

Click

12

Click

12
8
9
10
11
12
14
16
18
20
22
24
26

Click

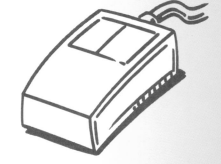

Click

Excerpt from the Harbor Real Estate Newsletter

Tips for the First-Time Home Buyer

Relax. Buying a home is stressful for anyone, and it is all the more anxiety-producing if it's your first time. Jot down all of your questions as you think of them, and then discuss them one by one with your real estate agent. Don't be afraid to be assertive about your concerns. If something about the house or the contract doesn't look right to you, it probably isn't.

5 ▸ Select the text whose size you want to change.

6 ▸ Click the **down arrow** to the right of the **Font Size** list in the Formatting toolbar.

7 ▸ Scroll through the list, and click the size that you want to use.

8 ▸ Click anywhere to deselect the text so that you can see the new size.

Task 3: Changing Paragraph Alignment

Changing Paragraph Alignment

Alignment refers to the way the right and left edges of a paragraph line up along the margins. By default, Word uses left alignment, which gives paragraphs a straight left edge and a ragged right edge. You usually use centering and right alignment for headings or other short lines of text. Occasionally, you may want to *justify* paragraphs so that both the right and left edges are straight. To change alignment, you use the four alignment buttons on the Formatting toolbar.

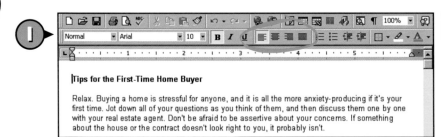

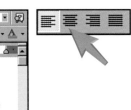

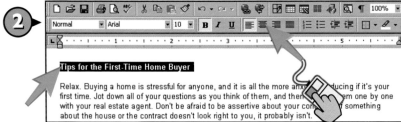

Click

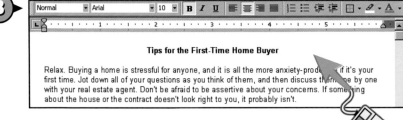

Click

1. The paragraph that contains the insertion point is left aligned, so the **Align Left** button looks like it's pushed in.

2. To center a paragraph, select it and click the **Center** button.

3. Click anywhere to deselect the paragraph.

Next Step

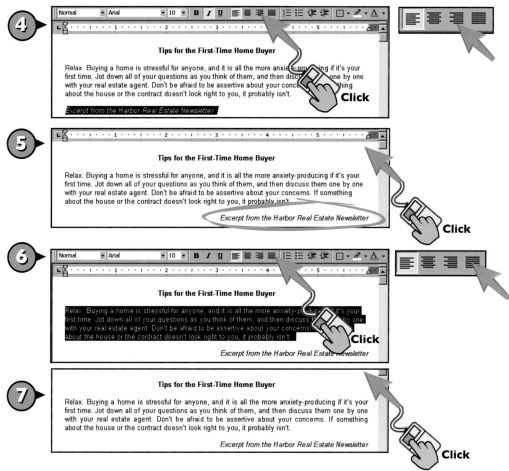

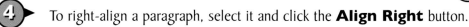

④ ▶ To right-align a paragraph, select it and click the **Align Right** button.

⑤ ▶ Click anywhere to deselect the paragraph.

⑥ ▶ To justify a paragraph, select it and click the **Justify** button.

⑦ ▶ Click anywhere to deselect the paragraph.

End Task

✔ Aligning paragraphs
If you are changing the alignment of a single paragraph, you don't actually need to select it first. You can just place the insertion point anywhere in the paragraph, and then click the alignment button. If you want to align several paragraphs at once, however, you need to select at least a portion of all of them first.

Task 4: Changing Line Spacing

Changing Line Spacing

Line spacing is the amount of space between lines within a paragraph. Word assumes single spacing, but you can change this setting to double spacing, which is great for rough drafts (you have room to write your edits between the lines), or one-and-a-half line spacing, which can make your text easier to read.

✓ **Use the keyboard to change line spacing**
If you don't like the hassle of displaying the Paragraph dialog box, you can change line spacing with the keyboard instead: Select the paragraphs and then press **Ctrl+2** for double spacing, **Ctrl+5** for one-and-a-half line spacing, or **Ctrl+1** for single spacing.

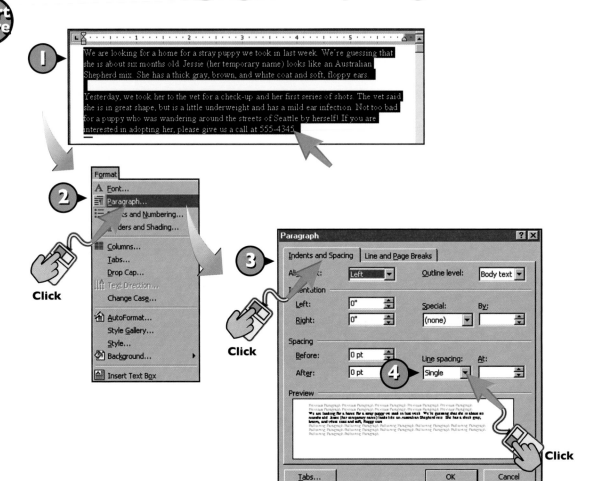

1. Select the paragraphs whose line spacing you want to change.

2. Choose **Format**, **Paragraph** to display the Paragraph dialog box.

3. Click the **Indents and Spacing** tab if it isn't already in front.

4. Click the **down arrow** to the right of the **Line spacing** list.

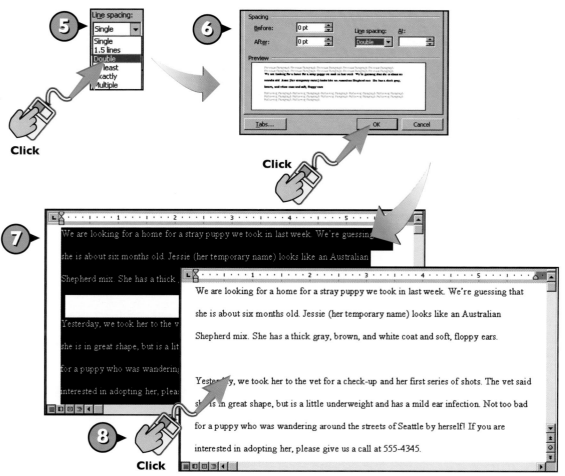

5 ► Click the desired spacing in the list.

6 ► Click the **OK** button.

7 ► Word applies the line spacing you chose to the selected paragraphs.

8 ► Click anywhere to deselect the text.

Task 5: Adding Indents

Indenting Paragraphs

Word lets you indent paragraphs from the left margin, the right margin, or both. You can also create a *first line* indent, which indents only the first line of a paragraph, or a hanging indent, which indents all the lines except the first. Word provides several ways to set indents. Here, you learn to add indents by dragging the *indent markers* on the ruler. To undo any indent you set, select the indented paragraphs and then drag the appropriate marker back to its original position on the ruler.

✓ **First line indent**
To create a first line indent, select the paragraphs and then drag the **First Line Indent** marker (the top triangle above the **Left Indent** marker). To create a hanging indent, select the paragraphs and then drag the **Hanging Indent** marker (the bottom triangle directly above the **Left Indent** marker).

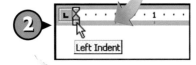

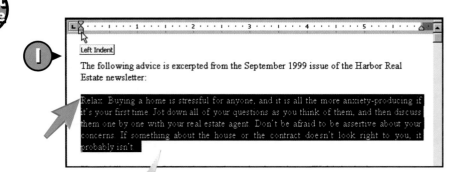

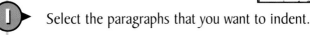

Click & Drag

Select the paragraphs that you want to indent.

To set a left indent, point to the **Left Indent** marker (the square underneath the two triangles). The ToolTip *Left Indent* appears.

Drag to the desired position on the ruler.

Release the mouse button. The paragraphs are now indented from the left.

Next Step

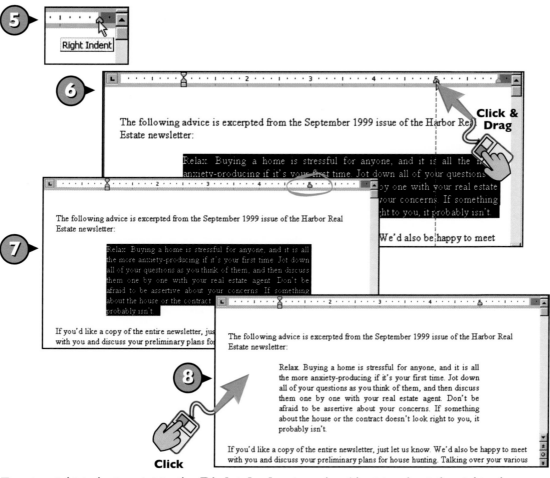

5 To set a right indent, point to the **Right Indent** marker (the triangle at the right edge of the ruler). The ToolTip *Right Indent* appears.

6 Drag to the desired position on the ruler.

7 Release the mouse button. The paragraphs are now indented from the right.

8 Click anywhere in your text to deselect the text.

Task 6: Creating Bulleted and Numbered Lists

Bulleted and Numbered Lists

Setting off items in a list with numbers or bullets is a great way to present information clearly. Word's bulleted and numbered list features add the bullets or numbers for you, and they even create hanging indents so that when text in an item wraps to the next line, it doesn't wrap underneath the number or bullet.

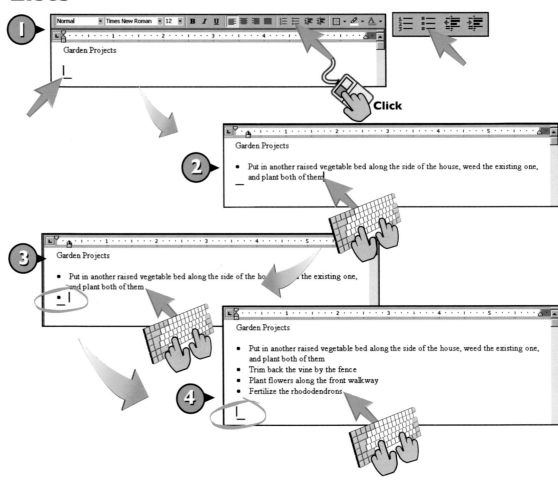

Start Here

Click

Garden Projects

Creating blank lines between items
If you want a blank line in between items in a bulleted or numbered list, press **Shift+Enter** and then press **Enter** at the end of each item (instead of just pressing Enter).

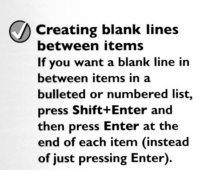

1 Click where you want the list to start, and then click the **Bullets** button on the Formatting toolbar.

2 Word inserts a bullet. Type the first item in the list.

3 Press **Enter**. Word inserts a bullet on the next line for you.

4 Continue typing items in your list. After the last item, press **Enter** twice to turn off the bullets.

Next Step

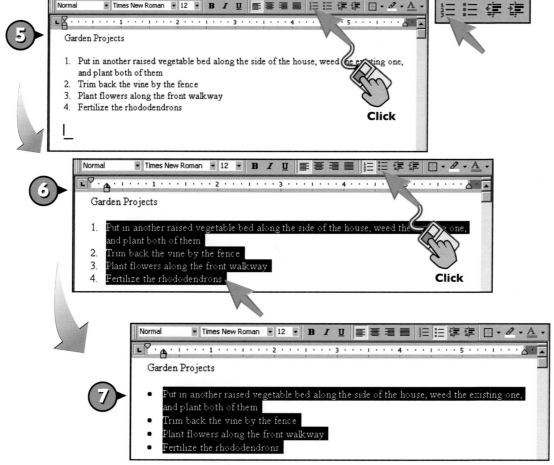

5 To create a numbered list, follow steps I through 4, but click the **Numbering** button on the Formatting toolbar in step I instead.

6 To switch from numbers to bullets (or vice versa), select the list, and then click the **Bullets** or **Numbering** button.

7 Word makes the change for you. Click anywhere to deselect the text.

✅ **Automatic renumbering**
One of the advantages of using Word's numbered list feature is that when you add, delete, or move items in a list, Word keeps the numbering sequential.

✅ **Turning off the Automatic feature**
You may notice that Word automatically turns on the bulleted or numbered list feature as soon as you type a line beginning with an asterisk (*) or a number and press **Enter**. If you like this behavior, great. If you don't, you can turn it off: Choose **Tools, AutoCorrect**, click the **AutoFormat As You Type** tab, clear the check boxes for **Automatic bulleted lists** and **Automatic numbered lists**, and click **OK**.

Setting a Custom Left or Right Tab

Word's default tab stops are fine for many documents (see "Inserting a Tab" in Part 3, "Editing Text"). But in some situations, you need to specify the exact type and position of your tab stops. Word provides four types of custom tabs: left (the default tabs are also left tabs), right, center, and decimal. You learn about left and right tabs here, and center and decimal tabs in the next task.

Task 7: Setting a Custom Left or Right Tab

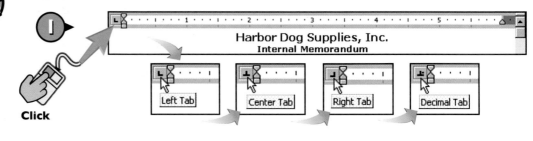

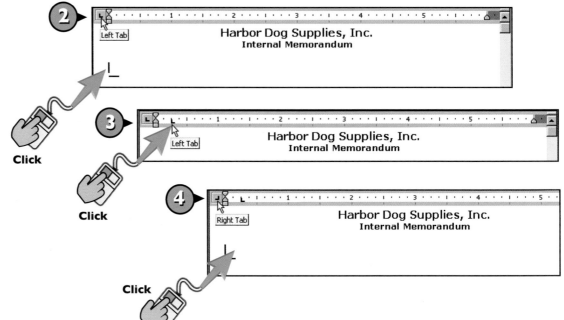

✓ **Viewing tab settings**
To see what custom tabs are in effect for any paragraph, click anywhere in the paragraph, and then look at the ruler.

1 Before you insert any type of custom tab, first click the **Tab Stop Indicator** button until you see the symbol for the tab you want.

2 To insert a left tab, display the left-tab symbol on the **Tab Stop Indicator** button, and click in the paragraph where you want to use the tab.

3 Click at the desired location on the ruler to insert the tab.

4 To insert a right tab, display the right-tab symbol on the **Tab Stop Indicator** button, and click in the paragraph where you want to use the tab.

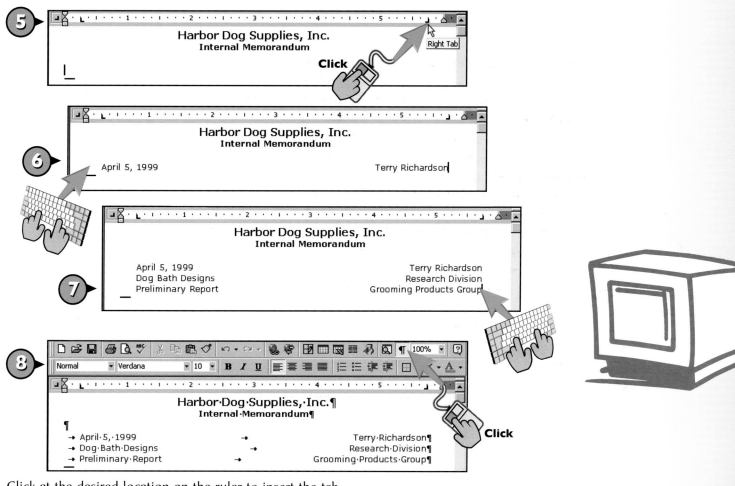

5 Click at the desired location on the ruler to insert the tab.

6 Press **Tab** to move to the first tab stop, and type your text. Then press **Tab** to get to the next tab stop (if any) and type your text.

7 Press **Enter** after typing the last block of text on the line, and type the remaining paragraphs that use the custom tabs.

8 Remember that the **Show/Hide** button lets you see where you pressed the Tab key (see "Using the Show/Hide Button" in Part 3).

Setting a Custom Center or Decimal Tab

Setting custom center and decimal tabs is exactly the same as setting left and right tabs. Center tabs let you center text over the tab stop, and decimal tabs align text along the decimal point. (Decimal tabs are most useful for typing columns of numbers.) If you haven't done so yet, look over the preceding task to get an overview of working with custom tabs before continuing with these steps.

Task 8: Setting a Custom Center or Decimal Tab

Start Here

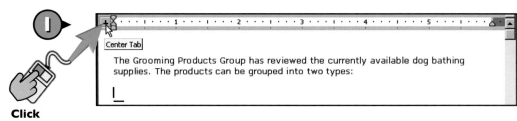

Click

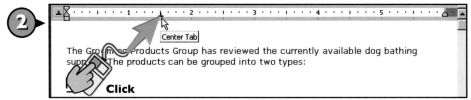

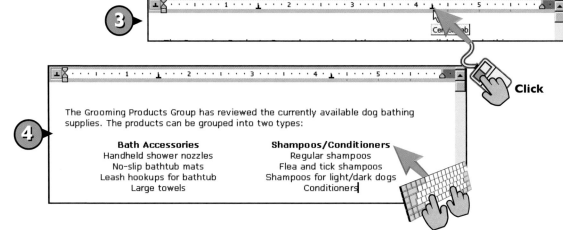

Click

1 To insert a center tab, display the center-tab symbol on the **Tab Alignment** button, and click in the paragraph where you want to use the tab.

2 Click at the desired location on the ruler to insert the tab.

3 Insert any additional tabs in the paragraph. In this example, a second center tab was added to the right.

4 Type your text using the custom tabs (see steps 6 and 7 in the preceding task).

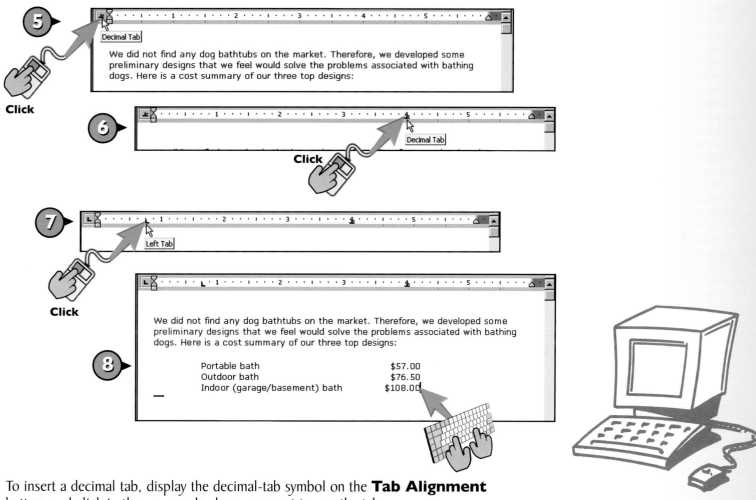

Click

Click

Click

We did not find any dog bathtubs on the market. Therefore, we developed some preliminary designs that we feel would solve the problems associated with bathing dogs. Here is a cost summary of our three top designs:

Portable bath	$57.00
Outdoor bath	$76.50
Indoor (garage/basement) bath	$108.00

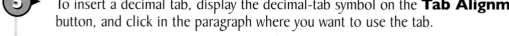

⑤ To insert a decimal tab, display the decimal-tab symbol on the **Tab Alignment** button, and click in the paragraph where you want to use the tab.

⑥ Click at the desired location on the ruler to insert the tab.

⑦ Insert any additional tabs in the paragraph. In this example, a left tab was added to the left of the decimal tab.

⑧ Again, type your text using the custom tabs as described in steps 6 and 7 in the preceding task.

End Task

Moving or Deleting a Custom Tab

When you work with custom tabs, you will frequently need to adjust their positions on the ruler. If you've already typed your text, it shifts as soon as you move the tab. Deleting a custom tab is even simpler: You just drag it off of the ruler.

✓ Restoring default tab settings

To restore the default tabs below a paragraph that contains custom tabs, click in the paragraph where you'd like the default tabs to begin, and delete the custom tabs as described in these steps. The default tabs will automatically reappear.

Task 9: Moving and Deleting a Custom Tab

Start Here

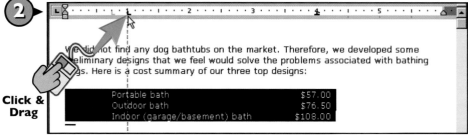

Click & Drag

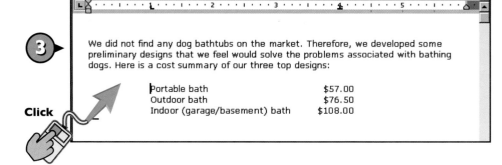

Click

To move a custom tab, select the paragraphs that contain the tab, and point to it on the ruler.

Drag the tab to the new position. A vertical dotted line shows you where the text will realign.

Release the mouse button and click to deselect the text. The text shifts to the repositioned tab.

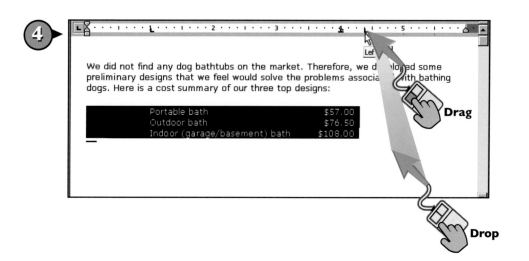

We did not find any dog bathtubs on the market. Therefore, we developed some preliminary designs that we feel would solve the problems associated with bathing dogs. Here is a cost summary of our three top designs:

Portable bath	$57.00
Outdoor bath	$76.50
Indoor (garage/basement) bath	$108.00

Drag

Drop

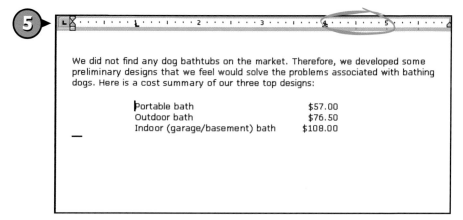

We did not find any dog bathtubs on the market. Therefore, we developed some preliminary designs that we feel would solve the problems associated with bathing dogs. Here is a cost summary of our three top designs:

Portable bath	$57.00
Outdoor bath	$76.50
Indoor (garage/basement) bath	$108.00

4 To delete a tab, point to it on the ruler and drag it straight down toward your document. Release the mouse button and click to deselect the text.

5 The tab is no longer on the ruler.

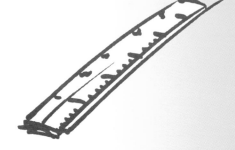

Task 10: Changing Margins

Changing Margin Settings

Word's default margins are 1 inch on the top and bottom of the page and 1.25 inches on the left and right. You may want to decrease the margins if you need to squeeze a bit more text onto the page, or increase the margins to give your document a more spacious feel. When you change the margins, Word applies the new setting to all the pages in your document.

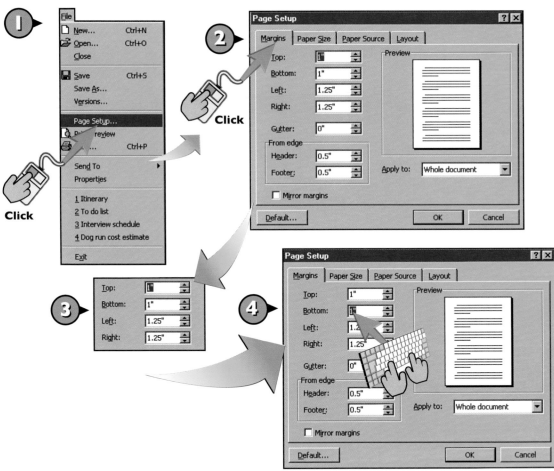

Click

Click

✓ **Preview new margins before printing**
If you want to see what your margins will look like before you print, use Print Preview (see "Previewing the Document" in Part 5, "Viewing and Printing the Document").

① Choose **File**, **Page Setup**. (It doesn't matter where your insertion point is.)

② In the Page Setup dialog box, click the **Margins** tab if it isn't already in front.

③ The **Top**, **Bottom**, **Left**, and **Right** text boxes let you change the width of all four margins.

④ Select the number in the text box for the margin you want to change. Type over the number with a new number in inches. (You don't have to type the " symbol.)

Next Step

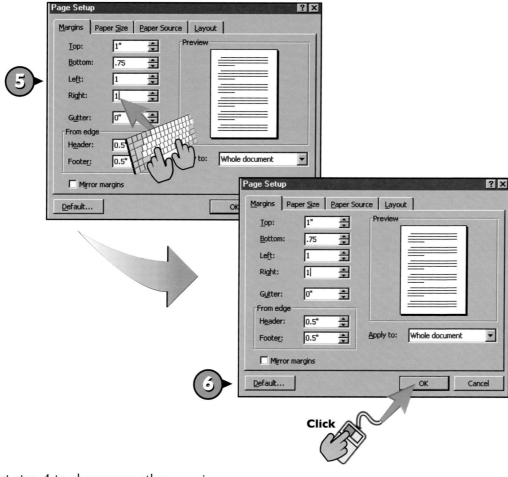

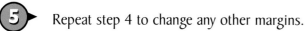

5 ▶ Repeat step 4 to change any other margins.

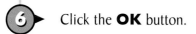

6 ▶ Click the **OK** button.

Task 11: Inserting a Page Break

Inserting a Page Break

When you fill up a page with text, Word inserts a *soft page break* to end the page and wrap text to the next page. There are times, however, when you need to end a page before it's filled with text. To do this, you insert a *hard page break*. For example, you can use a hard page break to separate a title page from the text that follows, or to start a new section of a report at the top of the next page.

Start Here

Post-Interview Phase - where impressions are formed of the applicant's qualifications and

This could be explained by the fact that people with high test scores, good grades, etc., on their credentials actually make better impressions in the interview, although studies have been done (Sparks & Manese, 1970) to show little support for this contention.

B.   **Self-Fulfilling Prophecy:**
An interviewer will form a pre-interview opinion of the applicant and will categorize them as "ideal, highly qualified" or "typical" or "unqualified," and the interviewer's subsequent conception of the applicant will then influence the subsequent

This could be explained by the fact that people with high test scores, good grades, etc., on their credentials actually make better impressions in the interview, although studies have been done (Sparks & Manese, 1970) to show little support for this contention.

B.   **Self-Fulfilling Prophecy:**
An interviewer will form a pre-interview opinion of the applicant and will categorize them as "ideal, highly qualified" or "typical" or "unqualified," and the interviewer's subsequent conception of the applicant will then influence the subsequent gathering and processing of information. This "cognitive categorization" means

Click

This could be explained by the fact that people with high test scores, good grades, etc., on their credentials actually make better impressions in the interview, although studies have been done (Sparks & Manese, 1970) to show little support for this contention.

--------Page Break--------

B.   **Self-Fulfilling Prophecy:**
An interviewer will form a pre-interview opinion of the applicant and will categorize them as "ideal, highly qualified" or "typical" or "unqualified," and the interviewer's subsequent conception of the applicant will then influence the subsequent gathering and processing of information. This "cognitive categorization" means

`Ctrl`+`↵Enter`

✓ **Preview page breaks**
To see the results of inserting a hard page break, use Print Preview (see "Previewing a Document" in Part 5).

1 In Normal view, Word displays a soft page break as a dotted horizontal line running across your document.

2 To insert a hard page break, click where you want to break the page.

3 Press **Ctrl+Enter**. Word inserts a hard page break at the insertion point.

Next Step

This could be explained by the fact that people with high test scores, good grades, etc., on their credentials actually make better impressions in the interview, although studies have been done (Sparks & Manese, 1970) to show little support for this contention.

―――――――――――――Page Break―――――――――――――

B.   **Self-Fulfilling Prophecy:**
        An interviewer will form a pre-interview opinion of the applicant and will categorize them as "ideal, highly qualified" or "typical" or "unqualified," and the interviewer's subsequent conception of the applicant will then influence the subsequent

This could be explained by the fact that people with high test scores, good grades, etc., on their credentials actually make better impressions in the interview, although studies have been done (Sparks & Manese, 1970) to show little support for this contention.

―――――――――――――Page Break―――――――――――――

B.   **Self-Fulfilling Prophecy:**
        An interviewer will form a pre-interview opinion of the applicant and will categorize them as "ideal, highly qualified" or "typical" or "unqualified," and the interviewer's subsequent conception of the applicant will then influence the subsequent

Del

Post-Interview Phase - where impressions are formed of the applicant's qualifications and

This could be explained by the fact that people with high test scores, good grades, etc., on their credentials actually make better impressions in the interview, although studies have been done (Sparks & Manese, 1970) to show little support for this contention.

B.   **Self-Fulfilling Prophecy:**
        An interviewer will form a pre-interview opinion of the applicant and will categorize them as "ideal, highly qualified" or "typical" or "unqualified," and the interviewer's subsequent conception of the applicant will then influence the subsequent

 In Normal view, the break appears as a horizontal dotted line with the words *Page Break* on it.

 If you need to remove a hard page break, place the insertion point directly on the break, and press the **Delete** key.

 The hard page break is removed and the soft page break returns.

Task 12: Adding a Border to a Paragraph

Adding a Border

You don't have to know anything about graphics to set off paragraphs with attractive borders, and you can even add a decorative border around the whole page. In the next task, you learn how to further enhance the appearance of a paragraph with shading.

✓ **Changing left and right borders**
If you don't want the right and left borders on a paragraph to extend all the way to the margins, set left and right indents (see "Adding Indents" earlier in this part).

✓ **Removing borders from a paragraph**
To remove borders from a paragraph, select the paragraph, choose **Format, Borders and Shading**, click the **Borders** tab, click **None** under **Setting**, and click **OK**.

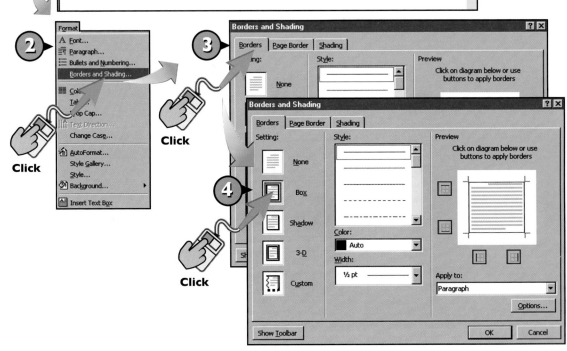

1 Select the paragraphs to which you want to add the border.

2 Choose **Format**, **Borders and Shading** to display the Borders and Shading dialog box.

3 Click the **Borders** tab if it isn't already in front.

4 Click the option that most closely matches what you want under **Setting**.

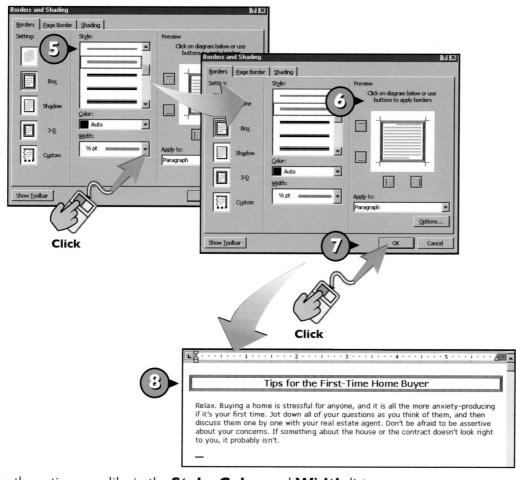

Click

Click

Tips for the First-Time Home Buyer

Relax. Buying a home is stressful for anyone, and it is all the more anxiety-producing if it's your first time. Jot down all of your questions as you think of them, and then discuss them one by one with your real estate agent. Don't be afraid to be assertive about your concerns. If something about the house or the contract doesn't look right to you, it probably isn't.

5 ▶ Choose the options you like in the **Style**, **Color**, and **Width** lists.

6 ▶ The **Preview** area shows the options you've chosen.

7 ▶ Click **OK**.

8 ▶ Word applies your borders to the selected paragraphs.

 **Add a border around the entire page**
To add a border around your entire page, click the **Page Border** tab in the Borders and Shading dialog box, and then select from the same set of options as those in the **Borders** tab.

 End Task

Task 13: Shading a Paragraph

Shading a Paragraph

If you really want to set a paragraph or two off from the rest of your text, adding a border might do the trick. Word gives you a wide selection of border styles and colors to choose from, and you can also add shading to the paragraph, as described in the next task.

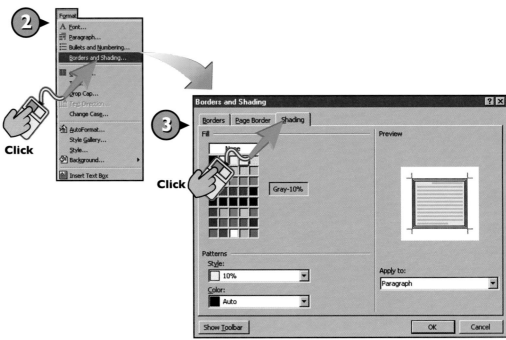

Click

Click

 Select the paragraphs to which you want to add shading.

 Choose **Format**, **Borders and Shading** to display the Borders and Shading dialog box.

 Click the **Shading** tab.

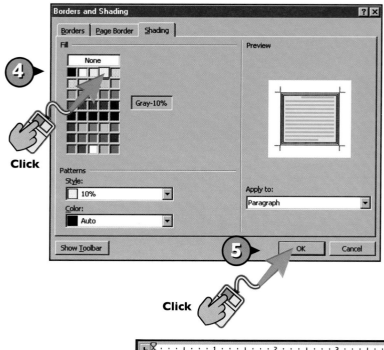

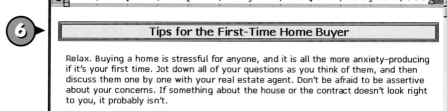

4 Choose the color you want to use under **Fill**.

5 Click **OK**.

6 The shading is applied to the selected paragraphs.

Task 14: Centering a Page Vertically

Centering a Page Vertically

Many people try to center text vertically on the page by moving the insertion point to the top of the page and then pressing Enter several times to force the text down. More often than not, you end up pressing Enter too many (or too few) times and then have to add or delete blank lines to position the text where you want it. A more straightforward method is to let Word center the page vertically for you.

 Start Here

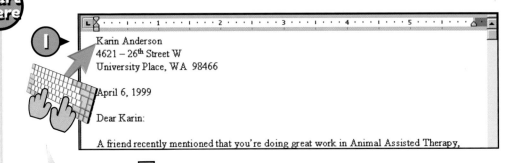

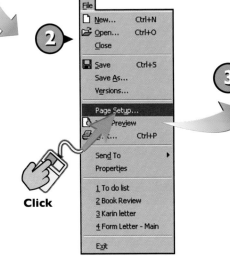

Click

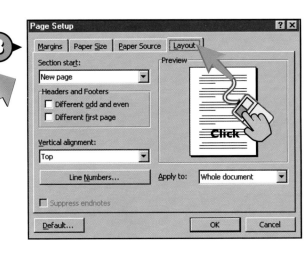

Click

 Preview the vertical centering of a page
To see what the vertical centering will look like when your document is printed, use Print Preview (see "Previewing a Document" in Part 5, "Viewing and Printing the Document").

 Press the **Backspace** or **Delete** key to remove any blank lines from above and below the text you want to center vertically.

Choose **File**, **Page Setup** to display the Page Setup dialog box.

Click the **Layout** tab if it isn't already in front.

 Next Step

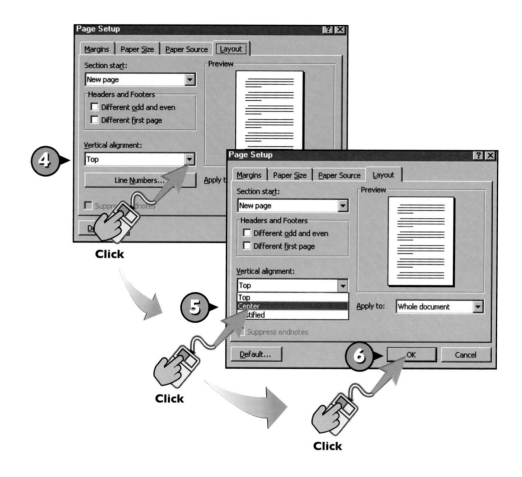

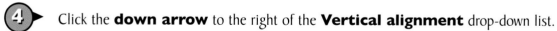

4 Click the **down arrow** to the right of the **Vertical alignment** drop-down list.

5 Choose **Center**.

6 Click the **OK** button.

Task 15: Numbering Pages

Adding Page Numbers

Word offers two methods for adding page numbers to your document. You can use the **Insert, Page Numbers** command, as described in this task, to tell Word what type of page number you want and where it should appear. Word then adds the page number *field* to the header or footer for you. The next two tasks teach you how to work with headers and footers directly. Adding pagination to the header or footer yourself gives you more control over the appearance of your page numbers.

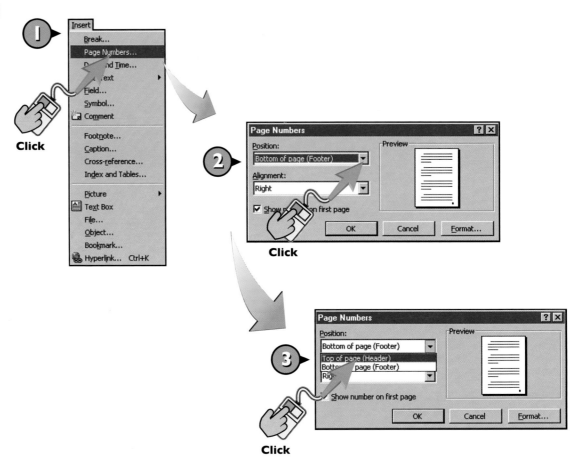

Click

Click

Click

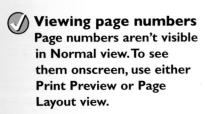

Viewing page numbers
Page numbers aren't visible in Normal view. To see them onscreen, use either **Print Preview** or **Page Layout** view.

1 ▶ Choose **Insert**, **Page Numbers**.

2 ▶ To place the number at the top of the page, click the **down arrow** next to the **Position** drop-down list. (Otherwise, leave the default setting.)

3 ▶ Choose **Top of page (Header)**.

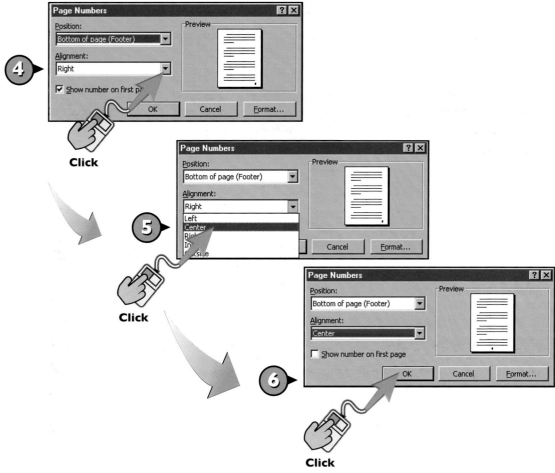

Click

Click

Click

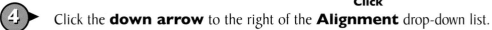

④ ▸ Click the **down arrow** to the right of the **Alignment** drop-down list.

⑤ ▸ Choose the alignment you prefer for your page numbers.

⑥ ▸ Click the **OK** button.

Task 16: Creating Headers and Footers

Adding Headers and Footers to Your Document

A header appears at the top of every page, and a footer appears at the bottom of every page. You might want to use headers and footers to display the document title, your name, the name of your organization, and so on. Word includes custom tabs in the header and footer so you can easily position your text.

Format the font in your headers and footers

You can format the font and font size of your header and footer text. Select the text and choose the formatting you want from the Font and Font Size drop-down lists in the Formatting toolbar. (See "Changing the Font and Font Size" earlier in this part.)

Start Here

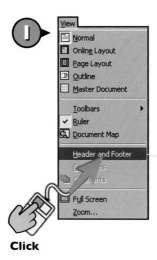

Click

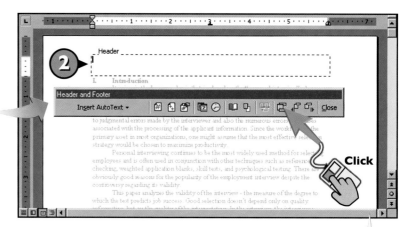

Click

Click

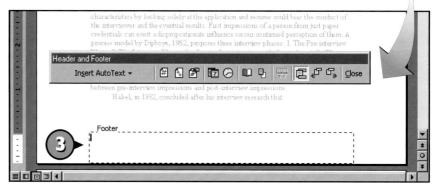

Choose **View**, **Header and Footer**. (It doesn't matter where your insertion point is when you issue the command.)

Word activates the header area and displays the Header and Footer toolbar. Click the **Switch Between Header and Footer** button.

Word activates the footer area.

Next Step

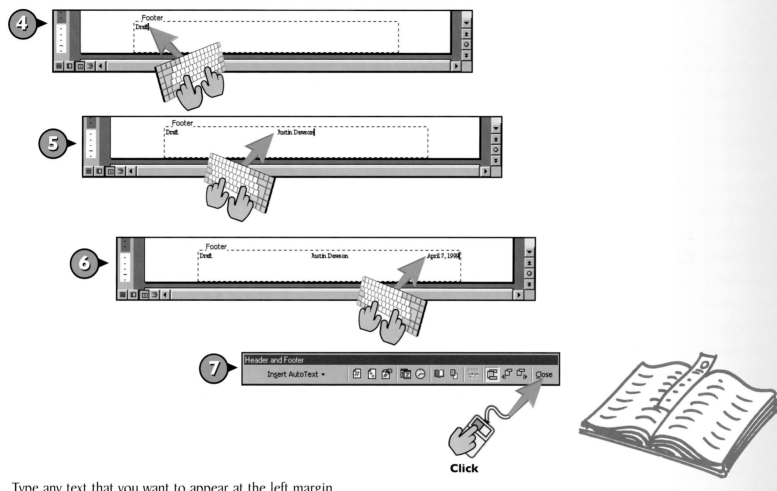

Click

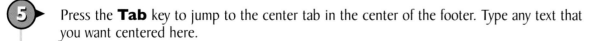

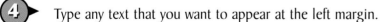

④ Type any text that you want to appear at the left margin.

⑤ Press the **Tab** key to jump to the center tab in the center of the footer. Type any text that you want centered here.

⑥ Press the **Tab** key again to move to the right tab at the right edge of the footer. Type any text that you want flush right here.

⑦ Click the **Close** button in the Header and Footer toolbar to return to viewing your document text.

End Task

Using the Header and Footer Toolbar

The Header and Footer toolbar makes it easy to insert commonly used blocks of text as a header or footer, as well as fields for the page number, the date, the time, and so on. Here, you take a quick tour of some of the options available on the toolbar. Feel free to experiment more on your own.

Task 17: Using the Header and Footer Toolbar

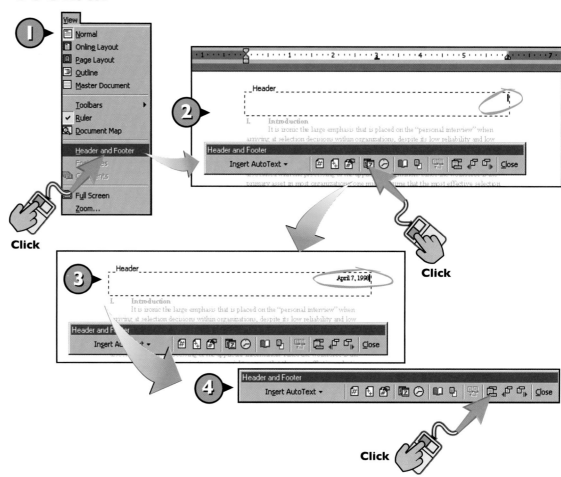

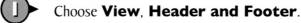

✓ Deleting fields
To delete a field, select it and then press the **Delete** key. When you click a field, it turns a light shade of gray. It isn't actually selected, however, until you double-click it or drag over it with the mouse.

1 ▶ Choose **View**, **Header and Footer**.

2 ▶ Press **Tab** twice to move to the right edge of the header area, and click the **Insert Date** button.

3 ▶ Word inserts the current date. (To insert the current time, click the **Insert Time** button to the right of the **Insert Date** button.)

4 ▶ Click the **Switch Between Header and Footer** button to move to the footer area.

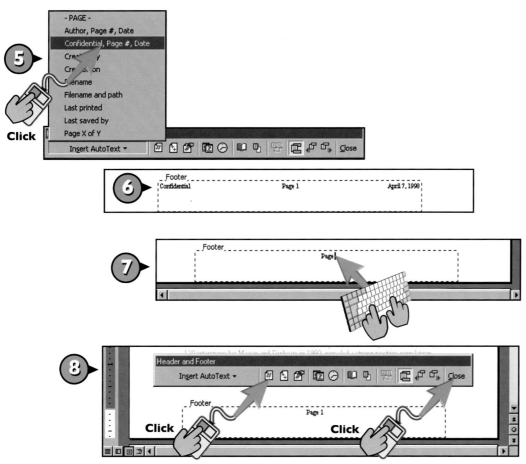

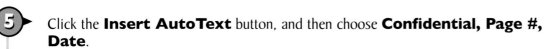

5. Click the **Insert AutoText** button, and then choose **Confidential, Page #, Date**.

6. Word inserts the AutoText entry in the footer. Select and delete this entry, and then try a few others.

7. Type **Page** and then press the **Spacebar**.

8. Click the **Insert Page Number** button, and then click the **Close** button in the Header and Footer toolbar.

End Task

PART 7

More Editing Techniques

You don't have to use any of the features described in this part, but they sure can help. All the skills you learn here will save you editing time and increase your efficiency. You learn how to ask Word to search a document for a particular word or phrase and replace it with something else, how to check your spelling and fix spelling errors automatically, how to insert the date automatically, and much more.

Tasks

Task #		Page #
1	Searching for Text	120
2	Finding and Replacing Text	122
3	Using Automatic Spell Checking	124
4	Checking Your Spelling with the Spell Checker	126
5	Using the Thesaurus	128
6	Inserting a Special Character	130
7	Inserting the Date	132
8	Using AutoCorrect	134
9	Using AutoText	136

7

Task 1: Searching for Text

Searching for Text

If you frequently type long documents, you have probably had the experience of scrolling through each page trying to find all the places where you used a particular word or phrase. Word can help you with this process, searching for text much more quickly and accurately than we humans can.

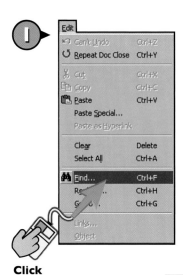

Click

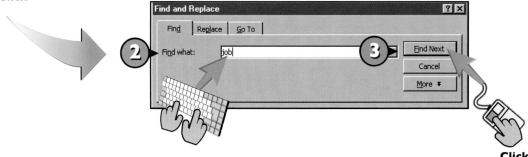

Click

✓ Using more options in your search

If you want to be more specific about what text you're looking for, click the **More** button in the lower-right corner of the Find and Replace dialog box to display more options. To hide the options again, click the **Less** button.

  Choose **Edit**, **Find** to display the **Find** tab of the Find and Replace dialog box.

  Type the text that you want to find in the **Find what** text box.

  Click the **Find Next** button.

 Next Step

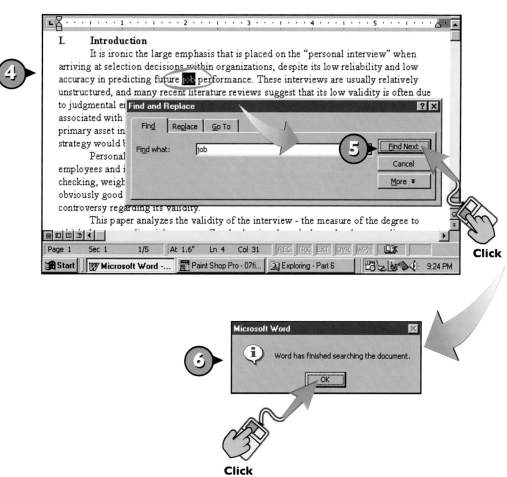

I. Introduction

It is ironic the large emphasis that is placed on the "personal interview" when arriving at selection decisions within organizations, despite its low reliability and low accuracy in predicting future **job** performance. These interviews are usually relatively unstructured, and many recent literature reviews suggest that its low validity is often due to judgmental er associated with primary asset in strategy would b

Personal employees and i checking, weigh obviously good controversy regarding its validity.

This paper analyzes the validity of the interview - the measure of the degree to

Find and Replace

Find | Replace | Go To

Find what: job

Find Next
Cancel
More ∓

(5)

Page 1 | Sec 1 | 1/5 | At 1.6" | Ln 4 | Col 31 | REC TRK EXT OVR WPH

Start | Microsoft Word -... | Paint Shop Pro - 07fi... | Exploring - Part 6 | 9:24 PM

Click

Microsoft Word

ⓘ Word has finished searching the document.

OK

(6)

Click

(4) Word highlights the first occurrence of the word.

(5) Continue to click the **Find Next** button to look for more matches.

(6) Click **OK** when Word informs you that it has found all the matches.

Task 2: Finding and Replacing Text

Finding and Replacing Text

Sometimes you not only need to find text, you also have to replace it with something else. Word's Replace feature takes the tedium out of making the same change in several places. Whenever you find yourself about to change something by hand throughout your entire document, stop and see if you could have Replace do the work for you.

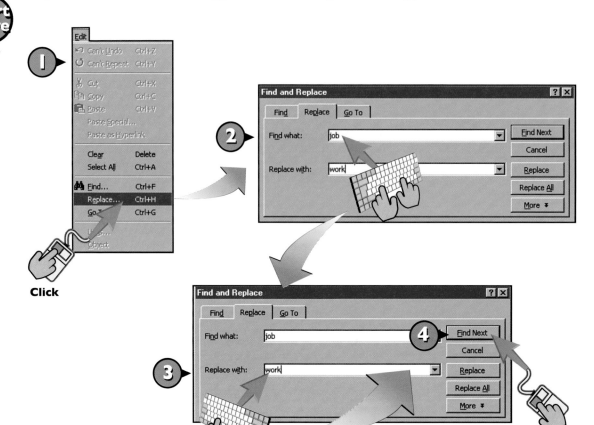

Click

Click

✓ **Using more options to replace text**
If you want to be more specific about what text you're looking for, click the **More** button in the lower-right corner of the Find and Replace dialog box to display more options. To hide the options again, click the **Less** button.

1 ► Choose **Edit**, **Replace** to display the **Replace** tab of the Find and Replace dialog box.

2 ► Type the text that you want to find in the **Find what** text box.

3 ► In the **Replace with** text box, type the text that you want to replace the **Find what** text.

4 ► Click the **Find Next** button.

Next Step

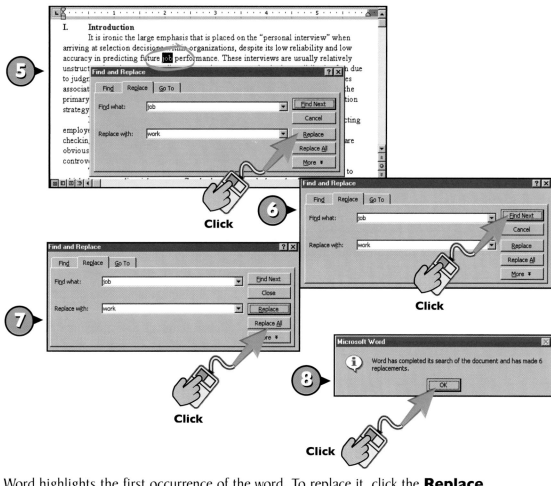

Click

Click

Click

Click

 Word highlights the first occurrence of the word. To replace it, click the **Replace** button.

 To skip this instance without making the change, click the **Find Next** button.

 Continue this process. If you don't need to confirm every replacement, click the **Replace All** button.

 Click **OK** when Word informs you that it has finished searching the document.

End Task

Using Automatic Spell Checking

Word's automatic spell checking monitors the characters you type and marks words that it doesn't find in its dictionary with red wavy lines. (By default, Word also checks your grammar and highlights possible problems with green wavy lines, but you can turn the grammar checking off and just check spelling.) Automatic spell checking lets you fix misspellings as you're typing; to correct spelling after you've typed the entire document, see the next task.

✓ **Turn off automatic grammar checking**
To turn off the automatic grammar checking, choose **Tools, Options**, and click the **Spelling & Grammar** tab. Clear the **Check grammar as you type** check box, and click **OK**.

Task 3: Using Automatic Spell Checking

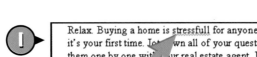

Start Here

Right Click

Click

Click

  To correct the spelling of a word marked with a red wavy line, right-click the word.

 A context menu appears with a list of possible spellings. If you see the one you want, click it.

Word makes the correction for you.

 If the mistake is one that you make frequently, click **AutoCorrect**.

Next Step

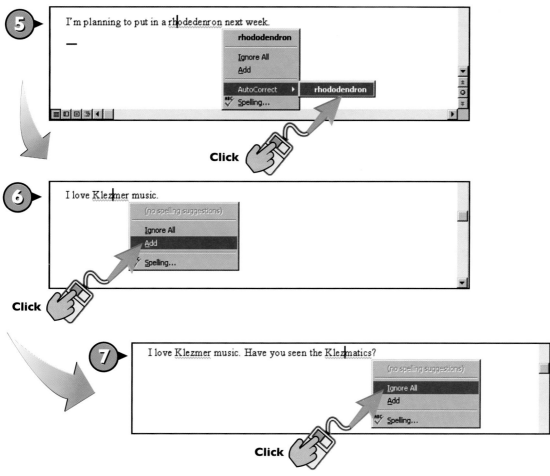

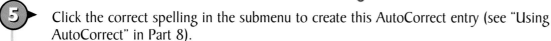

5 Click the correct spelling in the submenu to create this AutoCorrect entry (see "Using AutoCorrect" in Part 8).

6 If a word is spelled correctly and you use it frequently, click **Add** to add it to the dictionary so that Word won't catch it in the future.

7 If a word is spelled correctly but you don't use it that often, choose **Ignore All** to prevent Word from marking it as a misspelling in this document only.

Checking Your Spelling

The spell checker lets you check the spelling (and grammar) of an entire document all at once. You won't really need to use it if you use automatic spell checking to fix your spelling "on-the-fly" (see the preceding task). However, if you've disabled automatic spell checking, or if you're working in a rather large document, the spell checker will come in handy.

✅ **Turn off grammar checking**
If you don't want Word to look for grammatical problems during the spell check, clear the **Check grammar** check box in the lower-left corner of the Spelling and Grammar dialog box.

Task 4: Checking Your Spelling with the Spell Checker

Start Here

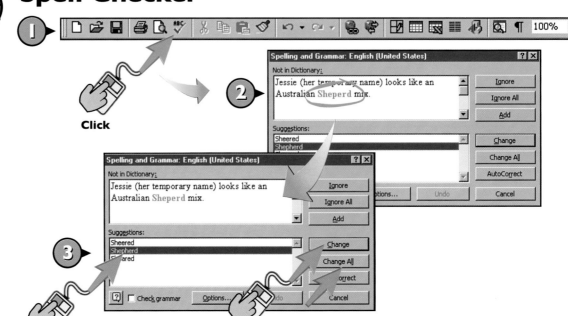

Click

Click

Click

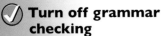

1️⃣ Click the **Spelling and Grammar** button on the Standard toolbar to start checking your document.

2️⃣ When Word finds a spelling error, it highlights it in red.

3️⃣ If you see the correct spelling, click it and click the **Change** button (or **Change All** to change it throughout the document).

4️⃣ Sometimes Word doesn't offer the correct spelling for a misspelled word.

Next Step

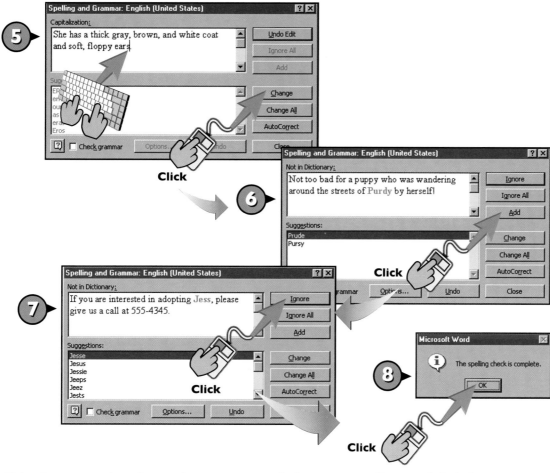

Click

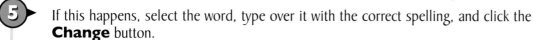

Click

Click

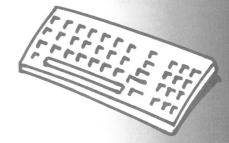

Click

5 If this happens, select the word, type over it with the correct spelling, and click the **Change** button.

6 If the word is spelled correctly and you plan to use it often, click the **Add** button to add it to the dictionary.

7 To leave the word "as is," click **Ignore** to ignore it once or **Ignore All** to ignore it throughout the document.

8 When Word tells you that it has finished the spell check, click **OK**.

End Task

Using the Thesaurus

If you find yourself
overusing a particular word
and want to find a good
synonym for it, or if you
want to get some ideas for
livening up your text,
Word's thesaurus can help
you.

Task 5: Using the Thesaurus

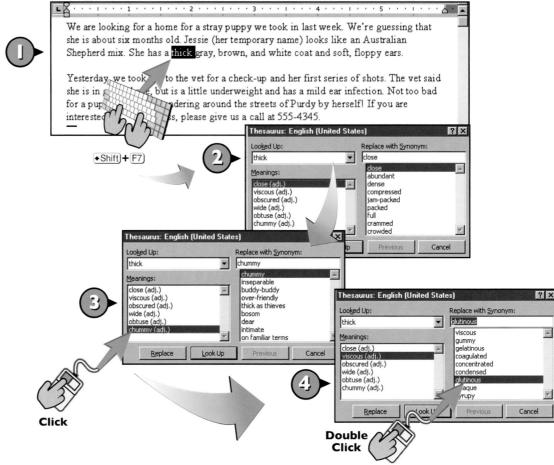

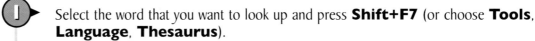

(1) Select the word that you want to look up and press **Shift+F7** (or choose **Tools**, **Language**, **Thesaurus**).

(2) Word displays the Thesaurus dialog box with the word you selected in the **Looked Up** list.

(3) Click the different meanings in the **Meanings** list to see synonyms for the various meanings of the word.

(4) To see the synonyms for a word in the synonyms list, double-click it.

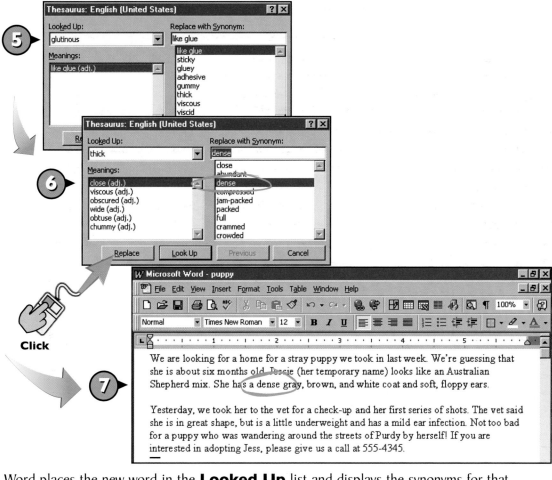

Click

5 ▸ Word places the new word in the **Looked Up** list and displays the synonyms for that word.

6 ▸ When you see the word that you want to use, click it and click the **Replace** button.

7 ▸ Word replaces the selected word with the one that you chose.

Task 6: Inserting a Special Character

Using Special Characters

Many everyday documents, such as letters and memos, require special characters here and there. For example, you might need to use the trademark symbol (^{TM}), a long dash (—), or the ellipses (…). As you'll see in steps 1 through 3, Word inserts many of these symbols for you automatically as you type. If it doesn't insert the one you need, you can likely find it in the Symbol dialog box.

✓ **Changing the size of symbols**
You can enlarge symbols that you've inserted in your document just like regular text. Drag over the symbol to select it, and then choose a larger point size from the **Font Size** drop-down list in the Formatting toolbar. (See "Changing the Font and Font Size" in Part 6.)

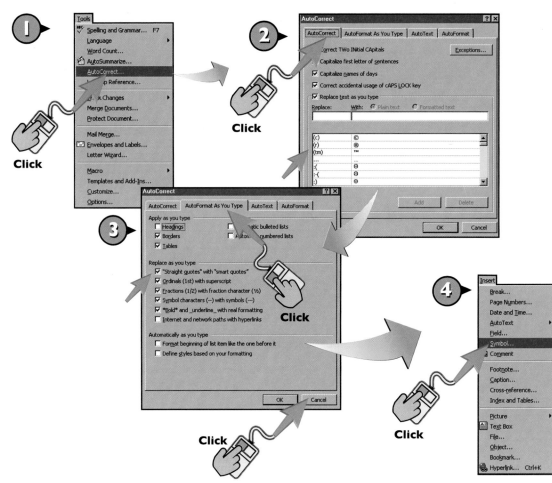

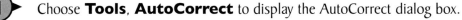

1. Choose **Tools**, **AutoCorrect** to display the AutoCorrect dialog box.

2. Click the **AutoCorrect** tab. When you type the characters on the left, Word replaces them with the symbols on the right. (See "Using AutoCorrect" in Part 8.)

3. Click the **AutoFormat As You Type** tab. The **Replace as you type** options insert many symbols for you as well. Click the **Cancel** button.

4. To insert a less commonly used symbol, click where you want the symbol to go, and choose **Insert**, **Symbol**.

Next Step

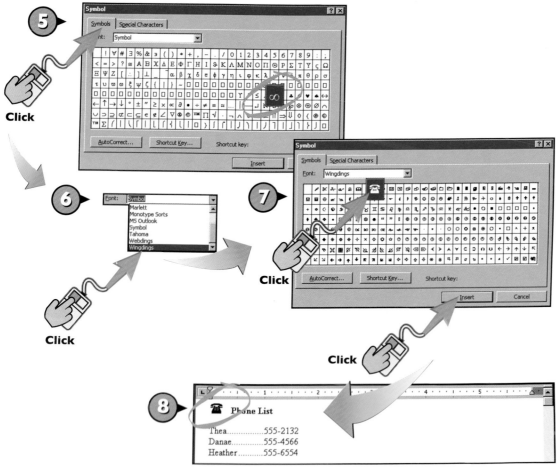

5 Click the **Symbols** tab. Look through the symbols in the grid. You can click them to magnify them.

6 If you don't see the symbol you want, display the **Font** drop-down list, and choose a different font set.

7 To insert a symbol, click it, click the **Insert** button, and then click the **Close** (X)

your document.

Task: 7: Inserting the Date

Start Here

Adding a Date to Your Document

Your computer has a clock that keeps track of the date and the time. Instead of typing the current date, you can have Word take this information from the computer and insert it for you. You can even insert the date as a *field*, which lets Word update it to the current date for you when you open the document in the future. Inserting a date as a field is useful in documents that you open frequently because the date is always current. The drawback to doing this is that you don't have a date within the document that verifies when the document was first created and saved.

✓ **Deleting the Date field**

To delete a date that you've inserted as a field, select it first and then press **Delete** or **Backspace**.

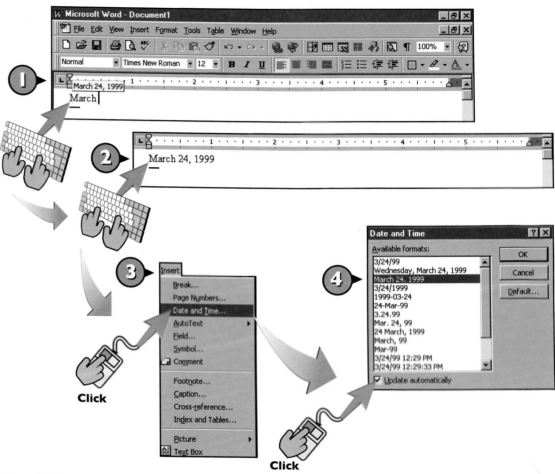

1. Type the first four letters or so of today's date. A yellow bubble containing the com[...] [...]te appears.

2. Press **Enter** to let Word fill in the rest of the date for you.

3. If you want to insert the date as a field, choose **In**[...]

4. Mark the **Update automati**[...]

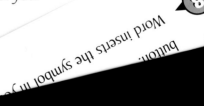

Word inserts the symbol in [...] button.

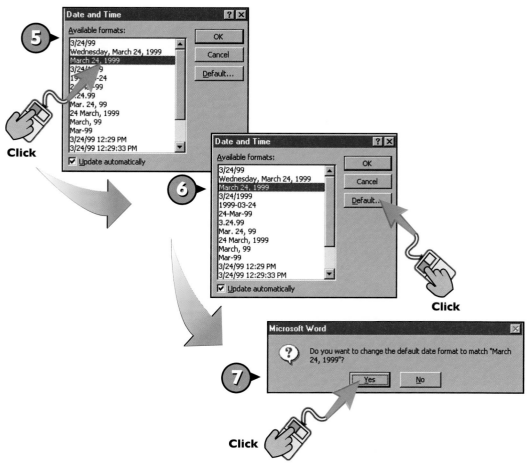

Click

Click

Click

⑤ Click the date format that you want to use.

⑥ If you want to use this format all the time, click the **Default** button.

⑦ Click **Yes** in the message box that appears, and click **OK** in the Date and Time dialog box. Word inserts the date in your document.

Task 8: Using AutoCorrect

Using AutoCorrect

Word's AutoCorrect feature fixes spelling errors for you automatically. It comes knowing about many commonly misspelled words, and you can add your own most irksome typos to the list. In addition, you can use AutoCorrect to automatically enter special symbols, long names, or phrases that you have to type frequently.

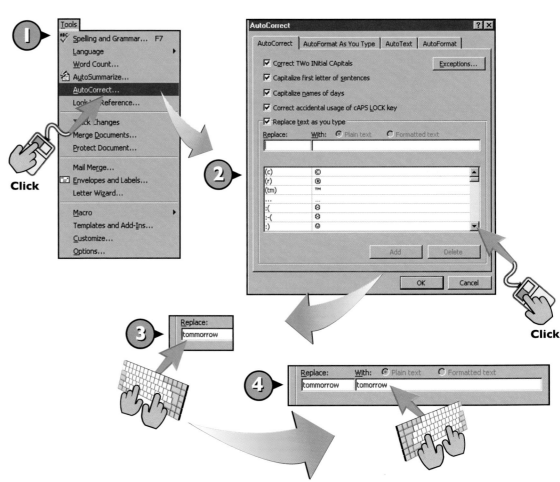

Start Here

Click

Click

✓ **Use AutoCorrect to insert repetitive text**
If you want to use AutoCorrect to insert a long name or phrase, type an abbreviation for the phrase in the **Replace** box (see step 3), and type the full spelling in the **With** box (see step 4). For example, you could type **napf** in the **Replace** box and **National Association of Poodle Fanciers** in the **With** box.

① Choose **Tools**, **AutoCorrect**.

② Scroll down the list at the bottom of the dialog box to see what AutoCorrect knows how to fix. Word replaces the items in the left column with the items in the right column.

③ Click in the **Replace** text box and type **tommorrow**.

④ Click in the **With** text box and type the correct spelling, **tomorrow**.

Next Step

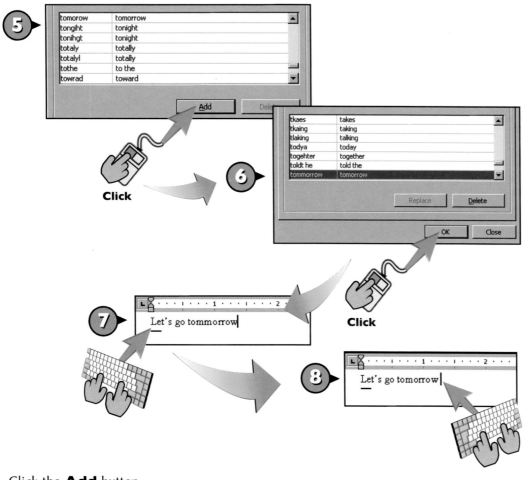

tomorow	tomorrow
tongiht	tonight
tonihgt	tonight
totaly	totally
totalyl	totally
tothe	to the
towrad	toward

Click

tkaes	takes
tkaing	taking
tlaking	talking
todya	today
togehter	together
toldt he	told the
tommorrow	tomorrow

Replace | Delete

OK | Close

6

7 Let's go tommorrow

Click

8 Let's go tomorrow

5 Click the **Add** button.

6 The entry is added to the list. Click **OK**.

7 Type **Let's go tommorrow**.

8 Press the **Spacebar**. Word automatically replaces *tommorrow* with *tomorrow*.

End Task

Task 9: Using AutoText

Using AutoText

AutoText is an extremely handy feature that lets Word "memorize" large blocks of text. After you've created an AutoText entry, you can insert it in your text by beginning to type the name of the entry. As soon as you've typed the first few characters, Word's AutoComplete feature takes over and inserts the entire block of text for you.

✓ AutoText reduces errors

One of the advantages of using AutoText is that you only have to proofread the block of text once before you create the AutoText entry. From then on, each time you insert the entry in a document, you can rest assured that it is error-free.

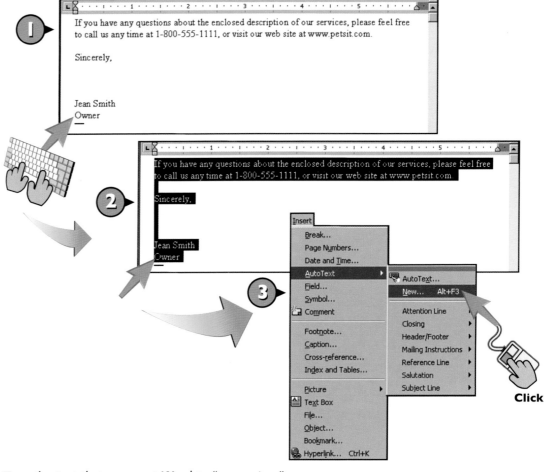

Start Here

Click

① Type the text that you want Word to "memorize."

② Select the text.

③ Choose **Insert**, **AutoText**, **New**.

Next Step

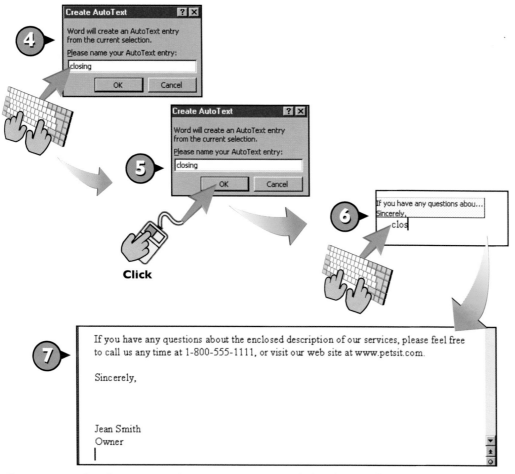

Click

If you have any questions about the enclosed description of our services, please feel free to call us any time at 1-800-555-1111, or visit our web site at www.petsit.com.

Sincerely,

Jean Smith
Owner

4 ▶ Type a name for the entry in the Create AutoText dialog box. (Choose a name that is at least four characters long.)

5 ▶ Click **OK**, and then click where you want to insert the text.

6 ▶ Type the first few letters of the name. As soon as you see the yellow bubble, press **Enter**.

7 ▶ Word inserts the AutoText entry in your document.

Columns and Tables

In this part, you learn two different ways of arranging columns of text on the page. Word's columns feature lets you create "newspaper-style" columns, in which the text wraps from one column to the next. You might use this type of column for your office newsletter or a brochure. The tables feature, in contrast, is great for creating columns of text that do not wrap. Tables are useful for creating everything from simple charts to resumes and invoices.

Tasks

Task #		Page #
1	Creating Columns	140
2	Formatting Columns	142
3	Creating a Table	144
4	Entering Text in a Table	146
5	Changing the Structure of a Table	148
6	Formatting a Table	150

Task 1: Creating Columns

Creating Columns in Your Document

If you would like to produce newsletters, bulletins, journal articles, and so on, you'll appreciate Word's capability to format text in multiple columns. When you use this feature, the text snakes from column to column. If you want to create columns of text that *do not* wrap from one column to the next, use either custom tabs (see Part 6, "Formatting Your Document") or a table (see the last four tasks in this part). If you don't want columns in part of your document, follow steps 1 through 5 to insert a *section break*. Otherwise, begin with step 6.

✓ Changing the number of columns

If you decide to change the number of columns in your document, simply repeat steps 6 through 8. If you want no columns, click the leftmost column in the grid in step 7.

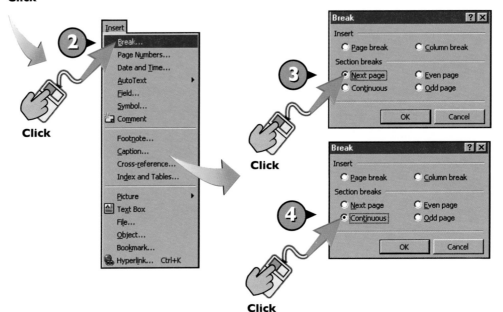

Click

Click

Click

Click

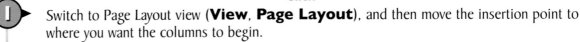

1 Switch to Page Layout view (**View**, **Page Layout**), and then move the insertion point to where you want the columns to begin.

2 Choose **Insert**, **Break** to display the Break dialog box.

3 To make the columns begin at the top of a new page, choose **Next page**.

4 To keep the columns on the same page as the text above them, choose **Continuous**.

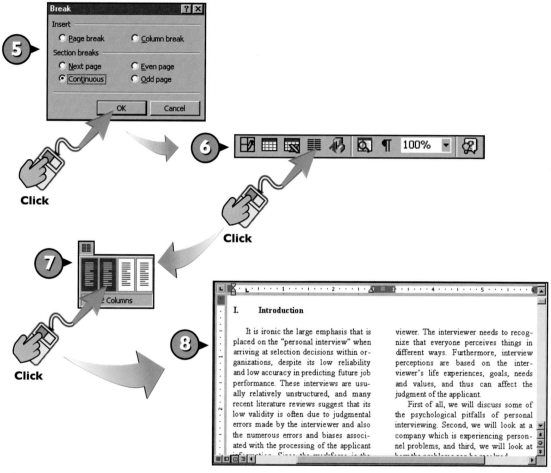

Break ? ✕

Insert
○ Page break   ○ Column break

Section breaks
○ Next page   ○ Even page
● Continuous   ○ Odd page

OK   Cancel

Click

100%

Click

2 Columns

Click

I.   Introduction

It is ironic the large emphasis that is placed on the "personal interview" when arriving at selection decisions within organizations, despite its low reliability and low accuracy in predicting future job performance. These interviews are usually relatively unstructured, and many recent literature reviews suggest that its low validity is often due to judgmental errors made by the interviewer and also the numerous errors and biases associated with the processing of the applicant information. Since the usefulness in the

viewer. The interviewer needs to recognize that everyone perceives things in different ways. Furthermore, interview perceptions are based on the interviewer's life experiences, goals, needs and values, and thus can affect the judgment of the applicant.

First of all, we will discuss some of the psychological pitfalls of personal interviewing. Second, we will look at a company which is experiencing personnel problems, and third, we will look at how the problems can be resolved

5 ▸ Click **OK**, and then make sure that your insertion point is in the section where you want the columns.

6 ▸ Click the **Columns** button in the Formatting toolbar.

7 ▸ Click the number of columns that you want in the grid.

8 ▸ Word creates the number of columns that you specified.

End Task

Formatting Columns

In addition to the standard formatting options described in **Part 6** of this book, "Formatting Your Document," Word gives you a few other choices for formatting text in multiple columns. Try them out and see what works well in your documents.

Task 2: Formatting Columns

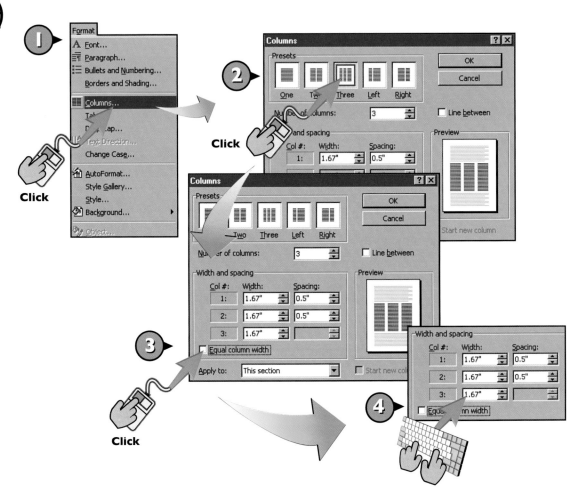

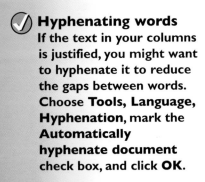

Hyphenating words

If the text in your columns is justified, you might want to hyphenate it to reduce the gaps between words. Choose **Tools, Language, Hyphenation,** mark the **Automatically hyphenate document** check box, and click **OK**.

1 ▶ Click anywhere in the multiple-column text, and choose **Format**, **Columns** to display the Columns dialog box.

2 ▶ If you like, click a preset format under **Presets** at the top of the dialog box.

3 ▶ If you have specific requirements for column widths, first clear the **Equal column width** check box.

4 ▶ Then enter the desired settings for each column under **Width and spacing**.

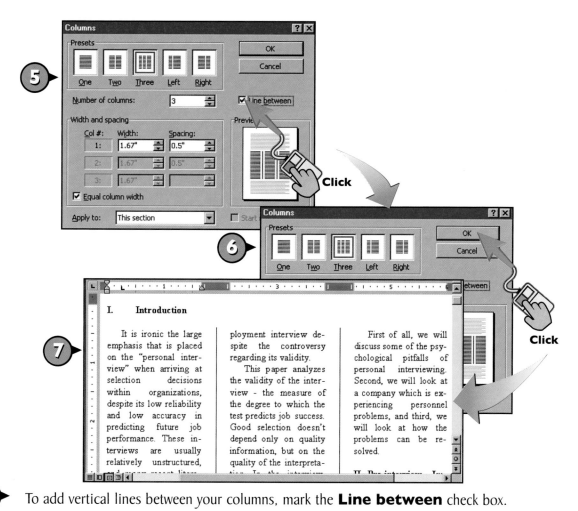

5 To add vertical lines between your columns, mark the **Line between** check box.

6 When you have made all your selections, click **OK**.

7 Word applies the settings you chose to your text.

✓ **Balancing the length of columns**
To balance the length of your columns on the last page of a document, press **Ctrl+End** to move to the end of the document, and choose **Insert, Break**. Mark the **Continuous** option button, and click **OK**.

Task 3: Creating a Table

Creating a Table

Word's table feature gives you a wonderfully flexible way of aligning text in a grid of rows and columns. You enter text into the individual boxes in the grid, which are referred to as *cells*. In this task, you learn to create a table using the **Insert Table** button on the Standard toolbar. In addition, you find out how to delete a table, in case you insert one that's not quite right and want to start over. The next three tasks teach you how to work with a table after you've created one in your document.

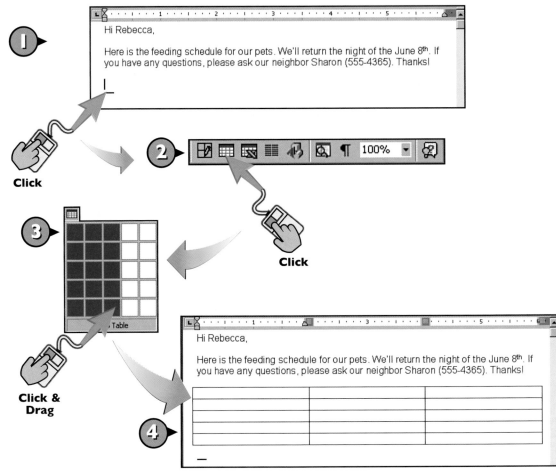

Start Here

Click

Click

Click & Drag

Hi Rebecca,

Here is the feeding schedule for our pets. We'll return the night of the June 8th. If you have any questions, please ask our neighbor Sharon (555-4365). Thanks!

1. Move the insertion point to the place where you want to insert the table.

2. Click the **Insert Table** button on the Standard toolbar.

3. The squares in the grid represent cells. Drag through the approximate number of rows and columns that you want, and then release the mouse button.

4. A table with the number of rows and columns you specified appears in the document.

Next Step

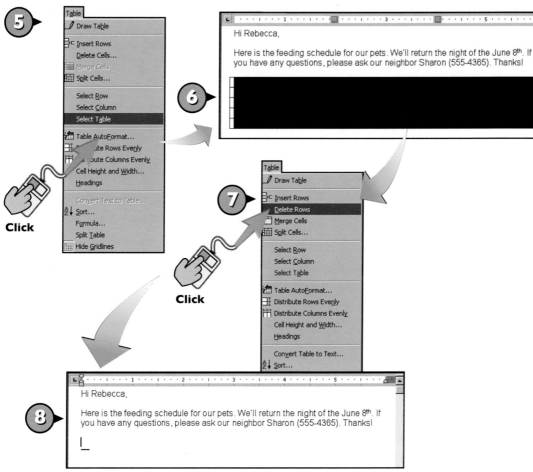

5 If you inserted a table accidentally and want to start over, make sure that the insertion point is in the table, and choose **Table**, **Select Table**.

6 The entire table is now selected.

7 Choose **Table**, **Delete Rows**.

8 The table is deleted from your document.

✓ **Using the Draw Table button**
You can also draw a table "by hand" by using the Draw Table button on the Tables and Borders toolbar. (You display this toolbar by clicking the Tables and Borders button on the Standard toolbar.) This method lets you create complex tables more easily, but it is a little more time-consuming than the method described in this task.

Entering Text in a Table

Typing text in a table is much like typing in a regular document, but navigating within a table is somewhat different. In this task, you first learn how to move the insertion point from cell to cell within a table, and then you get a few pointers about entering text.

✓ **Adding text above a table**

If you start a table at the very top of a document and then decide that you want to insert text above the table, click at the far left edge of the upper-left cell in the table and press **Enter**. Word inserts a blank line above the table; you can now click the blank line and type your text.

Task 4: Entering Text in a Table

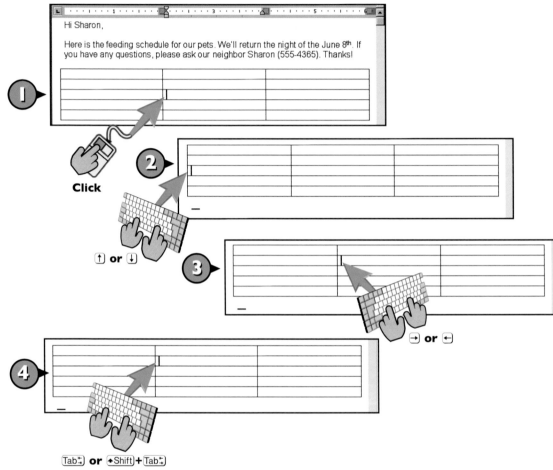

Click

↑ or ↓

→ or ←

Tab⇆ or ⬆Shift + Tab⇆

1. To move to a particular cell with the mouse, just click in the cell.

2. To move to the row above or below, press the **Up** or **Down arrow** key.

3. To move to the cell to the right or left, press the **Right** or **Left arrow** key. (If there is text in a cell, these arrow keys move the insertion point through the text.)

4. You can also press the **Tab** key to move into the cell to the right or **Shift+Tab** to move to the left. (If the destination cell contains text, it will get selected.)

Next
Step

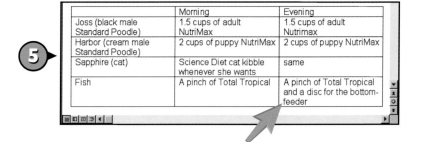

	Morning	Evening
Joss (black male Standard Poodle)	1.5 cups of adult NutriMax	1.5 cups of adult Nutrimax
Harbor (cream male Standard Poodle)	2 cups of puppy NutriMax	2 cups of puppy NutriMax
Sapphire (cat)	Science Diet cat kibble whenever she wants	same
Fish	A pinch of Total Tropical	A pinch of Total Tropical and a disc for the bottom-feeder

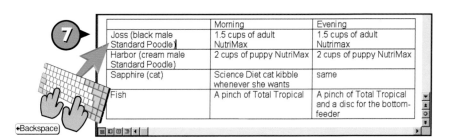

	Morning	Evening
Joss (black male Standard Poodle)	1.5 cups of adult NutriMax	1.5 cups of adult Nutrimax
Harbor (cream male Standard Poodle)	2 cups of puppy NutriMax	2 cups of puppy NutriMax
Sapphire (cat)	Science Diet cat kibble whenever she wants	same
Fish	A pinch of Total Tropical	A pinch of Total Tropical and a disc for the bottom-feeder

↵Enter

	Morning	Evening
Joss (black male Standard Poodle)	1.5 cups of adult NutriMax	1.5 cups of adult Nutrimax
Harbor (cream male Standard Poodle)	2 cups of puppy NutriMax	2 cups of puppy NutriMax
Sapphire (cat)	Science Diet cat kibble whenever she wants	same
Fish	A pinch of Total Tropical	A pinch of Total Tropical and a disc for the bottom-feeder

←Backspace

 When you type text in a cell, if the entry is too wide to fit in the cell, Word automatically wraps the text to the next line and increases the row height.

 Pressing **Enter** in a cell ends the paragraph and adds a blank line to that row.

 If you accidentally press **Enter** in a cell and want to remove the blank line, just press the **Backspace** key.

 Insert a tab within a cell
If you want to insert a tab within a cell, press **Ctrl+Tab** instead of **Tab**. (Pressing the **Tab** key by itself just moves you into the cell to the right.)

Changing the Table Structure

As you enter text in a table, you will almost certainly need to change its structure. This task describes the most common adjustments that you'll need to make. As you experiment with these techniques, keep in mind that Word does not prevent you from making a table too wide to fit on the page. If you're adding columns and changing column widths, check Print Preview periodically to make sure the table isn't running off the page.

✓ Using commands on the Table menu

Most of the commands in the Table menu are only active when the insertion point is in a table. If you notice that the commands are dim, it's a sign you accidentally clicked outside the table. Click inside the table and then display the Table menu again.

Task 5: Changing the Structure of a Table

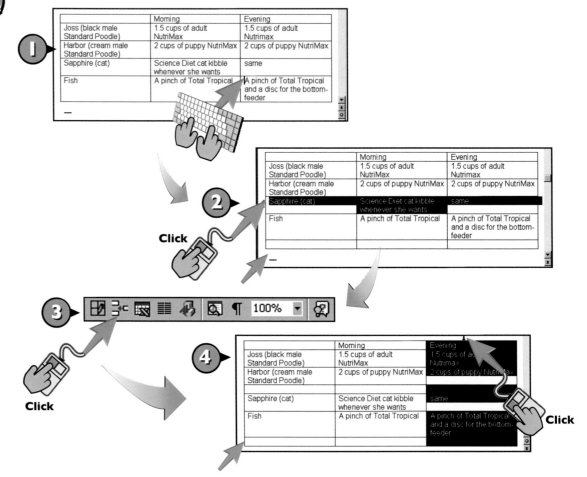

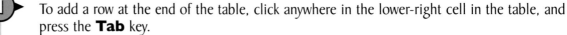

1 To add a row at the end of the table, click anywhere in the lower-right cell in the table, and press the **Tab** key.

2 A new row is added. To add a row in the middle of the table, select the row below the location of the new one by clicking to its left.

3 Click the **Insert Rows** button on the Standard toolbar. (The Insert Table button turns into Insert Rows when a row is selected.) A new row is added.

4 To insert a column, select the column to the right of where the new one will go by clicking at the top of the column (when you see the mouse pointer change to a black arrow).

Next Step

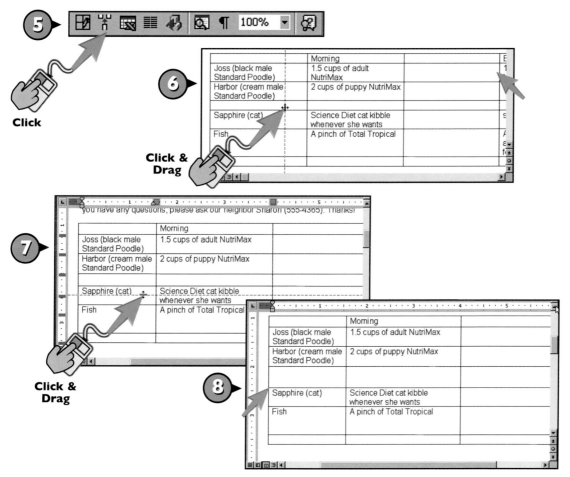

5 ▶ Click the **Insert Columns** button on the Standard toolbar. (The Insert Table button turns into Insert Columns when a column is selected.)

6 ▶ A new column is added. To adjust a column's width, point to its right border and drag it to the desired location.

7 ▶ The column is resized. To resize a row, point to its bottom border and drag it to the desired location.

8 ▶ The row is resized.

 Deleting a row or column
To delete a row or column, select it first (see steps 2 and 4), and then choose **Table, Delete Rows** or **Table, Delete Columns.**

Task 6: Formatting a Table

Formatting a Table

Formatting a table involves changing the appearance of the text and adding borders and shading. Be careful to select the exact cells that you want to format before using the commands described in this task, and remember that you can always use Undo if you make a change that you don't like.

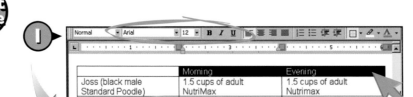

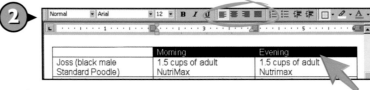

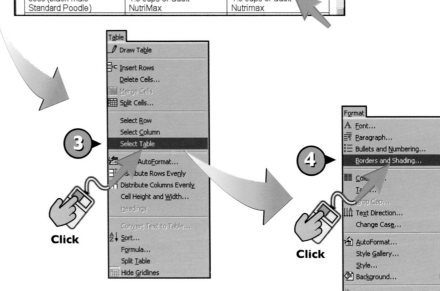

Click

Click

✓ **Add shading to cells**
If you want to add shading to some of the cells in your table, select the cells, and then choose **Format, Borders and Shading.** Click the **Shading** tab, click the color you'd like to use, and click **OK.**

1 ▸ To change text formatting, select the cells (or some text within a cell) and then use the familiar drop-down lists and buttons in the Formatting toolbar.

2 ▸ To change the alignment of text within cells, select the cells and then click the desired alignment button on the Formatting toolbar.

3 ▸ To change the border around the outside of the table, first select the entire table by choosing **Table**, **Select Table**.

4 ▸ Next, choose **Format**, **Borders and Shading**.

Next Step ▸

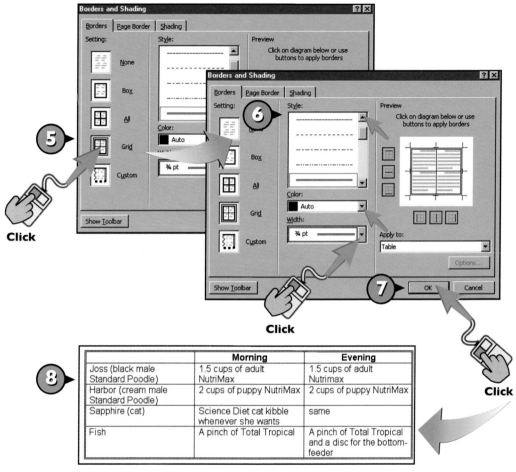

 Click

 Click

 Click

	Morning	Evening
Joss (black male Standard Poodle)	1.5 cups of adult NutriMax	1.5 cups of adult Nutrimax
Harbor (cream male Standard Poodle)	2 cups of puppy NutriMax	2 cups of puppy NutriMax
Sapphire (cat)	Science Diet cat kibble whenever she wants	same
Fish	A pinch of Total Tropical	A pinch of Total Tropical and a disc for the bottom-feeder

 Click

5 Click **Grid** under Setting to change only the outside border, or **All** to change all the borders in the table.

6 Choose the desired options from the **Style**, **Color**, and **Width** lists.

7 Click the **OK** button.

8 Word applies the border options you chose.

Adding Color and Graphics to Your Document

Working with color and graphics used to be out of reach for most everyone but desktop publishers. Now it takes only a click or two to spice up a document with a colorful title or a splashy graphic. In this part, you learn to add a colored highlight to text with Word's highlighter tool, how to change the color of the text itself, and how to insert, manipulate, and format graphical images.

Tasks

Task #		Page #
1	Adding Color to Your Text	154
2	Inserting a Graphic in Your Document	156
3	Moving and Sizing a Graphic	158
4	Formatting a Graphic	160
5	Adding Shapes	162
6	Creating Word Art	164

Task 1: Adding Color to Your Text

Coloring the Text in Your Document

Word offers a highlight feature you can use just as you would a highlighter pen. This tool comes in handy when you're editing text onscreen—it lets you call attention to blocks of text that you want to comment on, that need further revision, and so on. Word also lets you change the color of characters themselves (not the background behind the characters) by applying a font color. Although highlighting is useful regardless of whether you have a color printer, you're not as likely to use font colors unless you can print in color.

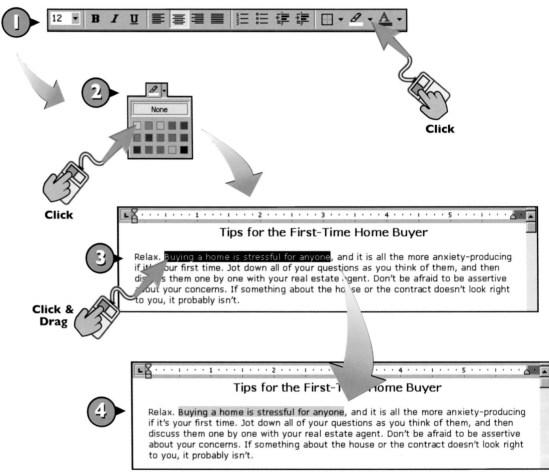

Start Here

Click

Click

Click & Drag

Tips for the First-Time Home Buyer

Relax. Buying a home is stressful for anyone, and it is all the more anxiety-producing if it's your first time. Jot down all of your questions as you think of them, and then discuss them one by one with your real estate agent. Don't be afraid to be assertive about your concerns. If something about the house or the contract doesn't look right to you, it probably isn't.

Tips for the First-Time Home Buyer

Relax. Buying a home is stressful for anyone, and it is all the more anxiety-producing if it's your first time. Jot down all of your questions as you think of them, and then discuss them one by one with your real estate agent. Don't be afraid to be assertive about your concerns. If something about the house or the contract doesn't look right to you, it probably isn't.

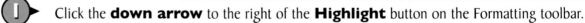

1 Click the **down arrow** to the right of the **Highlight** button on the Formatting toolbar.

2 Click the color that you want to use in the palette that appears.

3 The mouse pointer takes on the shape of a highlighter pen. Drag across the text, and then release the mouse button.

4 The text is now highlighted with the color you chose.

Next Step

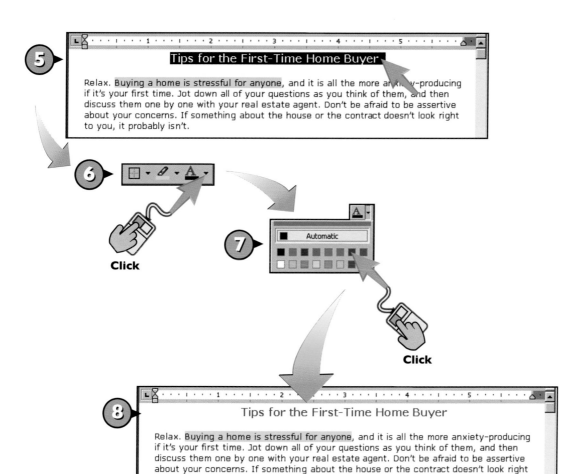

Click

Click

5 ▸ To change your font color, start by selecting the text.

6 ▸ Click the **down arrow** to the right of the **Font Color** button on the Formatting toolbar.

7 ▸ Click the desired color in the palette that appears.

8 ▸ Click anywhere to deselect your text and see the font color that you applied.

✓ **Remove highlighting and font color**
To remove highlighting, select the text, click the **Highlight** button in the Formatting toolbar, and then choose **None.** To remove font color, select the text, click the **Font Color** button in the Formatting toolbar, and then choose **Automatic.**

End Task

Adding Graphics to Your Document

Adding a graphic to your document is not as hard as you might think. In fact, it only takes a click or two. This task describes how to insert clip art images that come on the Microsoft Office CD, although you can certainly use any type of image—photographs, sketches, diagrams, and so on—and the file can be located in any folder on your computer system. After you've added a graphic to your document, you'll want to look over the next three tasks to learn how to adjust its location and appearance, among other things.

✓ **Use a graphic located on your hard disk**
If you want to insert a graphic from a folder on your hard disk instead of from the Microsoft Office CD, choose **Insert, Picture, From File**. In the Insert Picture dialog box, select the desired graphics file and click **OK**.

Task 2: Inserting a Graphic in Your Document

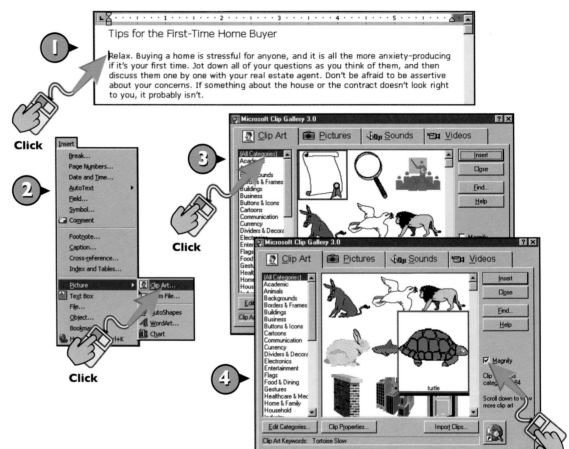

Move the insertion point to the approximate place you want to insert the graphic.

Place the Microsoft Office CD in your CD-ROM drive, and choose **Insert**, **Picture**, **Clip Art** to display the Microsoft Clip Gallery 3.0 dialog box.

In the **Clip Art** tab, click the various categories to browse the available images.

If you want to see an image more clearly, click it and then mark the **Magnify** check box.

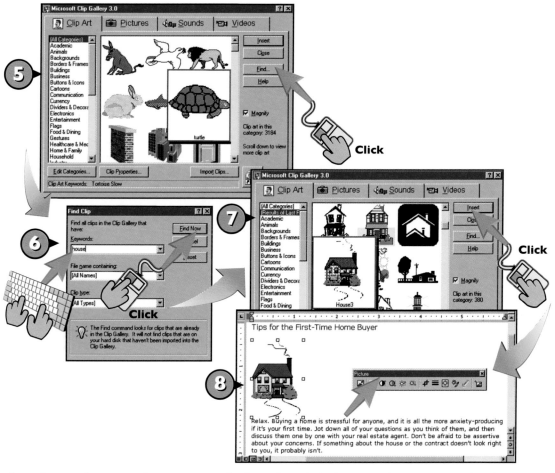

5 If you know what type of image you're looking for, click the **Find** button to display the **Find Clip** dialog box.

6 Type a word to describe what you're looking for in the **Keywords** text box (**house** in this example), and click the **Find Now** button.

7 Scroll through the search results, click the image that you want to use, and click the **Insert** button.

8 The graphic is inserted in your document, and the Picture toolbar appears to help you work with it.

Task 3: Moving and Sizing a Graphic

Changing the Size and Location of a Graphic in Your Document

After you've placed a graphic in your document, you need to tell Word how the text should wrap around the image. You also need to place the graphic where you want it to go, and adjust its size. You can accomplish all these tasks by using buttons in the Picture toolbar and by dragging with your mouse.

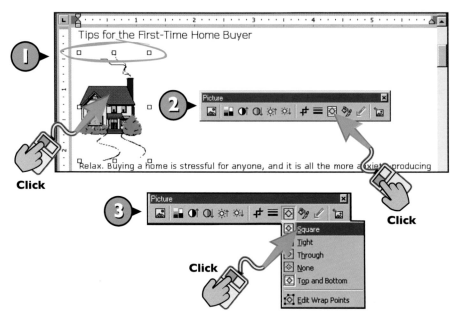

1. Click the graphic to select it. When it's selected, small white squares (called **selection handles**) appear around the image.

2. Click the **Text Wrapping** button on the Picture toolbar.

3. Choose the desired wrapping option (**Square** in this example).

4. The text now wraps along the side of the image.

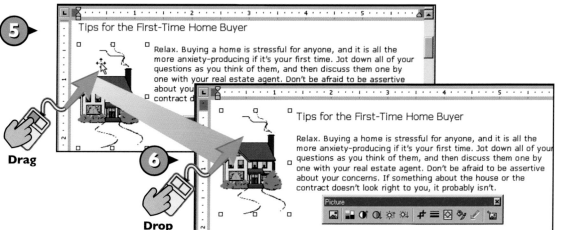

Drag

Drop

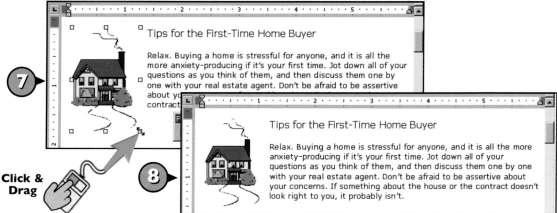

**Click &
Drag**

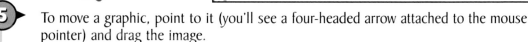

⑤ To move a graphic, point to it (you'll see a four-headed arrow attached to the mouse pointer) and drag the image.

⑥ The image has moved to a new location. (In this example, the text heading now wraps to the right of the image.)

⑦ To resize a graphic, point to a corner selection handle (the mouse pointer becomes a diagonal double-headed arrow) and drag to enlarge or shrink the image.

⑧ Click anywhere in the text to deselect the image and see its new size more clearly.

✓ **Understanding the text-wrapping options**
The text-wrapping options work as follows: **Square** wraps the text in a square shape around the image. **Tight** wraps the text right up to the outside edges of the image. **Through** is the same as **Tight**, but it also wraps inside any parts of the image that are open. **None** doesn't wrap the text at all—the image either appears in front of or in back of the text. Finally, **Top and Bottom** wraps the text above and below the image, but not along its sides (this is the default setting).

End Task

Task 4: Formatting a Graphic

Crop and Add Borders to Graphics

Word lets you format graphics in a wide variety of ways. In this task, you learn two techniques that will get you started: cropping and adding borders. You crop an image to remove a portion of it (the image's size and proportions remain unchanged). Adding borders around the outside of an image gives it definition and may give it the right "look" in a document.

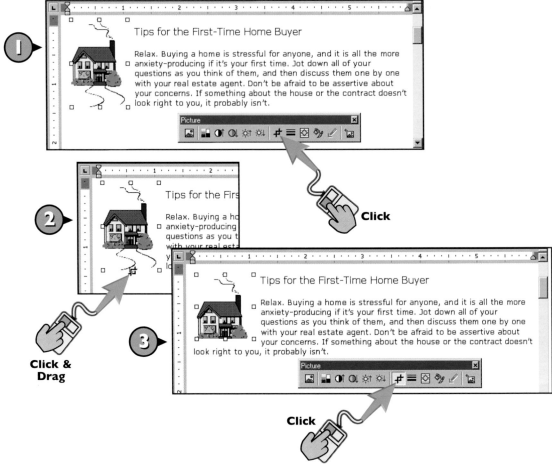

Click

Click & Drag

Click

(✓) **Display the Picture toolbar**
If you don't see the Picture toolbar, choose **View, Toolbars, Picture**.

1 Select your graphic (click anywhere on it) and click the **Crop** button on the Picture toolbar.

2 Point to a selection handle, start dragging, and release the mouse button when the desired portion is cropped out.

3 In this example, the lower part of the image is cropped out. Click the **Crop** button again to turn it off.

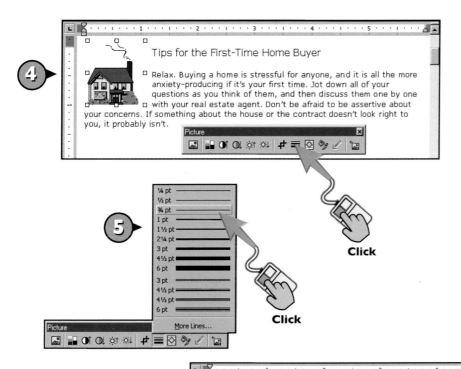

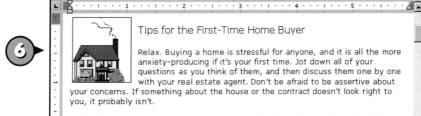

Click

Click

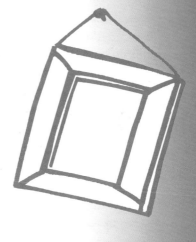

④ To add a border to an image, make sure it's selected, and click the **Line Style** button in the Picture toolbar.

⑤ Choose a line style from the menu that appears.

⑥ Word adds a border to the image. (Deselect the image so that you can see the border more clearly.)

Task 5: Adding Shapes

Adding Shapes to Your Document

Sometimes you don't need a complex graphic in your document—you just need something simple, such as an arrow or a box. Word's AutoShapes feature lets you quickly draw all manner of arrows, rectangles, ovals, callouts, banners, and so on. After you have inserted a shape, you can use many of the same methods you learned in the preceding two tasks to move and resize it, modify its borders, and so on. In this task, you add a shape to a document and then change its fill color.

✓ **Creating a perfect square or circle**
If you are using the rectangle shape and want to draw a perfect square, hold down the **Shift** key as you drag. This also works with the oval shape to get a perfect circle, the star shape to get a perfectly proportioned star, and so on.

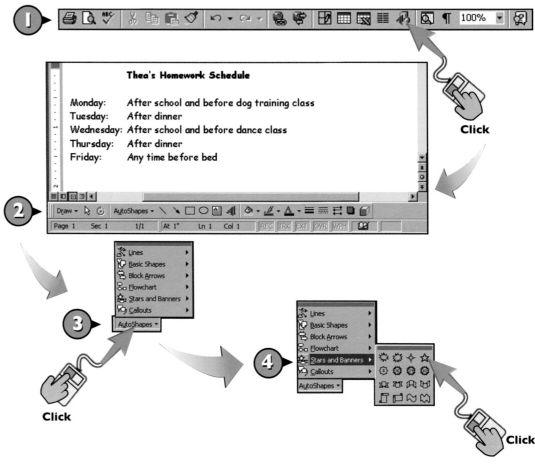

1 Click the **Drawing** button on the Standard toolbar.

2 The Drawing toolbar appears at the bottom of the Word window.

3 Click the **AutoShapes** button to display a menu with different categories of AutoShapes.

4 Point to a category, and then click the desired shape from the submenu that appears.

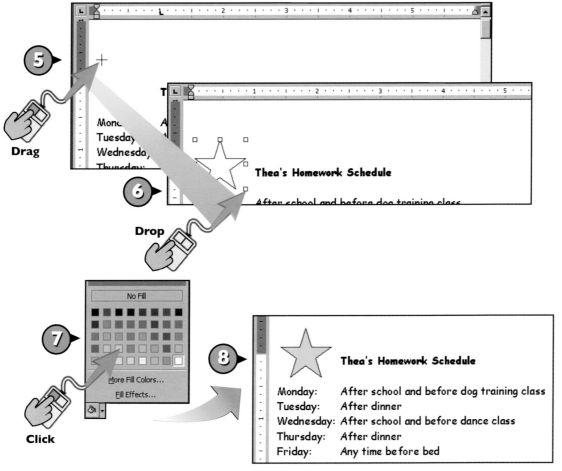

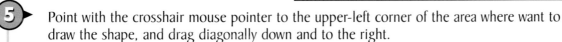

Thea's Homework Schedule

Monday:	After school and before dog training class
Tuesday:	After dinner
Wednesday:	After school and before dance class
Thursday:	After dinner
Friday:	Any time before bed

5 Point with the crosshair mouse pointer to the upper-left corner of the area where want to draw the shape, and drag diagonally down and to the right.

6 Release the mouse button to finish drawing the shape.

7 Keep the shape selected, click the **down arrow** to the right of the **Fill Color** button in the Drawing toolbar, and click a color.

8 The shape takes on the fill color you chose. (Deselect the shape to see it more clearly.)

Task 6: Creating WordArt

Using WordArt

When you add graphics to a document, you aren't limited to working with images separate from your text. WordArt lets you add flair to the text itself. It's perfect for creating splashy headings and titles. You start with a basic "look" for your word or phrase, and then tweak it to get the exact effect you want.

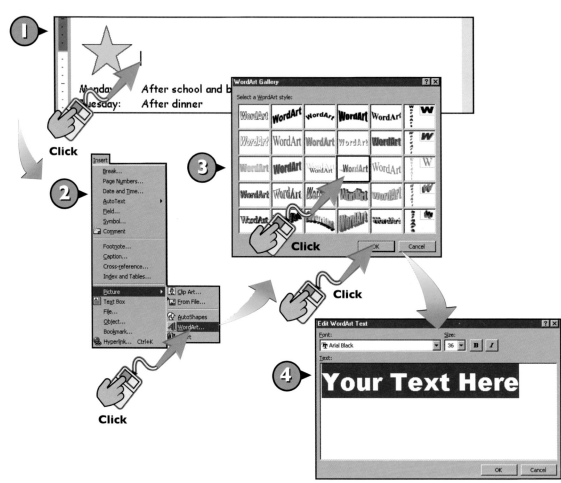

(1) Click where you want the WordArt image to go.

(2) Choose **Insert**, **Picture**, **WordArt**.

(3) The WordArt Gallery dialog box opens. Click the look that you want to start with, and click the **OK** button.

(4) The Edit WordArt Text window appears.

Next Step

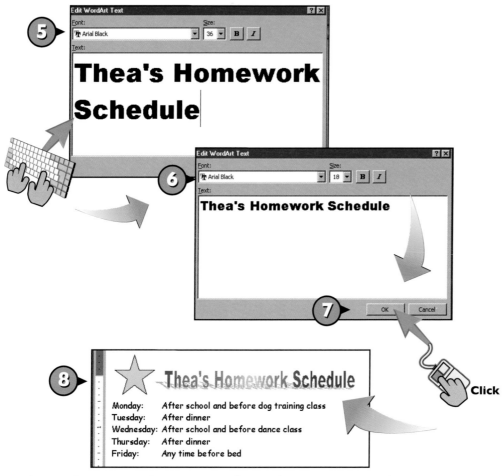

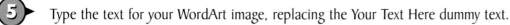

Click

5 ▶ Type the text for your WordArt image, replacing the Your Text Here dummy text.

6 ▶ Use the **Font** and **Size** drop-down lists and the **Bold** and **Italic** buttons to make additional adjustments to the text.

7 ▶ Click the **OK** button.

8 ▶ The WordArt image is inserted in your document. See "Moving and Sizing a Graphic," earlier in this part, for help with positioning and resizing it.

End Task

PART 10

Mail Merge

Mail merge automates the process of inserting personal information such as names and addresses into a document that you want to send to many people. You can use it to create such documents as personalized form letters for a mass mailing, cover letters for a batch of resumes, or marketing letters for publicity packages. Not only that, you can also use mail merge to print envelopes or labels to go with your letters. You should follow the steps in the first five tasks in this part (from "Starting the Main Document" to "Merging the Documents") in sequence. Each task picks up where the previous one left off. After you've run through these five tasks a time or two, you'll have no problem following the instructions in the last two tasks to merge your envelopes or labels.

Tasks

Task #   Page #

1 Starting the Main Document   168
2 Creating and Saving the Data Source   170
3 Entering Records into the Data Source   172
4 Completing the Main Document   174
5 Merging the Documents   176
6 Merging Envelopes   178
7 Merging Labels   180

Task 1: Starting the Main Document

Starting the Main Document

In this first phase of the mail merge process, you simply tell Word which document you want to use as the **main document**. You can either open an existing main document or start a new one. If you start a new one, as described in these steps, you don't have to type any of the document now; you simply save a blank document. In "Completing the Main Document," later in Part 10, you come back to the main document and enter both regular text and special **merge fields** telling Word where to insert each piece of information from the data source.

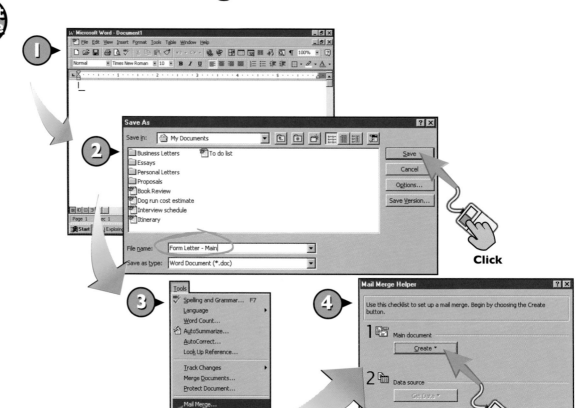

Click

Click

Click

1. Start a new, blank document in Word.

2. Save the document with a name such as **Form Letter – Main** to remind you that it's a main document.

3. Choose **Tools**, **Mail Merge** to display the Mail Merge Helper dialog box.

4. Click the **Create** button.

Next Step

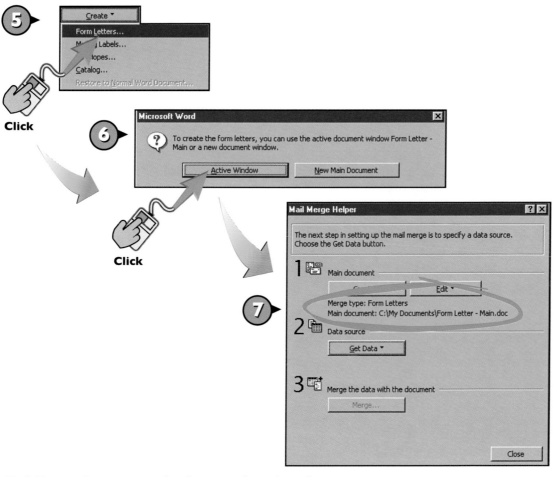

5 ▶ Click **Form Letters** in the **Create** drop-down list.

6 ▶ Click the **Active Window** button to tell Word that your main document is already open.

7 ▶ The Mail Merge Helper dialog box appears again with information about the main document. Continue with the next task.

Creating the Data Source for Mail Merge

In this second phase of the mail merge process, you tell Word which document you want to use as your *data source*. You can either create a new one or open an existing one. You learn how to create a new one here. In "Merging Envelopes" and "Merging Labels," later in this part, you learn how to open an existing data source. The key step in creating a data source is telling Word which *fields*, or pieces of information, you want to store. Typical fields are first name, last name, company, address, city, state, zip code, and so on.

Task 2: Creating and Saving the Data Source

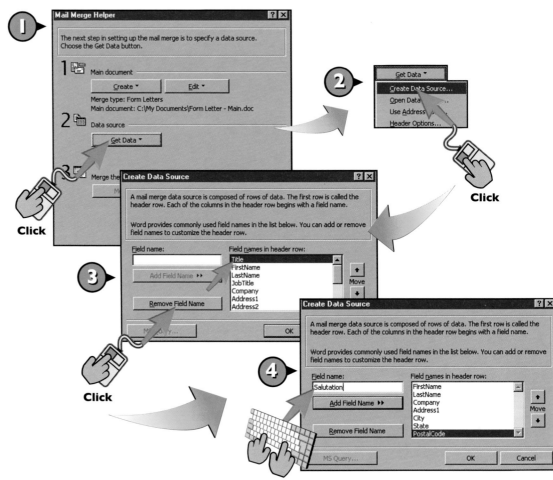

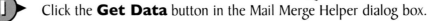

Click the **Get Data** button in the Mail Merge Helper dialog box.

Choose **Create Data Source** in the **Get Data** drop-down list to display the Create Data Source dialog box.

To remove a field that you don't want, click it in the **Field names in header row** list and click the **Remove Field Name** button.

To add a field, first replace the contents of the **Field name** text box with the name of the field you want to add.

Next Step

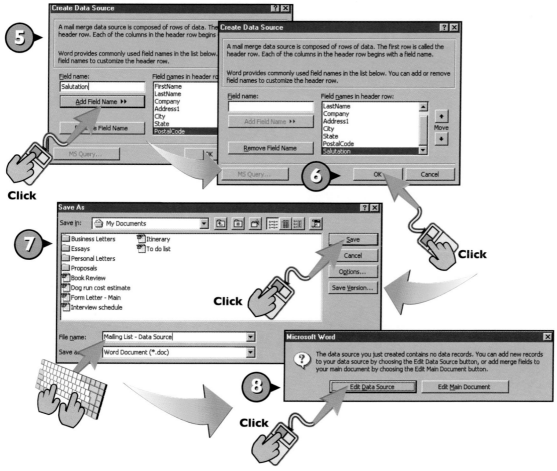

5 Then click the **Add Field Name** button to add the name to the **Field names in header row** list.

6 When your list of fields is the way you want it, click **OK**.

7 Word displays the Save As dialog box. Save your data source with a name such as *Mailing List – Data Source*.

8 When Word asks what you want to do next, click the **Edit Data Source** button and continue with the next task.

Adding Records to the Data Source

In this third phase of the mail merge process, you enter data into your data source. The data for each person is called a *record*. When you merge the documents later, Word will merge the information from each record into the main document to create your personalized form letters (or envelopes, or labels).

 Editing your data source

The easiest way to edit your data source in the future is to open it *through* the main document. First open the main document (File, Open). Then click the **Edit Data Source** button at the far-right end of the Mail Merge toolbar (see the next task) to display the Data Form. Edit the records, and then click **OK**. Save the main document, and click **Yes** when Word asks whether you want to save the data source.

Task 3: Entering Records into the Data Source

 Start Here

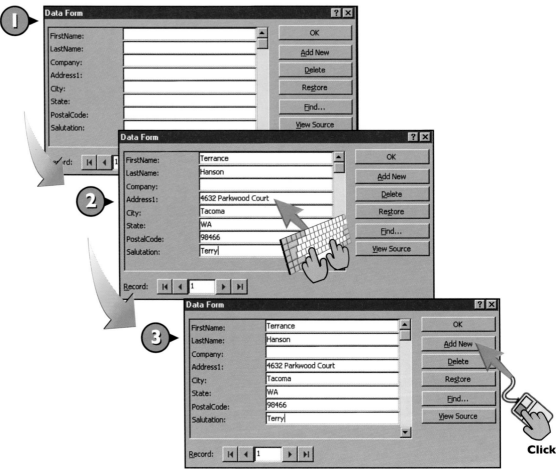

Click

① Word presents a blank Data Form with text boxes for all the fields that you defined in the preceding task.

② Enter the information for the first person in your list, using the **Tab** key to move from field to field.

③ Click the **Add New** button to add the next record. (Be careful not to click the **OK** button at this point.)

 Next Step

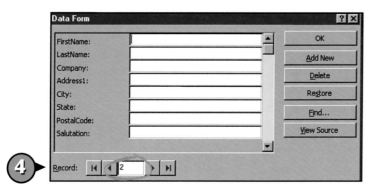

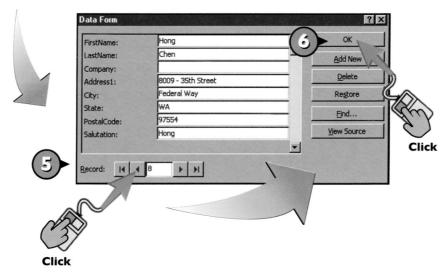

Click

Click

4 Word clears the Data Form to let you enter record 2. Continue entering records.

5 The **Record** arrows let you move forward and back in your data source so that you can edit records you've already entered.

6 When you've finished entering all the records, click the **OK** button.

ToolTips identify buttons
To find what the Record buttons do in the Data Form (see step 5), point your mouse at the button. A ToolTip will pop up and tell you the name of the button.

Task 4: Completing the Main Document

Finishing the Main Document

In this fourth phase of the mail merge process, you finish the main document. This entails typing and formatting the text, and inserting the merge fields that tell Word where to insert the data from your data source.

Start Here

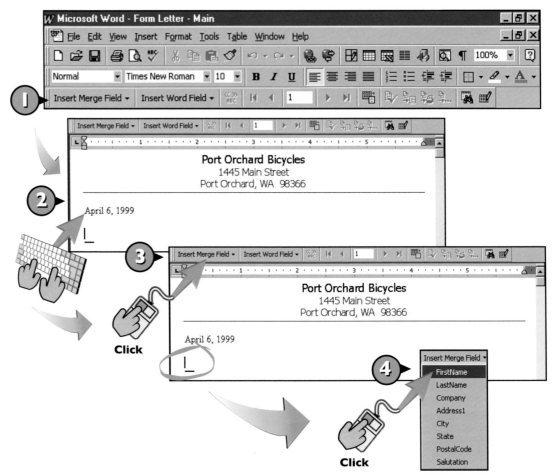

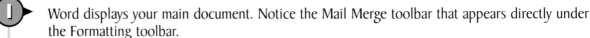

WARNING

When you close the main document (either before or after performing the merge), Word may ask whether you want to save the data source attached to the main document. If you see this message, click the **Yes** button! Otherwise, any changes you've made to records in your data source won't be saved.

1 Word displays your main document. Notice the Mail Merge toolbar that appears directly under the Formatting toolbar.

2 Type and format the text that you want to include above the recipient's address.

3 Place the insertion point on the first line of the address block, and click the **Insert Merge Field** button.

4 In the drop-down list that appears, click the first field in the address block.

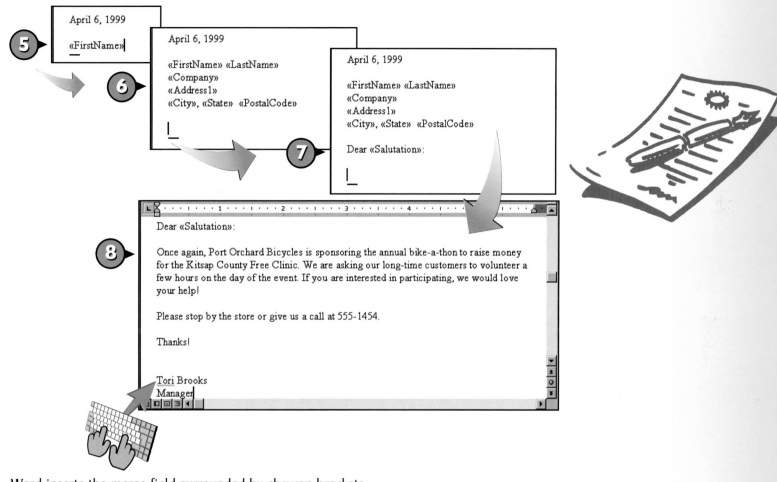

5 ► Word inserts the merge field surrounded by chevron brackets.

6 ► Insert the remaining merge fields in the address block, pressing **Enter** and adding spaces and commas where necessary.

7 ► If you have a salutation field, add it after **Dear** and follow it with a colon.

8 ► Type the remaining text and then save the main document. Leave it open for the next task.

Task 5: Merging the Documents

Producing the Form Letters

In this final phase of the mail merge process, you merge the main document with the data source to produce your form letters. In these steps, you first check to see whether the data will merge correctly, and then you merge the letters to a new document window and print them.

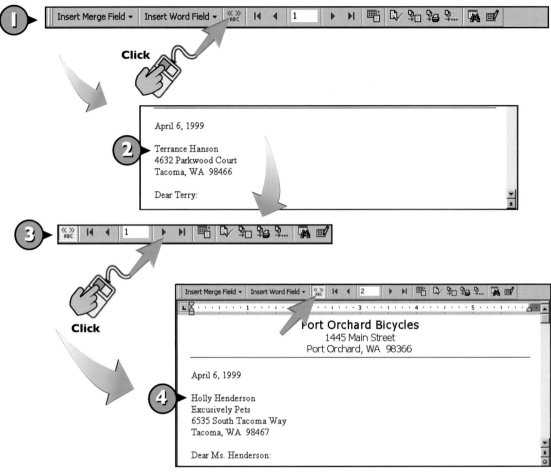

Start Here

Click

April 6, 1999

Terrance Hanson
4632 Parkwood Court
Tacoma, WA 98466

Dear Terry:

Click

Port Orchard Bicycles
1445 Main Street
Port Orchard, WA 98366

April 6, 1999

Holly Henderson
Excusively Pets
6535 South Tacoma Way
Tacoma, WA 98467

Dear Ms. Henderson:

Using your main document again
When you want to merge the same main document and data source in the future, just open the main document and follow steps 5 and 6 in this task.

1. Click the **View Merged Data** button on the Mail Merge toolbar.

2. Word displays the data from the first record.

3. Click the **Next Record** button on the Mail Merge toolbar.

4. Word displays the data from the next record. Click the **View Merged Data** button again to turn it off.

Next Step

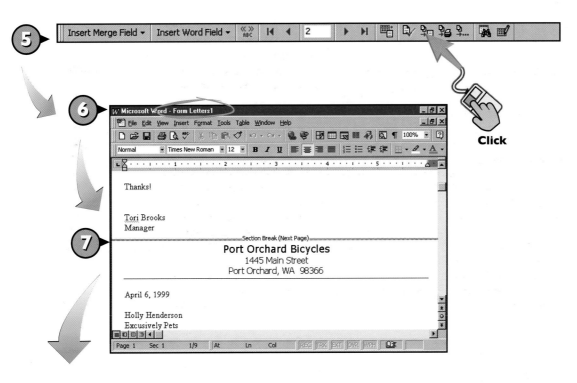

Click

Click

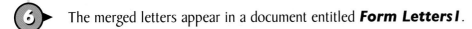

5 ▶ Click the **Merge to New Document** button on the Mail Merge toolbar to merge the documents.

6 ▶ The merged letters appear in a document entitled **Form Letters1**.

7 ▶ Scroll down the document. The letters are separated by **section breaks** that force them to print on separate pages.

8 ▶ Click the **Print** button in the Standard toolbar to print the form letters, and then close the document without saving it.

Task 6: Merging Envelopes

Printing Envelopes Using Mail Merge

The general steps for merging envelopes and labels are the same as for merging form letters (although the details are somewhat different). Consequently, you'll find it helpful to practice a few mail merges with form letters before proceeding with this task and the next. Also note that both of these tasks assume that you already have a data source, so you'll open an existing one rather than creating a new one.

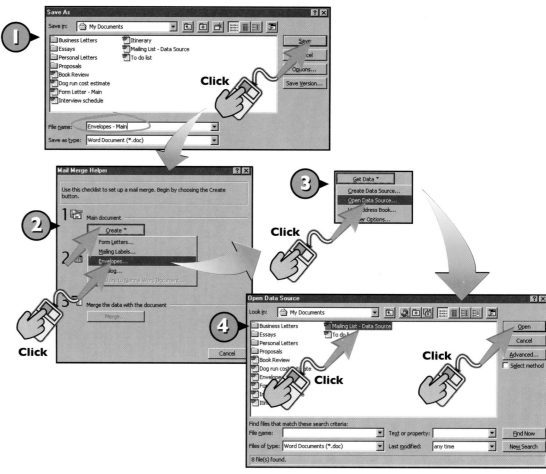

① ▶ Start a new document and save it with a name such as **Envelopes – Main**.

② ▶ Choose **Tools**, **Mail Merge**, click the **Create** button, and click **Envelopes**.

③ ▶ Click the **Active Window** button, and then click the **Get Data** button and choose **Open Data Source**.

④ ▶ Select your data source in the Open Data Source dialog box, and click the **Open** button.

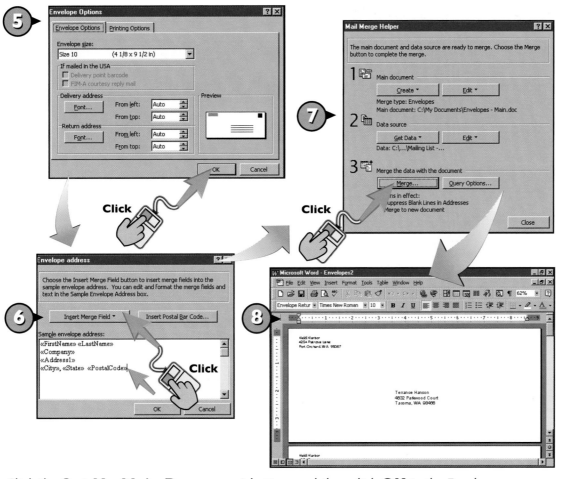

5 ▶ Click the **Set Up Main Document** button, and then click **OK** in the Envelope
Options dialog box.

6 ▶ Word displays the Envelope address dialog box. Use the **Insert Merge Field** button
to insert your merge fields. Click **OK**.

7 ▶ Click the **Merge** button in the Mail Merge Helper dialog box, and then click the
Merge button in the Merge dialog box.

8 ▶ The merged envelopes appear onscreen. Print the envelopes and close them without
saving. Then save and close the main document.

Printing Labels Using Mail Merge

As with merging envelopes (see the preceding task), it's easiest to merge labels if you practice a few mail merges with form letters first. And remember that this task assumes that you already have a data source, so you'll open an existing one rather than creating a new one.

Task 7: Merging Labels

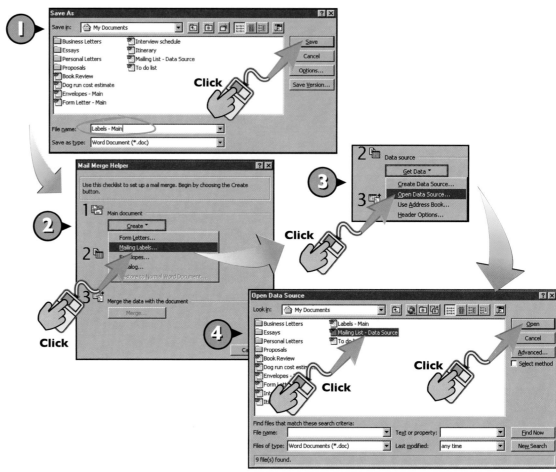

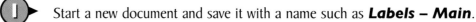

1 ▶ Start a new document and save it with a name such as **Labels – Main**.

2 ▶ Choose **Tools**, **Mail Merge**, click the **Create** button, and click **Mailing Labels**.

3 ▶ Click the **Active Window** button, and then click the **Get Data** button and choose **Open Data Source**.

4 ▶ Select your data source in the Open Data Source dialog box, and click the **Open** button.

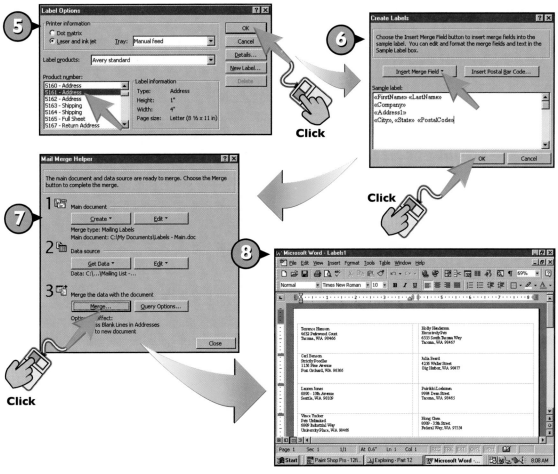

5 ▶ Click the **Set Up Main Document** button, and then choose the product number for your labels in the Label Options dialog box. Click **OK**.

6 ▶ Word displays the Create Labels dialog box. Use the **Insert Merge Field** button to insert your merge fields. Click **OK**.

7 ▶ Click the **Merge** button in the Mail Merge Helper dialog box, and then click the **Merge** button in the Merge dialog box.

8 ▶ The merged labels appear onscreen. Print the labels and close them without saving. Then save and close the main document.

alignment The way text aligns along the right and left sides of the page. You can individually set the alignment of each paragraph in your document.

alignment, centered The text is centered horizontally on the page.

alignment, justified Both the left and right edges of the text are straight. Word adds or removes space between characters to form the straight right edge.

alignment, left The left edge of the text is straight and the right edge is ragged. This is the default alignment option.

alignment, right The right edge of the text is straight and the left edge is ragged.

AutoCorrect A feature that corrects spelling errors as you type. You can also use AutoCorrect to enter long phrases automatically.

AutoText A feature that lets Word "memorize" long blocks of text that you use frequently so that you can quickly insert them in your document.

cell A box in a table, formed by the intersection of a row and a column.

check box A small box that you click to enable or disable an option in a dialog box. If the check box has a check mark in it, the option is currently enabled; if it's clear, the option is disabled. Check boxes are not mutually exclusive; you can mark several check boxes in a group.

context menu A menu that appears when you right-click something. The commands in a context menu vary depending on where you right-click.

copy and paste To place a duplicate of the selected text somewhere else in the current document or another document.

cut and paste To move the selected text somewhere else in the current document or another document.

default The assumed option, behavior, or formatting that remains in effect unless you specify otherwise.

dialog box A small window that appears when you issue a command followed by an ellipses (…) to get more information about how you want to carry out the command. Clicking the OK button in a dialog box issues the command; clicking the Cancel button cancels it.

drag To press and hold down your mouse button as you move the mouse pointer. You typically drag to move, draw, or select objects with the mouse.

drop-down list A list that stays hidden from view until you click the down arrow to its right. As soon as you select an option from the list, the list closes again.

end mark The small horizontal bar at the very end of a Word document. The end mark doesn't print.

field A holding place for information that can be updated. Typical fields in Word include the date field, which displays the current date, and the page number field, which displays the correct page number on each page in a document. *See also* **mail merge, merge field**.

font In the Windows environment, the term *font* refers to a typeface or character shape, such as Times New Roman or Arial.

I-beam The mouse pointer you see when it's resting over text. When you see an I-beam, you can click to move the insertion point, or drag to select text.

indent To push the text in a paragraph in from the margin. Word gives you four indent options (see the next four entries). You can individually set the indentation of each paragraph in your document.

indent, first-line   Only the first line of a paragraph is indented.

indent, hanging   All the lines in a paragraph except the first line are indented.

indent, left   All the lines in a paragraph are indented from the left.

indent, right   All the lines in a paragraph are indented from the right.

insertion point   The flashing vertical bar in a document window that indicates where text will be inserted or deleted when you type or delete text.

line spacing   The amount of vertical space between lines of text.

mail merge   The process of merging a "boilerplate" document (such as a form letter, label, or envelope) with a list of data (usually names and addresses) to generate personalized documents.

mail merge, data source   The file that contains the data you will merge into the "boilerplate" document (called the *main document*). *See also* **mail merge, main document**.

mail merge, main document   The actual document that you are producing, such as a form letter, label, or envelope.

mail merge, merge field   Fields that you insert in a main document telling Word where to insert the individual pieces of data (name, address, and so on) from the data source.

mail merge, record   All the information about one person in your data source. If you have the names and addresses of 50 people in your data source, your data source contains 50 records. Each record is composed of individual fields for the specific pieces of information, such as first name, last name, address, and so on.

memory   The temporary storage area in your computer that holds the programs and documents you currently have open (also called RAM, for *random access memory*). Memory is cleared each time you turn off your computer. If you want to return to a document later, you need to save it to disk.

option button   A small white circle that you click to choose an option in a dialog box (sometimes called a *radio button*). If the option button has a black dot in it, it is currently enabled; if it doesn't, it is disabled. Option buttons are mutually exclusive; you can mark only one option button in a group.

paragraph mark   This symbol (¶) indicates the end of a paragraph. A paragraph symbol is inserted each time you press the Enter key in a document. You can see where the paragraph marks in a document are by clicking the Show/Hide button on the Standard toolbar.

point   A unit of measurement for font size. Roughly speaking, the point size of a font measures its vertical height. There are approximately 72 points in a vertical inch. Standard business documents usually use a 10- to 12-point font.

restore   To return a window to the size it was before it was last minimized or maximized.

scroll arrows   The arrows at either end of a scrollbar that you can click to scroll through your document.

scrollbar   A long bar that lets you move through your document with the mouse. Word provides a vertical scrollbar on the right side of the document window and a horizontal scrollbar along the bottom of the document window.

scroll box   The small box on a scrollbar that you can drag along the bar to scroll in either direction.

select   To mark text in preparation for performing an action on it. Often called *highlighting*. When you select text, it takes on a black background. When you select a graphical image, ***selection handles*** appear around its edges.

selection handles   Small white squares around the edges of a graphical image that indicate the graphic is selected.

shortcut icon   An icon that opens a program, folder, or file. A shortcut icon is just a pointer to a program, folder, or file. When you delete a shortcut icon, you don't remove the item to which it points.

spinner arrows   Small up and down arrows to the right of a text box. Clicking these arrows increments the number in the text box up or down.

status bar   The bar at the bottom of the Word window. The status bar contains information such as the current page number, the total number of pages in your document, and so on.

tab   This term has several meanings: Many dialog boxes have tabs across the top. Clicking the tabs displays different sets of options. This term also refers to the character that is inserted in your document when you press the Tab key. Finally, the term *tab* refers to a tab stop (see the next six terms).

tab, center   A custom tab stop that centers text over the tab stop.

tab, custom   A tab stop that you insert in a document. When you add a custom tab, all the default tabs to its left disappear.

tab, decimal   A custom tab stop that aligns text along the decimal point.

tab, default   The tab stops that automatically appear in your document. Default tabs are spaced every half inch across the document, and they remain in effect unless you insert custom tabs (see *also* **tab, custom**).

tab, left   A custom tab stop that left aligns text at the tab stop. The default tabs are also left tabs.

tab, right   A custom tab stop that right aligns text at the tab stop.

taskbar   The bar on the Windows desktop (usually at the bottom of the screen) that contains the Start button at one end and the clock at the other. When a program such as Word is open, a button for it appears on the taskbar.

template   A rough "blueprint" for a document. A template usually contains some combination of formatting and text. Word comes with a wide variety of templates.

template, Blank Document   See **template, Normal**.

template, Normal   The Normal template (also called the *Blank Document template*) is the default template that Word uses for all new documents unless you specify otherwise. This template contains the formatting for a standard business document (Times New Roman, 10-point font, single spacing, 8 1/2- by 11-inch paper, and so on).

text box   A small box in a dialog box in which you can type text or numbers.

title bar   The bar across the top of a window that lists the name of the program and/or document that's open in the window.

toggle   A button or keyboard command that you click or press once to turn an option on, and again to turn it off.

ToolTip   A small "bubble" that appears when you rest your mouse pointer over a toolbar button or other screen element that gives you the name of the item. Also referred to as a *ScreenTip*.

wizard   A specialized template that asks you questions about what type of document you want to create, and then generates the document for you based on your answers.

zoom   To change the magnification of a document onscreen. You can zoom in to enlarge a document or zoom out to shrink it.

Index

Symbols

* (asterisks), bulleted/numbered
lists, 95
... (ellipses), menus, 18

A

addresses
  envelopes
    mail merge, 178-179
    printing, 78-79
  form letter data sources, mail merge,
  170-173
  mailing labels
    mail merge, 180-181
    printing, 80-81
aligning text, 88-89
  columns, *see* columns
  indents, 92-93
  lists (bulleted/numbered), 94-95
  margins, 102-103
  page numbers, 113
  tables, *see* tables
  tabs, 50
    moving tab stops, 100-101
    setting tab stops, 96-99
  vertically centering pages, 110-111
**asterisks (*), bulleted/numbered
lists, 95**
AutoComplete, 136-137
AutoCorrect
  adding entries, 134-135
  lists (bulleted/numbered), 95
  special characters, 130
AutoFormat As You Type, 130
  bulleted/numbered lists, 95
automatic hyphenation, columns, 142
automatic spell checking, 124-125

AutoShapes, 162-163
AutoText, 136-137
Avery labels, *see* labels

B

balancing columns, 143
bold text, 84-85
borders
  graphics, 161
  pages (margins), 102-103
  paragraphs, 106-107
  tables, 150-151
breaks
  pages
    balancing columns, 143
    creating columns, 140-141
    inserting, 104-105
    sections, mail merge documents, 177
bulleted lists, 94-95

C

centering text
  horizontally, 88
  setting tab stops, 98
  vertically, 110-111
clip art, 156-161
  borders, 161
  cropping, 160
  inserting, 156-157
  moving, 159
  resizing, 159
  selecting, 158
  text wrap, 158-159
Clippit, *see* Office Assistant
closing
  documents, 58-59
  Word, 11

color
  graphics, 163
  paragraph borders/shading, 107-109
  text, 154-155
columns, 138-139
  creating, 140-141
  formatting, 142-143
  see also tables
commands
  Edit menu
    Find, 120
    Go To, 34-35
    Replace, 122
  File menu
    Close, 58
    Exit, 11
    New, 62, 64, 66
    Page Setup, 102, 110
    Print, 76
    Save As, 56
  Format menu
    Borders and Shading, 106,
    108-109, 150
    Columns, 142
    Paragraph, 90
  Help menu, 24
  Insert menu
    AutoText, 136
    Date and Time, 132
    Picture, Clip Art, 156
    Picture, From File, 156
    Picture, WordArt, 164
    Symbols, 130
  Table menu, 148
    Delete Rows, 145
    Select Table, 145, 150
  Tools menu
    AutoCorrect, 130, 134
    Mail Merge, 168, 178, 180
    Options, 80
    Thesaurus, 128

View menu
    Header and Footer, 114
    Page Layout, 72
    Ruler, 17
    Toolbars, 21
    see also menus
context (right-click) menus, 16
copying text, 48-49
Create Data Source dialog box (mail merge), 170-171
Create Labels dialog box (mail merge), 181
creating documents, 62-67
    blank documents, 62-63
    templates, 64-65
    wizards, 66-67
cutting/pasting text, 46-47

D

data sources, mail merge
    creating, 170-171
    editing/entering records, 172-173
    envelopes, 178
    mailing labels, 180
    merging documents/data sources, 176-177
date/time, inserting, 132-133
    headers/footers, 116
decimal tabs, 98-99
deleting
    columns, tables, 149
    date/time, 132
    headers/footers, 116
    rows, tables, 149
    tab stops, 100-101
    tables, 145
    text, 44-45
        color, 154

dialog boxes, 18-19
    AutoCorrect, 130, 134-135
    Borders and Shading
        Borders tab, 106-107
        formatting tables, 151
        Shading tab, 108-109
    Break, Continuous option, 140-141, 143
    Columns, 142-143
    Create AutoText, 137
    Create Data Source, 170-171
    Create Labels (mail merge), 181
    Data Form, 172-173
    Date and Time, 132-133
    Edit WordArt Text, 164-165
    Envelope Address (mail merge), 179
    Envelopes and Labels
        Envelopes tab, 78-79
        Labels tab, 80-81
    Find and Replace
        Find tab, 120-121
        Replace tab, 122-123
    Find Clip, 157
    Help Topics, 24-25
    Label Options, 81
        mail merge, 181
    Mail Merge Helper
        envelopes, 179
        form letters, 168-170
        Get Data button, 170
        mailing labels, 181
    Microsoft Clip Gallery 3.0, 156-157
    New, 62
        templates, 64
        wizards, 66
    Open, 60-61
        searching for documents, 68-69
    Open Data Source (mail merge)
        envelopes, 178
        mailing labels, 180
    Options, User Information tab, 80
    Page Numbers, 112-113
    Page Setup
        Layout tab, 110-111
        Margins tab, 102-103

    Paragraph, Indents and Spacing tab, 90-91
    Print, 76-77
    Save As, 56-57, 59
        saving mail merge data sources, 171
    Spelling and Grammar, 126-127
    Symbol, 131
    Thesaurus, 128-129
    WordArt Gallery, 164-165
displaying
    headers/footers, 114
    ruler, 17
    toolbars, 21
        Picture, 157, 160
documents
    closing, 58-59
    creating, 62-67
        blank documents, 62-63
        templates, 64-65
        wizards, 66-67
    date/time, inserting, 132-133
        headers/footers, 116
    finding (Open dialog box), 68-69
    formatting, *see* formatting documents
    mail merge main documents
        completing, 174-175
        envelopes, 179
        mailing labels, 181
        merging documents/data sources, 176-177
        starting, 168-169
    navigating
        Go To command, 34-35
        keyboard, 32-33
        mouse, 30-31
    opening
        existing documents, 60-61
        new documents, *see* documents, creating
    printing, 74-77
        Print Preview, 74-75
    saving, 56-57
    switching between open documents, 63
    views, *see* viewing, documents

double spacing, 90-91
drag and drop, see moving
drawing
    shapes (AutoShapes), 162-163
    tables, 145

E

Edit menu commands
    Find, 120
    Replace, 122
Edit WordArt Text dialog box, 164-165
ellipses (...), menus, 18
entering
    mail merge records, 172-173
    text, 28-29, 36
        tables, 146-147
envelopes
    mail merge, 178-179
    printing, 78-79
exiting Word, 11

F

fields
    date/time, 132
    headers/footers, 116
        inserting, 114-115
    mail merge
        data sources, 170-173
        main documents, 174-175
File menu commands
    Close, 58
    Exit, 11
    New, 62, 64, 66
    Page Setup, 102, 110
    Print, 76
    Save As, 56
fill, paragraph shading, 109

finding
    clip art images, 157
    documents (Open dialog box), 68-69
    help topics, 22-23
    text, 120-123
        replacing, 122-123
fonts
    changing, 86
    color
        adding, 155
        removing, 154
    size, 86-87
    style (bold/italic/underline), 84-85
    symbols, 131
footers/headers, 114-117
form letters, see mail merge
Format menu commands
    Borders and Shading, 106, 108-109, 150
    Columns, 142
    Paragraph, 90
formatting documents, 84
    columns, 142-143
    graphics
        AutoShapes, 163
        clip art, 160-161
        WordArt, 165
    lists (bulleted/numbered), 94-95
    pages
        centering pages vertically, 110-111
        headers/footers, 114-117
        inserting page breaks, 104-105
        margins, 102-103
        numbering, 112-113, 117
    paragraphs
        alignment, 88-89
        borders, 106-107
        indents, 92-93
        line spacing, 90-91
        shading, 108-109
    tables, 150-151
    tab stops
        moving, 100-101
        setting, 96-99

    text
        bold/italic/underline, 84-85
        color, 154-155
        font/size, 86-87
        WordArt, 164-165
Formatting toolbar
    Align Left button, 88
    Align Right button, 89
    Bold button, 84
    Bullets button, 94
    Center button, 88
    Columns button, 141
    Font Color button, 154-155
    Font list, 86
    Font Size list, 87
    Highlight button, 154
    Italic button, 85
    Justify button, 89
    Numbering button, 95
    Underline button, 84

G

Go To command (Edit menu), 34-35
grammar check, 124, 126-127
graphics, 156-165
    borders, 161
    cropping, 160
    inserting
        clip art, 156-157
        drawing shapes, 162-163
        WordArt, 164-165
    moving, 159
    resizing, 159
    selecting, 158
    text wrap, 158-159
green wavy underlines, 124

H

hanging indents
lists (bulleted/numbered), 94
paragraphs, 92
hard page breaks, 104-105
hard returns, 37
headers/footers, 114-117
help, 22-25
Help menu commands, 24
Help Topics dialog box, 24-25
Office Assistant, 22-23
printing help topics, 24
hiding
ruler, 17
toolbars, 21
highlighting text, 154
see also selecting, text
hyphenation, columns, 142

I

images, *see* **graphics**
indenting text, 92-93
tabs, 50
moving tab stops, 100-101
setting tab stops, 96-99
see also aligning text
Insert menu commands
AutoText, 136
Date and Time, 132
Page Numbers, 112
Picture
Clip Art, 156
From File, 156
WordArt, 164
Symbols, 130
inserting
columns, tables, 148-149
date/time, 132-133
headers/footers, 116

graphics
clip art, 156-157
drawing shapes, 162-163
WordArt, 164-165
hard returns, 37
headers/footers, 114-117
merge fields, mail merge, 174-175
page breaks, 104-105
balancing columns, 143
creating columns, 140-141
page numbers, 112-113, 117
rows, tables, 148
special characters/symbols, 130-131
tables, 144
tabs, 50
setting custom tabs, 96-101
text, 36
AutoText/AutoComplete, 136-137
insertion point
entering text, 28-29, 36
moving, 30-35
Go To command, 34-35
keyboard, 32-33
mouse, 30-31
navigating tables, 146
italic text, 84-85

J-K

justifying text, 88-89

keyboard
navigating documents, 32-33
selecting text, 42-43
shortcut key combinations
Bold text, 84
Italic text, 84
line spacing, 90
Page Break, 104-105
Underline text, 84

L

labels
mail merge, 180-181
printing, 80-81
layout
Page Layout view, 72
page setup, *see* pages
letters
envelopes
mail merge, 178-179
printing, 78-79
form letters, *see* mail merge
mailing labels
mail merge, 180-181
printing, 80-81
see also documents
lightbulb icons, Office Assistant, 23
lines
borders, *see* borders
spacing, 90-91
lists (bulleted/numbered), 94-95

M

magnifying
Clip Gallery images, 156
documents (Zoom control), 73
mail merge, 166-181
data sources
creating, 170-171
editing/entering records, 172-173
envelopes, 178-179
mailing labels, 180-181
main documents
completing, 174-175
starting, 168-169
merging documents/data sources, 176-177
toolbar, 174

mailing labels
　mail merge, 180-181
　printing, 80-81
margins, 102-103
maximizing Word window, 12
memos
　creating from templates, 64-65
　creating with wizards, 66-67
　see also documents
menus
　... (ellipses), 18
　context (right-click) menus, 16
　pull-down menus, 14-15
　see also commands
Microsoft Clip Gallery 3.0 dialog box,
156-157
minimizing Word window, 12
mouse
　I-beam pointer, 28
　navigating documents, 30-31
　right-click (context) menus, 16
　selecting text, 40-41
moving
　graphics, 159
　tab stops, 100-101
　text
　　copying/pasting, 48-49
　　cutting/pasting, 46-47
　Word window, 13
　see also navigating

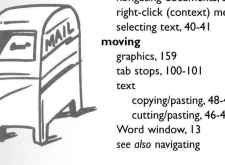

N

naming mail merge data sources, 171
navigating
　documents
　　Go To command, 34-35
　　keyboard, 32-33
　　mouse, 30-31
　tables, 146

New dialog box, 62
　templates, 64
　wizards, 66
numbered lists, 94-95
numbering pages, 112-113, 117

O

Office Assistant, 22-23
opening
　data sources, mail merges
　　envelopes, 178
　　mailing labels, 180
　documents
　　existing documents, 60-61
　　finding documents, 68-69
　　new documents, *see* documents,
　　creating
　Word, 10
Options dialog box, User Information
tab, 80

P

Page Layout view, 72
pages
　aligning text, *see* aligning text
　breaks
　　balancing columns, 143
　　creating columns, 140-141
　　inserting, 104-105
　headers/footers, 114-117
　margins, 102-103
　numbering, 112-113, 117
paragraphs
　alignment, 88-89
　　see also aligning text
　borders, 106-107
　combining, 37

　indents, 92-93
　shading, 108-109
　spacing, 90-91
　splitting, 37
　tabs, 50
　　moving tab stops, 100-101
　　setting tab stops, 96-99
pasting
　copying/pasting text, 48-49
　cutting/pasting text, 46-47
Picture toolbar, 157
　Crop button, 160
　displaying, 157, 160
　Line Style button, 161
　Text Wrapping button, 158-159
pictures, *see* **graphics**
point size (fonts), 86-87
pointer (mouse), I-beam, 28, 36
pop-up (right-click) menus, 16
previewing documents (Print
Preview), 74-75
printing, 76-81
　documents, 76-77
　envelopes, 78-79
　help topics, 24
　labels, 80-81
　mail merge documents, 177
　page setup, *see* pages
　Print Preview, 74
pull-down menus, 14-15

Q-R

red wavy underlines, 124
Redo button (Standard toolbar), 52
replacing text
　AutoCorrect, 134-135
　　special characters, 130
　Find and Replace, 122-123
　inserting text, 36, 45
　thesaurus, 129

resizing
 columns, tables, 149
 graphics, 159
 text, 86-87
 Word window, 12-13
restoring Word window, 12
ruler
 hiding/displaying, 17
 indenting paragraphs, 92-93
 tabs
  moving tab stops, 100-101
  setting tab stops, 96-99

S

saving
 documents, 56-57
 mail merge data sources, 171
ScreenTips, see ToolTips
scrolling documents, 30-33
searches
 clip art images, 157
 documents (Open dialog box), 68-69
 help topics, 22-23
 text, 120-123
  replacing, 122-123
sections, mail merge documents, 177
selecting
 graphics, 158
 tables, 145
 text
  keyboard, 42-43
  mouse, 40-41
shading
 paragraphs, 108-109
 tables, 150
shapes, drawing (AutoShapes), 162-163
shortcut (right-click) menus, 16

Show/Hide button (Standard toolbar), 51
sizing
 graphics, 159
 text, 86-87
 Word window, 12-13
soft page breaks, 104-105
spacing paragraphs, 90-91
special characters, inserting, 130-131
spell check
 automatic, 124-125
 manual, 126-127
 see also AutoCorrect
splitting paragraphs, 37
Standard toolbar
 Copy button, 48
 Cut button, 46
 Drawing button, 162
 Insert Columns button, 149
 Insert Rows button, 148
 Insert Table button, 144
 New button, 62
 Open button, 60, 68
 Paste button, 47
 Print button, 76
 Print Preview button, 74
 Redo button, 52
 Save button, 56
 Show/Hide button, 51
 Spelling and Grammar button, 126
 Tables and Borders button, 145
 Undo button, 52-53
 Zoom Control, 73
starting
 documents, see documents, creating
 Word, 10
switching between open documents, 63
symbols, inserting, 130-131

T

Table menu commands, 148
 Delete Columns, 149
 Delete Rows, 145, 149
 Select Table, 145, 150
tables, 138-139, 144-151
 adding rows/columns, 148-149
 creating, 144
 deleting, 145
  rows/columns, 149
 drawing, 145
 entering text, 146-147
 formatting, 150-151
 navigating, 146
 resizing columns, 149
 selecting, 145
 see also columns
Tables and Borders toolbar, 145
tabs, 50, 96-101
 custom tabs
  moving, 100-101
  setting, 96-99
 default tabs, 50
  restoring, 100
templates, creating documents, 64-65
text
 aligning, see aligning text
 AutoText/AutoComplete, 136-137
 columns
  creating, 140-141
  formatting, 142-143
 date/time, 132-133
 deleting, 44-45
 entering, 28-29, 36
  tables, 146-147
 finding, 120-121
 formatting
  bold/italic/underline, 84-85
  color, 154-155
  font/size, 86-87

text

graphics, wrapping text, 158-159
highlighting, 154
moving
copying/pasting, 48-49
cutting/pasting, 46-47
replacing, 122-123
selecting
keyboard, 42-43
mouse, 40-41
special characters/symbols, 130-131
WordArt, 164-165
thesaurus, 128-129
time/date, inserting, 132-133
headers/footers, 116
toolbars, 20-21
Drawing, AutoShapes button, 162
Formatting
Align Left button, 88
Align Right button, 89
Bold button, 84
Bullets button, 94
Center button, 88
Columns button, 141
Font Color button, 154-155
Font list, 86
Font Size list, 87
Highlight button, 154
Italic button, 85
Justify button, 89
Numbering button, 95
Underline button, 84
Header and Footer, 114-117
hiding/displaying toolbars, 21
Mail Merge, 174
Merge to New Document
button, 177
Next record button, 176
View Merged Data button, 176
Picture, 157
Crop button, 160
displaying, 157, 160
Line Style button, 161
Text Wrapping button, 158-159

Standard
Copy button, 48
Cut button, 46
Drawing button, 162
Insert Columns button, 149
Insert Rows button, 148
Insert Table button, 144
New button, 62
Open button, 60, 68
Paste button, 47, 49
Print button, 76
Print Preview button, 74
Redo button, 52
Save button, 56
Show/Hide button, 51
Spelling and Grammar button, 126
Tables and Borders button, 145
Undo button, 52-53
Zoom control, 73
Tables and Borders, 145
ToolTips, 20
Tools menu commands
AutoCorrect, 130, 134
Envelopes and Labels, 78, 80
Mail Merge, 168, 178, 180
Options, 80
Thesaurus, 128
ToolTips, 20
data forms, mail merge, 173
typefaces, see fonts
typing, see entering, text

U-V

underlined text
applying underline formatting, 84-85
wavy red/green underlines, 124
**Undo button (Standard toolbar),
52-53**

vertically centering pages, 110-111
View menu commands
Header and Footer, 114
Page Layout, 72
Ruler, 17
Toolbars, 21
viewing
documents
Page Layout view, 72
Print Preview, 74-75
Zoom control (Standard toolbar), 73
headers/footers, 114
ruler, 17
toolbars, 21

W-X-Y-Z

wavy underlines, 124
**Window menu, switching
documents, 63**
wizards, creating documents, 66-67
Word
exiting, 11
help, 22-25
Help Topics dialog box, 24-25
Office Assistant, 22-23
starting, 10
window
context (right-click) menus, 16
dialog boxes, 18-19
moving, 13
pull-down menus, 14-15
ruler, 17
sizing, 12-13
toolbars, 20-21
WordArt, 164-165
wrapping text, graphics, 158-159

Zoom control (Standard toolbar), 73